Fodor's

☞ **W9-CDX-399**

Canada's Great Country Inns
The Best in Food and Lodging
by Anita Stewart

Fodor's Travel Publications, Inc.
New York, London, Toronto

Canadian Cataloguing in Publication Data

Stewart, Anita
Canada's great country inns

ISBN 0-679-02183-3

1. Hotels, taverns, etc. - Canada - Directories.
2. Bed and breakfast accommodations - Canada -
Directories. I. Title.

TX907.5.C2S74 1992   647.9471'01   C90-095425-6

First Edition

Fodor's Canada's Great Country Inns

Art Director: Fabrizio La Rocca
Cartographer: David Lindroth
Map Editor: Robert Blake
Illustrator: Linda Montgomery assisted by Romana Huq
Design: Rochelle Udell, Fabrizio La Rocca, and Fortunato Aglialoro

Contents

Contents   *iv*

Foreword

While every care has been taken to ensure the accuracy of the information in this guide, the passage of time will always bring change, and, consequently, the publisher cannot accept responsibility for errors that may occur.

All prices and listings are based on information supplied to us at press time. Details may change, however, and the prudent traveler will avoid inconvenience by calling ahead.

Fodor's wants to hear about your travel experiences, both pleasant and unpleasant. When an inn or B&B fails to live up to its billing, let us know and we will investigate the complaint and revise our entries where the facts warrant it.

Send your letters to the editors of Fodor's Travel Publications, 201 E. 50th Street, New York, NY 10022; in Canada to: Random House of Canada Ltd., 1265 Aerowood Drive, Mississauga, Ontario, L4W 1B9.

About the Author

Anita Stewart, one of Canada's most celebrated travel and food writers, is author of the bestselling *Country Inn Cookbook* and the recently published *From Our Mothers' Kitchens*. She writes a column on cuisine for Toronto's *The Globe and Mail* newspaper and lives with her family in Elora, Ontario.

Introduction

Fodor's Canada's Great Country Inns . . . The Best in Food
and Lodging *is a complete vacation planner that tells you
not just where to stay but how to enjoy yourself when you
get there. We describe the country inns, of course, but we
also help you organize trips around them, with
information on everything from the history of a particular
region to local sporting and recreational activities like
salmon fishing, downhill and cross-country skiing, and
winery tours. Reviews are divided by province and, within
each province, by region.*

*All inns are not created equal, and age in itself is no
guarantee of good taste, quality, or charm. We therefore
avoid the directory approach, preferring instead to
discriminate—recommending the very best for travelers
with different interests, budgets, and sensibilities.*

*It's a sad commentary on other inns guides today that we
feel obliged to tell you our author visited every property in
person, and that it was she, not the innkeepers, who wrote
the reviews. No one paid a fee or promised to sell or
promote the book, in order to be included in it. Fodor's has
no stake in anything but the truth: a dark room with
peeling wallpaper is not called quaint or atmospheric, it's
called run-down; a gutted 18th-century barn with motel
units at either end is called a gutted 18th-century barn
with motel units at either end, not a historic inn.*

*What all the country inns in this guide offer is the promise
of a unique experience. Each is one of a kind, and each
exudes a sense of time and place. All are destinations in
themselves—not just places to put your head at night, but
an integral part of a weekend escape.*

So trust us, the way you'd trust a knowledgeable, well-traveled friend. And have a wonderful vacation!

***

A word about the service material in this guide:

A second address in parentheses is a mailing address that differs from the actual address of the property. A double room is for two people, regardless of the size or type of beds; if you're looking for twin beds or a king- or queen-size bed, be sure to ask.

All prices quoted in this guide are given in Canadian dollars. Rates are for two in the high season, and include breakfast; ask about special packages and off-season discounts. Mandatory taxes are extra. Most places leave tipping to the discretion of the visitor, but some add a service charge to the bill; if the issue concerns you, inquire when you make your reservation, not when you check out.

What we call a restaurant serves meals other than breakfast and is usually open to the general public. Inns listed as MAP (Modified American Plan) require guests to pay for two meals, usually breakfast and dinner. The requirement is usually enforced during the high season, but an inn may waive it if it is otherwise unable to fill all its rooms.

Michael Spring
Editorial Director

Eastern Canada

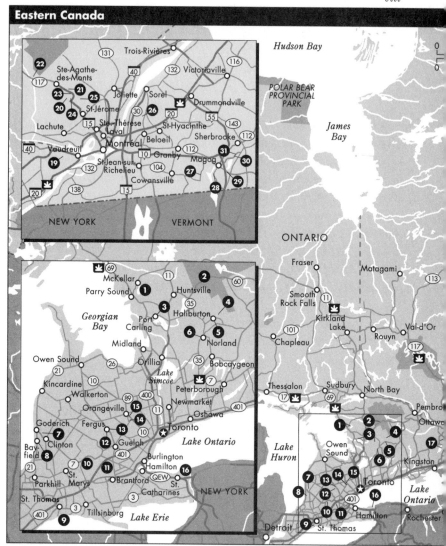

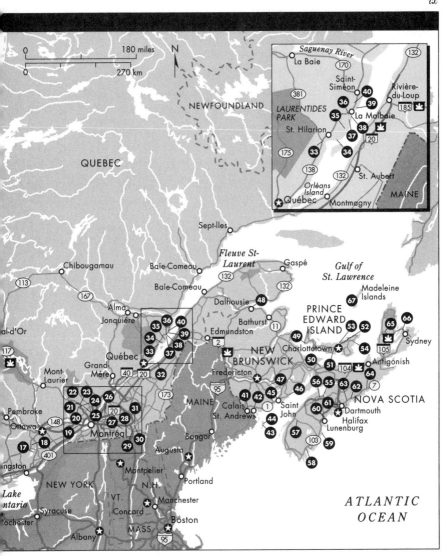

L'Eau à la Bouche, **23**

L'Été, **34**

L'Hôtel au Vieux Couvent, **67**

La Girandole, **27**

La Maison Otis, **33**

La Pinsonnière, **39**

Langdon Hall Country House Hotel, **11**

Le Clos Joli, **20**

Les Trois Tilleuls, **26**

Little Inn of Bayfield, **8**

Loon Bay Lodge, **41**

Manoir des Erables, **32**

Marquis of Dufferin Seaside Inn, **64**

Milford House, **57**

Millcroft Inn, **15**

Moore Lake Inn, **6**

Normaway Inn, **65**

Quaco Inn, **46**

Ripplecove Inn, **29**

Rossmount Inn, **42**

Salmon River House, **62**

Shadow Lawn Country Inn, **45**

Shaw's Hotel and Cottages, **53**

Sherwood Inn, **3**

Shorecrest Lodge, **43**

Sir Sam's Inn, **5**

South Shore Country Inn, **59**

The Steamer's Stop Inn, **47**

Strathgartney Country Inn, **51**

Tattingstone Inn, **56**

Waterlot, **10**

West Point Lighthouse, **49**

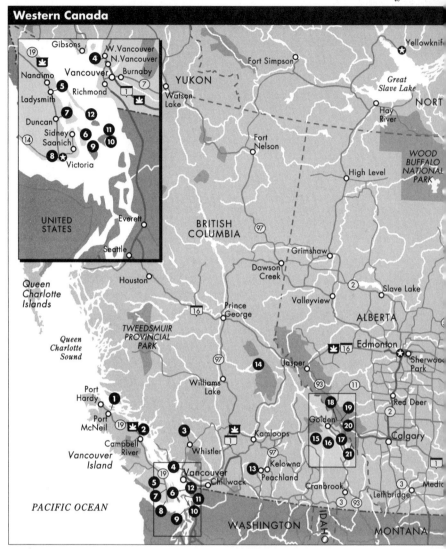

April Point Lodge, **2**
Baker Creek Chalets, **20**
Banbury House Inn, **22**
Bobbie Burns Lodge, **15**
Bugaboo Lodge, **16**
Cariboo Lodge, **14**
Cliffside Inn-on-the-sea, **9**

Durlacher Hof, **3**
Fairburn Farm, **7**
Fernhill Lodge, **11**
Hastings House, **6**
Hatheume Lake Resort, **13**
Lake O'Hara Lodge, **18**
Mount Engadine Lodge, **21**
Nimmo Bay Lodge, **1**

Oceanwood Country Inn, **10**
Park Royal Hotel, **4**
Post Hotel, **19**
Sooke Harbour House, **8**
Storm Mountain Lodge, **17**
Woodstone Inn, **12**
Yellow Point Lodge, **5**

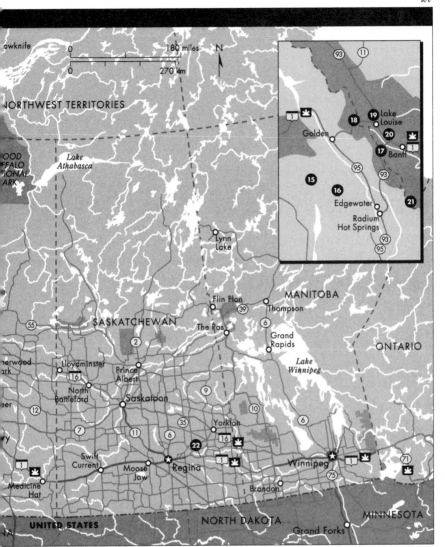

owknife

0 | 180 miles
0 | 270 km

N

NORTHWEST TERRITORIES

WOOD
BUFFALO
NATIONAL
PARK

Lake
Athabasca

55

SASKATCHEWAN

Lynn
Lake

Flin Flon
39

The Pas

MANITOBA

Thompson

Grand
Rapids

ONTARIO

Lloydminster
16

North
Battleford

2

Prince
Albert

Saskatoon

Lake
Winnipeg

12

7

9

10

11

35

Yorkton
16

6

Swift
Current

22

Regina

1

Winnipeg

1

71

Moose
Jaw

75

Medicine
Hat

1

Brandon

UNITED STATES

NORTH DAKOTA

MINNESOTA

Grand Forks

93 | 11

1

18

19 | Lake
Louise

Golden

20

17 | Banff

1

95

15

93

16

21

Edgewater

Radium
Hot Springs

93

95

Nova Scotia

Nova Scotia

The sea is a fact of life here. Over 4,600 miles (7,400 km) of sometimes jagged, sometimes sandy coast encircle the province, which tenaciously holds on to the rest of Canada by means of a narrow strip of land. It's a natural pier jutting out into the cold northern Atlantic.

Summer weather can be cool and foggy at times, so travelers should pack an extra sweater and rain gear. Generally though, the sun shines.

At least a decade ago, a very wise person in the tourism department looked at the marvelous seaside highways and recognized a million-dollar marketing opportunity. The province was then divided into regions to make the plan workable, and Nova Scotia's superb road system—known as "trails"—was inaugurated. Breaking the province into manageable chunks is an easy and interesting method of helping travelers find their way.

The Sunrise Trail begins in the northwest, along the Northumberland Strait across from New Brunswick. It is very rural. Veering southward is the Glooscap Trail, topping off the Bay of Fundy and its massive tides and wide mud flats. Farther down the Fundy Coast is the Evangeline Trail, passing through Annapolis Royal, Digby, and Yarmouth. Rounding the tip of the peninsula is the Lighthouse Route, with endless sandy beaches and shipbuilding villages. The Marine Drive begins just north of Halifax and continues up toward Cape Breton. This is one of the less-traveled routes, but one of my favorites—old-fashioned townsfolk, a solid working fishery, and lots of nooks and crannies to poke into. Finally, there's Cape Breton, the heart of the province and the place that is central to Nova Scotia's Scottish culture. There the Cabot Trail girdles the island, taking the visitor on one of the most scenic tours in eastern Canada. It rivals the Charlevoix in Quebec for raw highland beauty.

Nova Scotia is a province of horizons and of song. It has very little high-tech tourism, a fact that makes many travelers rejoice. It has been peopled over the past 3½ centuries by hard-working sea folk, miners, and loggers. Like most of Canada, the province uses its primary resources to fuel its economy. And like people in other parts of the country, Nova Scotians love a celebration. Beginning with North America's first feasting society, L'Ordre de Bon Temps, founded by Samuel de Champlain, the tradition of song, dance, and good food has continued to the present time, and Nova Scotia is now known as the province of festivals. There is something for everyone, from the Wooden Boat Festival in Mahone Bay, where boat builders still ply their craft, to the Bras d'Or Festival in Baddeck, which features some of the best Celtic music Canada has to offer. There are Highland Games and fiddling contests, county exhibitions and harvest festivals.

In 1991 the province was official host (for the fourth time) to the Gathering of the Clans. Nowhere in Canada is the Scottish influence so apparent as on Cape Breton Island. It began in 1773 when a small ship, the Hector, *landed in Pictou with a load of Highland refugees. In the Iona area of Cape Breton, some residents still speak Gaelic. At St. Ann's, not far from Iona, is the Nova Scotia College of Celtic Arts and Crafts, the only institution in North America that gives instruction in the Gaelic language, music, and, of course, bagpipes. When I think of Cape Breton, I can hear the music—at times skirling, at times lilting, and always coming from the hearts of the players.*

***

For information or reservations, call Nova Scotia's Check-Inn Service:

From the continental United States: *tel. 800/341–6096.*

From Canada: *tel. 800/565–0000.*

You may write to **Nova Scotia Dept.** *of Tourism, Box 456, Halifax, Nova Scotia, Canada B3J 2R5.*

Experts estimate that between 3½ and 4½ million people have some connection to Nova Scotia. It has been a refuge or stopping-off place for centuries. If you think that you may be able to trace your ancestry to these shores, here are some of the places where you can begin your search.

The Public Archives of Nova Scotia (6016 University Ave., Halifax, N.S. B3H 1W4, tel. 902/424–6060) is the province's main archival repository. There are books, documents, manuscripts, letters, and a large library of microfilm.

The Shelburne County Genealogical Resource Centre (Box 668, 24 Dock St., Shelburne, N.S. BOT 1W0) has a wealth of information on Loyalist history, early Welsh settlers, and pre-Loyalist immigrants. There are church records, vital statistics from newspapers from the last century, data from tombstones, land grants, and more.

The Nova Scotia Highland Village (Box 58, Iona, N.S. BOA 1L0) on Route 223 offers information on Scottish settlers to Cape Breton Island. Family names from church and census records are available.

La Société Saint Pierre (Box 430, Chéticamp, N.S. BOE 1H0), on the Cabot Trail, has information on Acadian names such as Deveau, LeBlanc, Aucoin, Chaisson, Boudreau, and Lefort.

Cape Breton Island
Gowrie House Country Inn

Ciad *mile fialte!* (One hundred thousand welcomes!) This is the motto of Cape Breton Island. Settled by Micmac Indians, the French, and then the Scots, it is home to a tough, resilient people who love their island passionately. The great thing is that they are willing to share its beauty with all of us "come-from-awayers."

Gowrie House Country Inn, now one of the finest small inns this side of Quebec, was solidly built in 1830 by Samuel, the first of a long line of Archibalds who held various powerful political positions in what was to become the Dominion of Canada. The home was named after their ancestral home in Scotland, Blair-Gowrie. Their businesses included shipbuilding, mining, fishing, and shipping. They were also general merchants, insurance agents, and brokers for the sale of Cape Breton coal. Supporting Sir John A. Macdonald, Canada's first prime minister, probably didn't harm the family's bankbook either.

In 1975, Clifford Matthews and Ken Tutty bought the house. In 1982 the slow process of renovation began, and by 1984 it was a lovely bed-and-breakfast. That year a friend who knew of Clifford's skill in the kitchen volunteered Clifford and Ken's services to prepare a dinner for the local Opimian Society. After that there was no looking back. All their advertising was of the best sort, word of mouth.

Both the innkeepers have collected magnificent antiques for years and years. Ask to see their stoneware jugs from the early 19th century. Some are museum quality—in fact, at sales they have been known to bid against museums in their quest to expand their collections. One of their sofas was snatched from under the nose of a buyer from New Brunswick's King's Landing Historical Site. Some of their pieces have been "retired from active service" because of their delicacy and value, but most are used to furnish the guest rooms. Six rooms located upstairs in the main house have shared baths. Four private suites, complete with fireplaces, small refrigerators, sinks, and tiny microwave ovens are in the coach house at the end of the garden. These new rooms had Clifford and Ken scouring their attic again for antiques and hooked rugs to hang on the walls. Their decor could be characterized as "country pine," although it is anything but rustic.

Cape Breton art has also been part of their lives. Paintings by Sheila Cotton, Lindee Climo, and Paul Clark grace their halls. One of Ken's favorites, *Angel on the Head of a Pin* by Taiya Barrs, is a finely detailed work that he describes as both "unusual and lovely."

Because so many visitors wish to make the trek to Fortress Louisbourg, no lunch is served. However, breakfast, which is included in the price of your room, may consist of a bowl of fresh strawberries with cream, warm blueberry coffee cake, hot muffins, scrambled eggs, and bacon. You won't leave for your journey even remotely hungry.

There are several excellent little cafés in which to grab a bite at noon; or, you can eat food prepared from authentic 18th-century recipes at the tavern inside the fortress itself.

But you must return for dinner.

Begin with a thin slice of leek-and-Roquefort tart baked in rich pastry and broiled, or the ratatouille crepes. It is imperative that at least one person in your party tries Clifford's fabulous seafood chowder, which Ken swears they really cannot afford to serve. And there's another Maritime specialty, cream of fiddlehead soup. Poached fresh Newfoundland salmon, in season; grilled local lamb marinated in cumin, curry, cardamom, and soy; and roasted tender chicken breasts stuffed with crumbs, sweet Italian sausage, and fresh herbs are among the main courses. All meals are accompanied by seasonal vegetables from the area's gardens.

Their *salade niçoise*, which is served in a giant cream-puff shell, may be a meal in itself, but save room for dessert because their chocolate hazelnut torte is nutty and crisp, with cream-filled layers. Freshly grated coconut is folded into the coconut-cream cheesecake, while a raspberry glaze tops the more traditional New York style.

Since the inn is not licensed, bring your own wine. Shop in either of the two Sydney outlets or at Louisbourg.

Fortress Louisbourg is the largest reconstruction project ever completed in Canada. In 1713, the French founded the fortress at this strategic location on the coast. Because of the growing population of the French, the British became apprehensive that they might lose power. In 1745 and 1758 they captured the fort. After the second victory, they destroyed the huge bastion. The ruins moldered away for over two centuries before the Canadian government began the massive restoration project. It now is a living, working community with more than 100 costumed animators. Even the fabrics that were used to create the garb for the residents

were carefully researched and painstakingly reproduced. Plan on spending at least half a day here; because the fortress is on the coast, a sweater or light jacket may be needed.

Because the region was rich in coal, the mines of the Sydney area have kept much of industrial North America in business. At the Miners' Museum in Glace Bay, retired miners guide you into the Ocean Deeps Colliery. Again, it's a good idea to take a sweater because you tour far into the bowels of the earth, where it is both cool and damp.

Farmers' Markets are held in Sydney on Saturdays from July to October from 9 A.M. to noon. In Glace Bay, they are on Thursdays from noon until 2 P.M. In Sydney Mines, they are on Tuesdays from 11 A.M. until 2 P.M.

Art collectors will be interested in the split-ash and birch basketry exhibited by the Micmac Indians. They are available at the reserve store and, according to Tutty, are "very well done." He recommends the work of Mr. Poulet. The Mi'kmaq Arts and Crafts Business Association has been formed to allow the elders to teach their skills to younger band members. Located in Ekasoni on the East Bay of the Bras d'Or Lakes, it is a short drive from Gowrie House.

* * *

Gowrie House Country Inn may be reached by following Highway 105 east. At Exit 21, follow Route 305 north to Sydney Mines. It is five minutes from the Newfoundland ferries.

Address: *139 Shore Rd., Sydney Mines, N.S. B1V 1A6, tel. 902/544-1050.*
Amenities: *Breakfast is included. Special dietary requirements can be accommodated if prior arrange-*

ments are made. Small meetings can be arranged in the nonsummer months.
Rates: *double $52–$65, double suites $85. MC, V.*
Restrictions: *Small, well-behaved pets are O.K. Limited wheelchair accessibility. No smoking in the rooms or dining room. Fine in sitting room. Inn closed Nov.–Apr. Dinner served only June–Sept., Tues.–Sun. Reservations requested.*

The Normaway Inn

Cape Breton Island means three things—song, stories, and salmon.

The Scots, at least on this island, have a vast musical and bardic heritage that is part of their everyday life. They have passed down their traditions orally; hence, a motherlode of legends has been circulating on Cape Breton for centuries. Storytelling is an art. The salmon, like those of the Highlands, swim in cold rivers and, by law, can only be landed by the traditional fly-casting methods.

At the Normaway Inn, tucked between the hills of the Margaree Valley, you will have an opportunity to experience all of these. Innkeeper David MacDonald was born and raised in Cape Breton. It's a difficult place to run an inn. Long, vicious winters and fairly short summers mean that innkeeping is undertaken for reasons other than accumulating great wealth. MacDonald does it because he's a Cape Bretoner and this is his home.

Throughout the summer the small barn on the property is the scene for sporadic *ceilidhs* (pronounced kaylees), where fiddlers, step dancers, and Celtic singers from the area raise the roof. Guests are encouraged to participate—and to this end. Other evenings, guests are taught the joys of step dancing, "with moderate success," according to MacDonald.

Ghosts and forerunners, visions that come before a particular event, people the tales of Archie Neil Chisholm, master storyteller, historian, and fiddler, who is periodically coaxed to the inn. If the light is waning, ask him to recount the tale about the *bochdan* (a satanic spirit) at the dance or the witch's evil eye. You may not sleep too well.

Salmon fishing is exquisite in the rocky Margaree River. At the inn a little map printed on cardboard shows the location of most of the best salmon pools on that stretch of river. You can hike, wade, or even drive to some. Equipment and waders are available, as are guides and licenses. Fisherfolk come for weeks to fish the Margaree. The inn has just introduced excellent, and affordable, introductory salmon- and trout-fishing packages.

The area is marvelous for cycling, and mountain bike tours can be arranged. Follow the river road for flatter terrain; more serious cyclists can head for the hills.

Normaway has a tennis court, and there are hiking trails through its 250 acres of fields and forests. There are canoe rentals in Margaree and cold ocean swimming at Margaree Harbour.

If you expect porridge when you visit an inn with such a strong Scottish connection, then you are dead-on. Breakfast is a hearty event, with steaming hot oatmeal and thin crispy oatcakes ready for butter and jam. A speciality called Eggs Hughie D' uses the Normaway's super porridge bread under poached eggs and back bacon with cheese and tomato sauce (sounds sort of strange, but it's delicious!).

Cook Ruth Ann Hart was taught to cook by her mother. Her dishes reflect that home-style training, and though the menu is not large, it is quite good. Salmon and Cape Breton lamb are specialties. Her fisherman's soup is excellent. Dinner is often accompanied by live music.

The inn has 26 rooms, some in the main lodge and some in a series of small cabins. A few need a little extra attention in terms of decor, but they are very comfortable.

Outside the Margaree Valley, you can explore the geological formations of Port Hood Island and discover its many legends. Take a whale cruise from the Acadian town of Chéticamp and visit their hooked rug and tapestry museum, the Dr. Elizabeth LeFort Gallery. A schooner based in Baddeck will unfurl her sails for an easy cruise of the Bras d'Or Lakes.

The Alexander Graham Bell National Historic Park is also located in Baddeck, near his summer home, Beinn Bhreagh. Bell's inventive genius outdistanced the telephone. A warm humanitarian, he made important contributions to medicine, the teaching of the deaf, genetics, and marine engineering. In 1909, the flight of his *Silver Dart* marked the first airplane flight in the British Empire. The park is open year-round, and admission is free.

North America's only Gaelic college, at St. Ann's, 37 miles (59 km) away from Normaway, has a summer concert series and week-long programs

for adults who want to learn the art of bagpiping and drumming in the privacy of their own valley. The Great Hall of the Clans, the Craft Centre, and the Scottish Tearoom are open from mid-May until mid-October. For information on their summer programs, call 902/295–3411 or write The Gaelic College of Celtic Arts and Crafts, Box 9, Baddeck, N.S. B0E 1B0.

Last but certainly not least is the Bras d'Or Festival of the Arts (winter tel. 902/295–2066, July–Aug. tel. 902/295–2787), which sings and dances its way through the summer, using a collection of nationally and internationally known musicians and players. If you are able to attend, you may catch a glimpse of a life style that has nurtured a people and caused them to sing what has become their anthem:

"We are an Island, a rock in the stream. We are a people, as proud as there's been. In soft summer breeze, or in wild winter wind. The home of our hearts, Cape Breton."

Kenzie MacNeill,
from the song "The Island"

***

The Normaway Inn is 20 miles (32 km) from Junction 7 on the Trans-Canada highway at Nyanza. Once you're on the Cabot Trail, turn off between Lake O'Law and N.E. Margaree and travel 2 miles (3 km) on the Eygpt Road to the inn.

Address: *Box 121, Margaree Valley, N.S. B0E 2C0, tel. 902/248–2987, off-season tel. 902/564–5433. Season: Mid-June–mid to late October.* **Amenities:** *Modified American Plan. Dinner and breakfast included. Special dietary requirements can be accommodated with prior notification. Meeting space for groups from 12 (in the inn) to 40 (in the barn).*

Rates: *double $175 daily; double $1,025 weekly (the week can be non-consecutive days). Discounts of up to $200 are provided for stays of two, four, and seven days. En Route, MC, V.*

Restrictions: *Pets allowed in cabins. Limited wheelchair accessibility. No smoking in the dining room. Closed late Oct.–mid-June.*

The Eastern Coast
Bayview Pines Country Inn

Bayview Pines Country Inn is located just outside the town of Mahone Bay on the way to Indian Point. The inn is on a hill, so all its eight rooms have a view of the sea. It is clean and well run, with private baths and a lovely veranda on which to relax. The 14 acres of pastureland and forest are all that remain of the 320 acres of the Andrews family homestead. The current owners, the Norkluns, can point you in a variety of interesting directions—from a three mile (five km) stroll on Oakland Commons, to a full day's excursion to a lobster shack.

A light breakfast featuring homemade bread is included in the rate, but hot breakfast carries a surcharge of several dollars.

A moderately priced limited lunch and dinner menu is available to guests at Bayview Pines. The inn is not licensed to serve alcoholic beverages.

Mahone Bay's Wooden Boat Festival is just one reason to visit the area. The beauty of the harbor with its three churches standing sentry, as they have done for 150 years, is another one. The top-quality pewter made by Amos Pewterers and clothing made by Suttles and Seawinds are two more. The intricate gingerbread designs on the verandas of the old houses built in the middle of the last century almost finishes the list. Finally, there is the burning ghost ship, the *Teazer*, that drifts in the harbor for a chosen few to see.

The town of Mahone Bay was founded by a sea captain who came with a band of "foreign Protestants" from Germany to settle the fertile areas and provide food for the garrison in Halifax. The name Mahone (pronounced muh-HONE) is taken from the old French word that describes the type of vessel used by pirates, *mahonne*. Little wonder—this whole area was at one time rampant with smugglers.

***

Bayview Pines Country Inn may be reached off Highway 103 south of Halifax. Take Exit 10 and Route 3 to Mahone Bay, then follow signs to Indian Point. It is three hours from Yarmouth, 45 minutes from Halifax, and 20 minutes from Lunenburg.

Address: *R.R. 2, Indian Point, Mahone Bay, N.S. B0J 2E0, tel. 902/624-9970*
Amenities: *Continental breakfast included. Limited meeting facilities. Diabetic diets are available with prior notice.*
Rates: *single $48–$58; double $56–$66; celebration suite $81. Special honeymoon package available. MC, V.*
Restrictions: *Pets are allowed in two rooms that open to the outdoors. It is requested that they not be left in the room alone. No smoking in bedrooms. Not accessible for wheelchairs.*

Camelot Inn

No one is less pretentious than Ms C. M. "Charlie" Holgate. If you want to stay in the lap of luxury, Camelot is not your inn. But if you like old stuffed chairs and a place where you can really put your feet up by the fireplace, this is it.

Although Charlie calls herself "the old broad who runs the place," she is much more. In 1991, she was chosen as the Tourism Industry of Canada's Person of the Year. She can regale you with stories of the region, and she makes her guests laugh. "People are the important part of innkeeping. I'm convinced that I never was supposed to make money," she says.

In 1971, Charlie moved to Camelot from her previous home in Northern Ontario. The five acres beside the Musquodoboit (pronounced mus-quo-daw-bit) River gave her a woodsy place much like the one she had left. The small inn has five bedrooms that share baths, all overlooking the river and its salmon pool.

Charlie's meals are substantial, and during the summer she harvests most of her vegetables directly from her rather large organic garden. If you're lucky she'll have a plate of dynamite lemon curd tarts to serve at teatime. Breakfasts are generous and home cooked with homemade bread and jams, hot cereal, and blueberry pancakes.

Because she doesn't provide meals to the general public, she asks that her guests reserve for dinner by noon the previous day—but knowing Charlie, she'll probably bend the rules a bit if you ask nicely.

The mouth of Musquodoboit Harbour has the largest wintering flocks of Canada geese and black ducks in the Atlantic provinces. Other waterfowl and shore birds use the area, and piping plovers are known to nest here. Martinique Beach, just down the road from Camelot, is a game sanctuary where tourists can find copious amounts of information on the area's birds.

Inland from Camelot is a granite-boulder-strewn wildland—one of the few remaining in this rapidly growing province. It is noted for its fishing, rock climbing, and back-country canoeing.

The river itself is home to beaver, otter, and mink. They are there because of the salmon that swim in these waters. Fly-fishing is encouraged on the Musquodoboit, but down at the various government wharves, all you need is a hook on a piece of string.

Nova Scotia is famous for its country crafts and antiques. The Old Anderson House (tel. 902/889-3099) is an artist-run cooperative around the harbor from Camelot on Petpeswick Inlet. Charlie calls them "the bag ladies" because, even before the days of cloth shopping bags, the women who were running the business made their own fabric bags in which to pack their customers' purchases. For wrapping paper they used old tissue-paper dress patterns.

***

Camelot Inn is on Route 7E, about 40 minutes along the Marine Drive from Halifax.

Address: *Camelot Inn, Musquodoboit Harbour, N.S. B0J 2L0, tel. 902/889-2198.*
Accommodations: *1 with double,*

single, and cot; 1 with double, and single bed; 2 with twin beds; 1 small bedroom with single bed.
Amenities: *European Plan. Huge home-cooked breakfast is available for a modest sum. Special diets can be arranged if advance notice is given.*
Rates: *single $32–$44; double $51–$56; twin $48; family room (3–4 persons) $63–$75. MC, V.*
Restrictions: *Pets are allowed if they are well behaved. Not wheelchair accessible. No smoking upstairs in rooms.*

Salmon Fishing Tips From a Master

Bill Bryson, the former outdoors expert at Nova Scotia Dept. of Tourism, has been fishing the river systems of eastern Canada for more than 50 years. He has a lot to say about the art of fly-fishing for salmon, the most exciting fish you will catch in the Maritimes.

Regarding tackle, he advises that if you are going to be fishing the Margaree River in the early runs, a 10 foot rod with 9- to 10-weight line is probably necessary. You will have to throw into the wind, the salmon can be 20- to 30-pounders, and the waters flow strongly. Otherwise, an 8½- to 9½-foot rod with 7- to 9-weight line is adequate.

Floating line is usually chosen with long, 10- to 20-foot leaders. Reels, especially in the early spring runs when the fish are powerful and energetic, should hold 200 yards.

The variation in tied flies is most noticeable between Cape Breton and the rest of Nova Scotia. It is best to check with the local fishermen or sporting-supply stores to determine which style to use.

Both wet and dry flies can bring success, but technique varies considerably. Dry flies are fished on a free drift, casting after the bait has moved only a few feet.

The season for salmon begins in mid-May and lasts until the end of October. About the first of June, the big ones start to run, albeit in smaller numbers than their junior cousins. The best salmon runs are in the eastern part of the province, where the rivers are short and relatively small.

To reach the salmon pools, take one of many well-worn paths. Local fishermen are helpful and friendly as long as the visitor approaches the river with respect.

Two excellent books on the subject are *Atlantic Salmon Flies and Fishing* by Joe Bates, Jr., and *Atlantic Salmon* by Le Wulff.

For more information and a complete "Fishing Guide to Nova Scotia," contact Nova Scotia Dept. of Tourism (p. 4); for up-to-date reports on salmon runs and weather conditions, call 902/424-4709, 902/424-4153, or fax 902/424-2668.

***

Cooper's Inn and Restaurant

In 1783, because of the Loyalists' flight, Shelburne, Nova Scotia, became the third-largest town in North America, with a population of 10,000. Americans came with little knowledge of the sea, and because the land was not good enough to farm successfully, the population dwindled until it reached 3,000, about what it is today. Then began an era when the sturdy Loyalist houses were burned for their nails and hardware—wood was free. Luckily, many were spared, and now Shelburne is known for the quality and quantity of its architectural treasures.

Walking along Dock Street, with sailing boats flitting back and forth across the harbor, is a stroll back in time. Eighteenth-century houses are still used as residences. One of the few working cooperages left in Canada is the oldest surviving business in town. Across the lane is the 1785 home of George Gracie, a blind New York merchant who fled the revolution. Now called Cooper's Inn and Restaurant, the 13-room waterfront property has been so lovingly restored that innkeepers Gary and Cynthia Hynes won an award from Heritage Nova Scotia. The reconstruction took months of research—including three just attempting to find the original floor plan. Skilled carpenters had to be employed, because the building had been framed using pole construction: Flat boards are extended vertically to form the walls. The blown-glass windows were repaired, and although it meant chipping out all the old mortar and bricks, the fireplace facing was saved.

Gary and Cynthia have Nova Scotian roots but met while working in the upscale Toronto restaurant scene. On their wages they realized that living and raising a family there was next to impossible, so they moved to the East Coast. After camping in a friend's backyard, they found the property in Shelburne, and with the energy and optimism of young people escaping the rat race, started to work.

Gary, the soon-to-be chef, and Cynthia, the soon-to-be mother, were in heaven: Lobster was $2.50 a pound, swordfish was fresh off the boats at the dock, fishermen would sell you their ration of Georges Bank scallops on their way to the tavern, and there was hardly a breath of snow in the winter.

They have a contract with a woman who lives on McNutt's Island, at the end of the harbor, to grow vegetables like green beans and patty-pan squash organically. In her seaside garden she cultivates the more unusual salad greens like shiso and radicchio. Meanwhile, her lambs graze on ocean grasses, and according to Gary, the meat does have the slightly salty tang of the much-touted French *pré-salé* animals.

Breakfast is homemade muesli and fresh berries, inn-made whole-grain breads and muffins, yogurt, and a Bodum pot of coffee.

Dinner is a long-drawn-out, wonderful affair. You might begin with a terrine of Nova Scotian smoked trout with mustard *crème fraîche* or a small serving of inn-made fettucini with tomato and *chèvre*. Main courses range from Georges Banks scallops in a ginger-and-peppercorn cream, to lobster saffron risotto, which is a roasted fresh lobster, shelled and served on a bed of saffron-scented rice. There is always fresh fish of the day with herbed *buerre blanc*. And in mushroom season, chanterelles appear in many dishes.

One dessert in particular stands out. It is as close to eating a slab of chocolate truffle as many of us will ever get, served with three sauces—caramel, cardamom, and chocolate. To save us from ourselves, Gary also makes fresh berry ice creams and a "light" lime cheesecake with raspberry purée.

Their somewhat short wine list reflects Gary's training as a sommelier. He has chosen carefully and he tries to feature local vintages.

This is a self-motivated vacation with no signs pointing the way. There are undiscovered beaches to explore where, unless it's 90°F (32°C) in the shade, you will not see another person. Craftsmen and decoy makers abound. One boat builder, 96-year-old Sydney Mahaney, works on his dory Tuesday and Thursday every summer at the J. C. Williams Dory Shop.

Also in the summer, the cooperage is open for visitors, who can see oak staves being shaped by hand into barrels. Although most of them are used as bait barrels for the lobster fishery, some are heading to Cape Breton Island, where Canada's first Scotch distillery has opened near Mabou. Sadly, it will be about five years before their first batch of Glenorra is finished and ready for a taste—but what a party that will be!

The Shelburne County Museum Complex is located down the dock from the cooperage. It's part of an ongoing and vigorous community program of restoration. The town is a rich repository of genealogical information. There are many strong ties to the New England region. In an annex of the Museum Complex on Dock Street is a resource center with indexed microfiche files of early local newspapers, and church and census records. Thousands have passed through the town on their way to or from other parts of North America.

Among the festivals in Shelburne are the International Pumpkin Contest; the Shelburne County Lobster Festival, where the town's claim to being the "lobster capital of the world" is made; the Captain Morgan's Founders Day Regatta; and the Heritage Home Tour. For more information, contact the Shelburne County Tourist Bureau (Box 280, Shelburne, N.S. B0T 1W0).

***

Cooper's Inn and Restaurant is located 2½ hours south of Halifax and 1¼ hours east of Yarmouth off Highway 103.

Address: *Box 959, Dock St. and Mason La., Shelburne, N.S. B0T 1W0, tel. 902/875-4656.*
Amenities: *Breakfast is included. Special diets prepared "all the time." Very small meetings can be arranged in the parlor. One guest room is reserved as nonsmoking. All rooms have a harbor view. Crib and cot are available for people traveling with small children.*

Rates: *$65 (double with king-size bed and sunset view; other with double bed); $55 (smaller, with old fashioned claw-foot tub). AE, MC, V.*

Restrictions: *No pets. Rooms not wheelchair accessible; dining room is. Closed Canadian Thanksgiving (early Oct.)–Apr.*

Halliburton House

Halliburton House is named after Sir Brenton Halliburton, an American banished from the U.S. with his family because of their Loyalist leanings. Sir Brenton went on to become a leading citizen of Halifax and the longest serving chief justice of the Nova Scotia Supreme Court. One of only two inns in major Canadian cities in this book, Halliburton House is gracious and elegant, a hostelry of distinction.

The inn is a seven-bedroom house that was built around 1829 at a cost of four thousand pounds. The house came complete with a wine cellar and was built of the best materials and in the most substantial manner. It went through a number of incarnations before it was purchased in 1984 by Charles Lief and William McKeever, the present innkeepers. By 1985, they had the building registered as a Nova Scotia Heritage Property, as are so many of the superb old stone structures in the immediate vicinity. The cobblestone streets lead a short distance into the old waterfront district. There the *Bluenose II*, built down the coast in Lunenburg, docks all summer long. As the province's goodwill ambassador, she sails the world, but if she's in port she is available to take travelers on cruises under full sail (tel. 902/422-2678) three times a day except Mondays. Next to her slip is the area known as the Historic Properties, a collection of former warehouses and commercial buildings that have been reborn as small shops, galleries, and restaurants. The Port of Wines, of the Nova Scotian Liquor Commission, is the prettiest such store in Canada, filled with rare and special vintages. Another place that is pleasant to browse in is the Nova Scotia Government Bookstore at 1700 Granville Street, especially for amateur and professional historians.

Just up the steep hill from the inn is the Citadel, where a massive fortress was built to keep watch over Halifax, which was one of the world's major ports. The old clock, ordered by Edward, Duke of Kent, in the late 1700s, still keeps perfect time.

The Halliburton House began as a bed-and-breakfast inn serving meals to guests by request only, but the food was so good that people kept pestering them to open for dinner. The inn is a charter member of A Taste of Nova Scotia, a province-wide program that highlights restaurants and inns providing regional food for travelers. The Halliburton House menu notes items that are special examples of the best that Nova Scotia has to offer.

Haligonians say that breakfast at Halliburton is the best in the city. It can be a light affair with home-baked muffins and gourmet preserves, fresh seasonal fruits (the blueberries are tops), and cereals. Or it can be a dish of eggs Halliburton, poached eggs on thin slices of Nova Scotian smoked salmon; inn-made polenta with fresh maple syrup; Maritime eggs, which are served on cod cakes; smoked mackerel; or authentic cheese blintzes.

For lunch, try the steaming seafood chowder, country pâté, and maple chicken.

In the evening, the choices are more extensive and a little more refined. The salmon pâté comes garnished with three caviars and small dollops of sour cream on a lacy, crisp potato pancake. The salmon is served, much in the native tradition, on a cedar plank, but updated with a basting of tarragon butter. Fresh Digby scallops swim in a saffron cream sauce and are served on squid-ink linguine.

The inn's signature dessert doesn't really say "Nova Scotia" but is quite wonderful. A "bag" of Belgian chocolate holds scoops of inn-made ice cream in a bath of *crème anglaise.* Crisp apples from the Annapolis Valley are used in the apple fritters, which are served with a caramel-and-rum sauce.

At this point, guests can either collapse in their antique-filled rooms or throw on a sweater and go out for a long walk. In the evenings this beautiful city is well lighted and very safe—cheap, too, because all you can do is look in the windows.

Allow at least two days to see Halifax properly. From the Neptune Theatre and the Art Gallery of Nova Scotia to the Maritime Museum of the Atlantic and the strolling buskers who sing and strum their way throughout the Historic Properties, the city is compact and quite walkable from a base such as Halliburton House.

***

Halliburton House may be reached by air (Halifax International Airport), by ferry (Saint John, New Brunswick, to Digby; Bar Harbor, Maine, to Yarmouth; or Portland, Maine, to Yarmouth), or by car, by driving through New Brunswick toward Amherst and then down into the heart of Nova Scotia. The inn is located in downtown Halifax near Spring Garden Road.

Address: *5184 Morris St., Halifax, N.S. B3J 1B3, tel. 902/420–0658 fax 902/423–2324.*
Amenities: *European Plan. Special diets can be accommodated with prior notification. Meeting facilities include a very well appointed board room or conference room for up to 35 people. Two private dining rooms also can host special functions.*
Rates (excluding taxes): *single $89–$119; double $99–$129; suite $139. AE, DC, EnRoute, MC, V.*
Restrictions: *No pets. Not wheelchair accessible. No smoking in main dining rooms but allowed in library.*

The Marquis of Dufferin Seaside Inn

This could be the quintessential Nova Scotian inn by the sea—a painted clapboard lodge with a wide porch overlooking the island-dotted Atlantic Ocean, boats bobbing at the dock and sea gulls wheeling in the breezy depths of the marine blue sky.

Owners Michael and Eve Concannon were voted Innkeepers of the Year in 1988. Little has changed. They are still a popular pair among their guests and neighbors alike. Their path, like that of many Canadian innkeepers, was somewhat long and circuitous in leading to this special part of the eastern shore. Michael began as an aerospace engineer (he has since graduated to boat building) and Eve was a teacher. They came to Canada from Great Britain to take part in the ill-fated Avro Arrow project in Toronto, and when that was scrapped they moved to Philadelphia, where they lived for 23 years. It was the beauty and relative isolation they experienced on the beach at Taylor Head Provincial Park that enticed them to move to Port Dufferin in 1982 and open their inn.

The main building of the Marquis of Dufferin, now a registered Nova Scotian Historic Property, was constructed in 1859 by sea captain Henry Balcom for his son, Samuel, a local merchant and politician. Over the ensuing century, it has served as the home of a lighthouse keeper, as a Royal Canadian Air Force mess hall, and as a bed-and-breakfast. Guests are housed in a more recent motellike building beside the old house. Michael is justifiably proud of the eight rooms in that facility, with all of their newly built private balconies facing the sea.

The Marquis of Dufferin is known for its fine Maritime country cooking. Clara Hiltz has been in the kitchen for as long as I've known the Concannons. Clara makes the place tick with her no-nonsense approach to seafood and her honest style. Since she can't bear to make the same thing over and over, menus are never quite the same. But you will always find paper-thin slices of Willy Krauch's famous smoked salmon and his smoked mackerel pâté. Clara's cream of carrot and split-pea-with-barley soups are perennial favorites. Michael has contributed his Hebridean poached salmon to the kitchen repertoire, and fish casserole from Eve's mother often makes an appearance. For meat lovers, and there are many in this small community, they serve steak-and-kidney pie and a shepherd's pie made properly, with ground lamb. The only secret recipe is the one used to prepare their succulent Atlantic scallops.

For dessert, there are lots of homemade pies and a delicious English sherry trifle.

Lunch is never served at the Marquis, but the Concannons will pack picnics for their guests. However, the alternative would be to create your own: Stop at Willy Krauch's for some smoked fish, perfect for a picnic after a shoreline hike. Then head for the deli at Sheet Harbour for the rest of the fixin's. If you would like a bottle of Nova Scotian wine to wash down Willy's smoked salmon, there's also a liquor store in town.

To understand the coastline, you must take a drive to Sober Island for a superb coastal hike. Connected to the mainland by bridge, the island juts out into the open ocean. Or you can swim or stroll at Taylor Head Provincial Park, the Concannons' favorite. The wide sandy beach rarely has anyone on it. Pick out shells and driftwood, or simply relax.

If you wish to stay close to the inn, Michael, who is now building his second wooden boat, will take you on a cruise on his 22-foot sailboat. You can escape for three hours or a day around the shore islands where you can see the hidden nesting places of eider ducks and roseat terns. Seals, dolphins, and even sharks are commonly sighted. Because of his affinity for the sea, Michael has collected nine other boats of various shapes and sizes that guests can skipper free of charge.

Scuba divers who have their own gear can dive for scallops right off the shore in front of the inn.

If you want an even more serious challenge, drive to Tangier, where Scott Cunningham of Coastal Adventures (tel. 902/772-2774) can introduce you to sea kayaking. The eclectic Cunningham is a biologist by training, and he takes novices and experts alike on all-day or even overnight (gear is provided) trips exploring the hundreds of small islands that dot the Atlantic. It provides a once-in-a-lifetime chance to observe seabirds, like eider ducks, in their own environment. Although close to

the mainland, it's still another world away.

The area's huge abundance of wild mushrooms remains largely undiscovered, except to a handful of local mycologists. Over 105 different kinds have been identified, many of them edible. Chanterelles, angel wings, and boletus *edulis* can all be collected in the autumn. But caution should also be exercised because the deadly amanita also spreads its wings in the maritime forests.

***

The Marquis of Dufferin Seaside Inn is 80 miles (130 km) from the Halifax airport, on Route 7, also known as Marine Drive. If you are sailing the coastline, it also may be reached by sea. Drop anchor in Beaver Harbour, and the Concannons will send a boat to shuttle you ashore.

Address: *R.R. 1, Port Dufferin, Halifax County, N.S. B0J 2R0, tel. 902/654-2696.*
Amenities: *8 units with full bath, balcony, ocean view, buffet breakfast. Charter-boat rates: minimum charge of $50. Meeting facilities are in the boat shed, which will accommodate up to 30 people.*
Rates: *single $63; double and twin $75; $10 per person supplement. MC, V.*
Restrictions: *Well-behaved pets welcome. Inn not suitable for small children. No smoking in the dining room, although it is allowed on the veranda. No restrictions in the rooms. Closed Oct.–May.*

Salmon River House

Salmon River House is located at a bridge, named, naturally, the Salmon River Bridge. (In reality, the "river" is merely a narrowing in Jeddore Harbour and hence has a tide and lots of fish.) Built in the mid-1800s, the inn was first operated as a travelers' hotel in 1920 by Sandy and Cora Myers. Sandy, a local character, acted as a fishing and hunting guide, but what he really excelled at was telling stories. Over the years little was done to the structure of the inn. Then in 1988, Adrien and Norma Blanchette purchased it. The restoration was completed in 1989 without destroying the inn's maritime feel. There are six large guest rooms; one of them, the Honeymoon Suite, features a double whirlpool bath and a canopied waterbed.

Adrien is the chef and Norma is the baker. Innkeeper Charlie Holgate of Camelot recommended their great Maritimes food. Potato-thickened seafood chowder warms you on the foggiest days. Lobster stew swims under a cheesy crumb crust. Mussels are treated like escargot: bathed in garlic butter, grilled, and served as an appetizer. Steak is on the menu for the locals who love it. When crab is called for in a recipe, real crab meat is used.

The key to their success is their choice of ingredients: The lobster is from Jack's, across the inlet. The mussels and scallops are cultured in Ship Harbour. Smoked salmon and mackerel come from Willy Krauch, the master of Danish-style wood-smoked fish, who has been supplying the finest delicatessens in New York City and Boston for decades. Fresh vegetables, in season, come from the Dartmouth Farmers' Market.

Norma calls herself "an entrenched Canadian," though she hails from Cheshire, England. Hence, her menu wouldn't be complete without a real English tea. Cream scones, tiny sandwiches, Twinings tea, fruit, and cookies are all served in the afternoon in the sun room. There may be a plate of ginger muffins, and there is always a selection of friend Janet Kane's seasonal jams, from black currant to apple.

The bridge at Salmon River was one more link in the opening of the eastern shore of Nova Scotia. When it was christened in 1853, the first vehicle across was the Musquodoboit Harbour mail coach. Over the years, the bridge has been destroyed twice. The first time was by a Presbyterian minister who was probably pondering some weighty parish concern. Clattering across in 1920, he nearly drowned when his horse and carriage went through the water-rotted boards. The second time, a ship broke away from her moorings in a typical maritime gale, crashed through the bridge, and ran aground on the north shore of the harbor.

The fishing at the bridge is excellent. According to Adrien, from June to September the water almost boils with mackerel trying to push their way through the narrows. All a would-be fisherperson needs to do is stand on the span and jig. You are sure to catch something.

At the head of the river, where salt- and fresh water mix, sea trout abound. Fishermen catch up to three pound (1.4 kg) fish with lures or they bait their hooks with mussels that cling to the oceanside rocks.

In the spring the Blanchettes give their guests a special rake and head them toward the nearby shoreline to harvest a bucket of wild mussels. After cleaning them at the inn, Adrien builds a campfire near the water and steams them open. A chilled glass of Nova Scotian wine, perhaps a Chardonnay from Jost Vineyards, is the perfect complement.

Launch a canoe and head upriver into the interior of Nova Scotia, where there's nothing but forest. Your company will be loons, blue herons, and a few eagles. A harbor seal or two might swim by, looking for lunch.

The largest surface-cultivated mussel farm in the world is just up the road, in Ship Harbour. Aquaculture is very big business in every Maritime Province, and this project allows the visitor to view firsthand its day-to-day operation. From the highway you can see the white buoys that dot the ocean surface and mark the location of specially designed nets called "collectors." By growing entirely on the ocean surface, the shellfish achieve maturity or market size more quickly than normal. Their meat is said to be very sweet and they contain no pearls or grit. To arrange a tour, call Little Harbour Fisheries (tel. 902/423-6610).

***

Salmon River House is located on its own 30-acre piece of rural Nova Scotia, 55 minutes north of Halifax on Route 7. It is four hours from the Yarmouth Ferry, 2½ hours from the Amherst Border Point, and three hours from Cape Breton.

Address: *Salmon River Bridge, R.R. 2, Head of Jeddore, Halifax County, N.S. B0J 1P0, tel. 902/889-3353.*
Amenities: *European Plan, but all meals are available at the inn. Special dietary requirements can be accommodated if prior notice is given. The dining room can be used for small meetings. Canoe/boat rental available.*
Rates: *single $50–$60; double $65–$95. Off-season rates available on request. MC, V.*
Restrictions: *No pets. No smoking is allowed. One bedroom and the dining room are wheelchair accessible.*

South Shore Country Inn

This small (four-bedroom, one-suite) inn at Broad Cove is located on the Lighthouse Route that winds down the south shore of the province. This coastline is what most of us envision when we think of the Maritimes—wide sand beaches with driftwood tossed helter-skelter on them, islands dotting the endless blue horizon, sturdy Cape Islander boats at anchor on a foggy day or nets drying in the sun.

The inn, more than 150 years old, is a typical family house that has had additions tacked onto it over the years as the number of children swelled. It took Avril Betts and John Abbonizio more than three years to renovate and restore it to a style that is reminiscent of an English country place. Because of its location, it makes a reasonably priced base for an in-depth exploration of much of what the shore at this end of the Lighthouse Route has to offer.

The sea is a two-minute walk away—it once was within sight of the inn, but the trees have grown. From there it's a three-hour oceanside hike to Green Bay, where MacLeod's Canteen specializes in homemade soups and fish-and-chips. The small canteens that dot the summer beaches on this shore often provide the least expensive and best food around. The one at Risser's Beach, a few miles north of the inn, is renowned. For any hike along the shoreline, good running shoes are recommended be-

cause sometimes the terrain is rocky. You might like to try your shovel at clam digging on Cresent Beach or unfurl your sailboard for a long run on the ocean.

Antiquing is another major opportunity for visitors to the area. Although many dealers have been in business for years, the prices have not risen accordingly. There is lots of maritime memorabilia: ships wheels, lanterns, fishing gear, and so on. But you will also find treasures from the farms of the region—from butter churns to furniture.

If you drive up the coast to Lunenburg, catch the little carry ferry at LaHave, which takes all of five minutes and costs 50 cents. If you have time (we missed the ferry!), there is a super little bakery and maritime outfitters that has air fills for divers who have their own gear and wish to explore the offshore islands and old wreck sites.

Avril also recommends the Broad Cove Community Suppers that are the bargain of the book—$5–$6 for adults, half-price for children. Unless you have a second helping, the women who have made the chowder and baked the ham or steamed the lobster will be disappointed. These dinners are held only five times a year, but if I were making vacation plans, I'd schedule them around the Broad Cove Community Suppers.

Another local tradition is the "pig 'n' whistle," a dance that is held every Saturday night at the Firehall, two miles (3 km) up the road. A deejay from the area is usually in charge, but if you are very lucky, there will be a neighborhood band of fiddlers playing some Nova Scotian tunes from the province's rich rural musical heritage.

Because Avril wants to make her guests' stay as comfortable as she can, she has equipped each room at South Shore Country Inn with a telephone, television, hair dryer, and curling iron. Robes are available on request. She serves a full breakfast that is included in the price of the room. Lunch is served daily, if you make it back, and always includes a seafood chowder. Dinner features the freshest fish Avril can find that day—perhaps a halibut baked in a mushroom cream sauce. Steak-and-kidney pie is one of her specialties, as is a "real" shepherd's pie. And speaking of pies—she always has six varieties fresh from the oven. It may be her own English recipe using the small purple plums from her neighbor's tree or a combination of fresh gooseberries and raspberries. Avril's three-course, homemade dinners, in 1992, cost a whopping total of $16 (including our infamous GST), a great value no matter how you slice the pie.

The inn is not licensed, so if you want a drink, you can bring your own and serve yourself at dinnertime.

***

South Shore Country Inn is centrally located on the Lighthouse Route about 1½ hours south of Halifax. Take Highway 103 toward Yarmouth and then take either Exit 15 or 16.

Address: *Broad Cove, Lunenburg County, N.S. B0J 2H0 Fax and Telephone: 902/677-2042.*

Amenities: *Breakfast is included. Meeting space for 10–12 in the dining room. Special diets not a problem but a call ahead would be a good idea. "We do it all the time," says Avril. Dining room is wheelchair-accessible and one ground floor suite is suitable for those who use walkers.*

Rates: *High season: $58.85 (double twin), $64.25 (king), $42.25 (single). Rates lower in off season. Ten % discount for 7-day stay. AE, DC, MC, V.*

Restrictions: *Pets by prior arrangement only. Open year-round, but Jan.–May by reservation only.*

The Bay of Fundy
Blomidon Inn

Mud Creek—it's hard to believe when you drive into Wolfville, with its tree-lined streets and gracious old mansions, that it ever had such an ignominious name. But it did, and every summer there's a festival called Mud Creek Days—a real old-fashioned fair.

Blomidon Inn always seems to be bathed in sunlight. Its wide veranda greets you even before you meet the innkeepers, Jim and Donna Laceby, recent winners of a well-deserved Innkeeper of the Year Award. This is the property they purchased when their children started to leave the other family inn at Amherst to go to college. It's a blessing for Nova Scotia, because the once-magnificent Blomidon had been on a downhill slide. Now, three years and lots of money later, the inn has regained most of its original splendor. It is again an imposing three-story mansion overlooking grassy terraces and flower-strewn gardens.

In 1877, Captain Rufus Burgess built Blomidon. He named it after Cape Blomidon, the legendary home of Glooscap, the great god of the Micmac Indians. From the top floor you can see the promontory (unless it's cloaked in fog), which overlooks the highest tides in the world. Burgess filled Blomidon with exotic woods from all over the world until it became a most civilized Victorian retreat.

The Lacebys have renovated all 26 guest rooms and spiffed up the rest of the inn. The candlelighted dining room serves excellent food, including a particularly delicious rum-soaked cake. Blomidon's lucky chefs are able to choose their produce from the farms and gardens of the Annapolis Valley, the most fertile region in the Maritimes. The fish, including the inn's specialty, salmon, is locally caught.

In late May, the apple and peach blossoms are at their best and there simply is no traffic. Spring and autumn are quieter and more reflective (and sometimes rainier) than the summer season.

If you want to experience the unequaled tides that poke inward to the Minas Basin from the Bay of Fundy, drive to Halls Harbour across the valley or simply walk to The Look Off, near the inn, from where you can oversee the valley and the basin in the distance.

When Captain Burgess built Blomidon, the trees in Wolfville were small. The view of the Minas Basin and its incredible tides was unobstructed. There, a little more than a century before, Acadians had been loaded like cattle onto ships bound for who knows where. After Longfellow published his famous poem "Evangeline," it was to this region—specifically to Grand Pré, which had been an Acadian village from 1680 to 1755—that hundreds of visitors came on a trek something akin to a pilgrimage. Grand Pré National Historic Site is located here; it has a stone church of French design that stands as a memorial and an exhibition on the Acadian deportation. It is open year-round, but the building is only accessible from mid-May until mid-October. (For more about the Acadians, *see* pp. 55–56)

After the deportation, a number of New England planters took over the Acadian lands. In 1790 they built the Church of the Covenanters, which still stands complete with box pews, sounding board, and a pulpit that reaches halfway to the ceiling.

***

Blomidon Inn is located near downtown Wolfville, about 35 minutes from Annapolis Royal and 1½ hours from Halifax.

Address: *127 Main St., Box 839, Wolfville, N.S. B0P 1X0, tel. 902/542–2291 fax 902/542–7461.*
Amenities: *Both bed-and-breakfast and Modified American Plan available. Bed-and-breakfast includes afternoon tea and Continental breakfast, while MAP includes afternoon tea, breakfast, and table d'hôte. Special diets can be handled if advance notice is given. Meeting-room capacity is 30–35 people with audiovisual equipment available. Board room has capacity for 10 seated. Wheelchair access to one specially equipped bedroom. Outside access to dining room. One nonsmoking dining room.*
Rates: *B&B single $59–$99, suites $109; double $69–$109, suites $119; special rates Nov.–Apr. MC, V.*
Restrictions: *No pets. Closed Dec. 25–26.*

The Tides of Fundy

The tidal surge in this region is the highest in the world. The daily rise in the South Pacific can be a mere foot (30 cm), while it is almost nonexistent at the Atlantic end of the Panama Canal. Yet twice a day, tides in the Bay of Fundy rise 53 feet (16 m); 3,680 billion cubic feet of water ebb and flow from the bay every day of the year.

As the water enters the wide mouth of the bay, it is squeezed into a narrowing space as it pours up the basin. This forces the water to rise very high along the shoreline as the tide comes in, and to recede a long way as the tide goes out. The most dramatic tidal effect occurs in the Minas Basin. When the tide is out, boats list on their keels and clam digging is at its best on the wide sandy beaches.

The tidal bore is a secondary phenomenon that occurs when the oncoming tide is compacted so tightly by a narrow passage that it actually turns in upon itself to form a wave.

North America's only tidal power generating station (tel. 902/532–5454) is at Annapolis Royal; it supplies the region with much of its hydroelectric power. There are displays and tours.

Tidal times and directions are usually available from local tourism bureaus.

Milford House

Milford House is unique among Nova Scotian inns. It was built more than 120 years ago as a fishing and hunting club by some wealthy Americans—among them a man named Gillette, whose cabin is still in the forest. In 1909 it was the major outfitting place in Eastern Canada, with 30 guides on staff. It is still owned by a group of 50 to 60 guests who allow their private woodsy retreats to be rented out on a weekly basis—sort of a Victorian predecessor to condominiums. It's an emotional investment for the owners and has never paid dividends. Any extra money is reinvested in maintenance and upgrading.

Located east of Annapolis Royal, South Milford (pop. 23 on a good day) is in wilderness that few identify with Nova Scotia. Freshwater lakes sparkle in the evergreen forests. The fishing is good and the canoeing is excellent. Milford House was constructed for easy access to a whole chain of lakes and hiking trails. Over the years the guest/owners have placed picnic tables on their favorite hidden beaches. Instead of portaging, paddlers pick up other canoes that are waiting for them. Beavers and loons abound—at last count there were 11 nesting pairs of the latter.

Each of the 27 cabins has at least two bedrooms. Some are insulated, but most are not. They have private indoor bathrooms, a few with the old claw-foot soaker tubs. The refrigerator and kitchen area in each is small, but you need only enough space to chill your soda (or beer) and a few lunch supplies. Every cabin is on one of two lakes and has its own little dock. All day long people can be seen lounging on the very private covered porches that face the water. Even the family pet can have a vacation, although Bob Howell admits that "the squirrels and chipmunks are quite arrogant to city animals."

Bob, who has been a guest himself since childhood, says that he likes to watch corporate lawyers and business executives, fresh from a takeover battle in some smoggy North American city, sitting on their decks. They'll have a beer in one hand, a book (which, invariably, they aren't reading) in the other. When they're asked what they are doing, their answer is always "Nothing, absolutely nothing." A Milford summer is like that.

Breakfast and dinner are taken in the dining room, where Moses and Betty Green are in charge. The food is excellent and home cooked. If you catch a few speckled trout, Moses will cook them for you. Every day bread is baked, and last year the staff was kept on for an extra four days at the end of the season to put up jams and pickles. No Nova Scotian table is complete without a bowl of chowchow, a spicy tomato pickle that is delicious with meat.

Betty or one of the staff will pack a marvelous picnic lunch for you to take over to Hal's Rock, an island in Gang Lake where there's a perfect swimming spot. Or you can simply explore the lake system to find your own special place on which to spread a blanket.

Moses and Bob are obsessive about serving the freshest of fish. This is the place to eat Digby scallops, famous for their succulent sweetness. Most of the produce is from the Annapolis Valley just north of the inn or from the inn's own vegetable/herb garden. Betty bakes all the pastries. There are plate-size Danishes for breakfast and deep-fruit pies and biscuits for dinner.

The lodge does not have a liquor license, but guests are allowed to bring their own.

A fleet of canoes lies ready to be launched, and instruction is available. Bud Miller, the former manager and a true fixture of the inn, now acts as a fishing guide and storyteller par excellence. He'll make sure you have a fishing license, then take you to one of his favorite places to catch largemouth bass or yellow perch.

There's great nonchlorinated swimming in one of the lakes, with a couple of rafts from which to dive, as well as tennis, volleyball, a playground, and croquet.

Near Milford, for those who actually can tear themselves away, there are several historic sites. The Habitation (the first settlement at Port Royal), which in 1991 celebrated its 50th anniversary of reconstruction, is at the top of my list. Fort Anne National Historic Park, with its dungeon and an ancient graveyard sprawling nearby, is another afternoon jaunt. Also in Annapolis are the Historic Gardens, where 10 acres have been intensively cultivated and planted with flowers that can be connected to a particular period in time. Of special interest are the Acadian collection and the Rose Garden. Brier Island, at the south tip of Digby Neck, has whale watching, while down in Yarmouth, some "crazy Nova Scotian fishermen friends" of Bob Howell's can be cajoled into taking people deep-sea fishing.

In the other direction, toward central Nova Scotia, sprawls Kejimkujik National Park, where, during the summer, there are guided nature walks and an interpretative center.

If you decide to book yourself for a week of R and R at Milford House, you almost always have to make a reservation a year in advance. The two winterized cottages, which are rented to cross-country skiers and other frost-proof adventurers, have kitchenettes and, like all the cabins, good working fireplaces with a huge woodpile.

Milford is an extraordinarily friendly place; staying here is rather like joining a large family at its summer reunion. Pack your sense of humor and a smile—you'll come back with a dozen new friends.

***

Milford House is 14 miles (21 km) from Annapolis Royal on Route 8. A car ferry runs from Saint John, New Brunswick, to Digby several times a day, while Yarmouth, Nova Scotia, can be reached from both Bar Harbor and Portland, Maine. It is a 2½ hour drive southwest from Halifax.

Summer Address: *South Milford, R.R. 4, Annapolis Royal, N.S. B0S 1A0, tel. 902/532-2617.*
Winter Address: *36 Lawson Ave., Dartmouth, N.S. B2W 2Z3, tel. 902/462-8106.*

Amenities: *Modified American Plan. Special diets are handled easily. Request prior notice from guests. Meeting facilities are available for 25–35 people. The library in the main lodge serves as the meeting room, and guests can stay in various cabins on the property.* **Rates:** *Weekly $800–$870 per couple; daily $133–$145 per couple. Reduced rates for young children. Rates do not include tipping. V.*

Restrictions: *Pets are fine if they don't mind being intimidated by the wildlife and are well behaved. At the moment, not wheelchair accessible. No smoking in dining room because most other guests frown on it. There are no real established rules. Closed early Oct. (after Canadian Thanksgiving)– mid-June. Native Nova Scotians know that autumn is the best time to visit.*

The Order of Good Cheer - L'Ordre de Bon Temps

Whether you are piped across the northern border near Amherst or sail to Nova Scotia by ferry, you are honored with membership in the society of the Order of Good Cheer. Although it appears to be just another smart marketing gimmick, it indeed has great significance to the whole of North America. In fact, it has been said to be of greater import than the first thanksgiving meal shared between the Pilgrims and the Indians. The Order of Good Cheer is this continent's first feasting society.

Nova Scotian winters are wild and wonderful if you are sipping mulled cider, perhaps zapped with dark rum, beside a roaring fire, or are dressed warmly enough to really enjoy the outdoors. But in 1604, when Samuel de Champlain attempted to settle on a small island in the mouth of the St. Croix River in the province of New Brunswick, an optimistic beginning turned into a nightmare. Men sickened and died of "land sickness" (scurvy), and as winter set in the Frenchmen were completely unprepared for the huge blocks of ice that prevented them from crossing to the mainland for food and fuel. Rock-hard cider was doled out by the pound, and by the end of that winter 35 of the 79 had died miserably.

Undaunted, the remaining settlers crossed the Bay of Fundy, bringing most of their buildings with them, and settled in Port Royal (now Annapolis Royal). There they built the Habitation. To the east of the settlement Champlain made his own personal garden, with streams of running water with trout in them. That winter 12 of the remaining men died.

Summer of 1606 brought fresh supplies from France and an energetic, if not law-abiding, young barrister, Marc Lescarbot. With his enthusiasm and the men's determination, The Order of Good Cheer was founded at the beginning of the 1606-07 winter to help alleviate the men's sufferings under such horrible conditions.

Lescarbot's greeting says it all:

Come, then, chefs, cooks, and boys—all who make good cheer.
Scullions and pastry cooks, let soup and roast appear,
Ransack the kitchen shelves, fill every pot and pan
And draw his own good portion for every eater man!
I see the men are thirsty, *sicut terra, sine aqua*

Bestir yourselves, be brisk.
Are the ducks on the spit?
What fowl have lost their heats?
The goose, who cares for it?

***

One man was appointed "governor" of each feast; two days before the event, he was required to organize a hunting and fishing party to gather supplies. Every day, all through the long, blustery maritime winter, the Order made "good cheer." Prepared foods were paraded into the dining hall, much to the delight of the men and the chiefs of the various Indian bands who were included as guests. Speeches, singing, dancing, and even drama were probably part of the celebration. The chances are that the peace pipe was passed, as tobacco smoking was part of the Micmac tradition. The noblemen served the meal, which was unheard of in France, and they learned the pleasures of working with their hands by tilling the gardens. Their love of life and sense of adventure truly came alive. Champlain wrote:

This spot was completely surrounded by meadows, and there I arranged a summer house with fine trees, in order that I might enjoy the fresh air. I constructed there likewise a small reservoir to hold salt-water fish, which we took out as we required them. I also sowed there some seeds which throve well; and I took therein a particular pleasure, although beforehand it had entailed a great deal of labour. We often resorted there to pass the time, and it seemed as if the little birds thereabouts received pleasure from this; for they gathered in great numbers and warbled and chirped so pleasantly that I do not think I ever heard the like.

***

The plague of scurvy retreated; a strong and permanent bond of friendship was forged between the French and the Micmacs, and the infant that was New France was cradled gently in the folds of the rich Annapolis Valley in Nova Scotia.

***

Many thanks to Professor Jo-Marie Powers of the University of Guelph, who put her extensive research on the founding of The Order of Good Cheer at my disposal and who delivered a paper on the Order at the Oxford Symposium in Oxford, England, in September 1990.

Tattingstone Inn

The gracious old university town of Wolfville has many mansions. Tattingstone was among them when innkeeper Betsy Harwood visited in 1967. Because the town reminded her of her native Cleveland, it was love at first sight. She eventually settled in Halifax, where she owned a successful restaurant, but over the years, her connection to Wolfville grew stronger, as well as her desire to live there.

When Tattingstone came on the market, Betsy was immediately drawn to it because of its unusual plantings. The house was built by an architect whose wife adored plants, and the yard held mature gingko and catalpa trees, variegated maples and a butternut. It was perfect.

Using local tradespeople, Betsy designed her dream inn. An avid gardener, Betsy felt a conservatory was a must, preferably facing the garden. New gardens were created and old ones were rejuvenated. Last year, Betsy planted a hundred irises in her perennial border, and 35–40 varieties of old roses: many of them are pure white climbers that will entwine on the walls of the inn. There is also a grape arbor, and the gardens are laden with many varieties of herbs. Her collection of oil paintings and fine art, which had been scattered between the Halifax restaurant and her house, were permanently placed here. A heated pool and tennis court were added. All 10 rooms were constructed with private

baths—those in the main house in Georgian style; the Carriage House is more modern. The small shed at the back of the main house became Toad Hall, as cozy a suite as any in the Maritimes. The inn was then filled with antiques and reproductions.

Romance fills the air with the scent of flowers—it's a perfect honeymoon getaway. Guests can relax by the fire, play the grand piano in the music room, or simply curl up with a book in the library. Muscle aches will disappear in the steam room.

The morning begins with a full hot breakfast of locally smoked bacon, whole-grain toast from a Wolfville bakery with some of Betsy's inn-made pear-ginger jam, fresh eggs, and, of course, Annapolis Valley fruit.

The day may be spent exploring the region. If it's Saturday, a farmers' market is open from 9 A.M. to 1 P.M. throughout the summer. Grand Pré National Historic Park celebrates the Acadian experience with a memorial to Longfellow's heroine, Evangeline. Because of Acadia University, a healthy arts and theater community has developed. Check with Betsy to find out what is happening while you are in town.

Highly recommended is a hike on Cape Split with its panoramic views of the Bay of Fundy and the Minas Basin. Bicycle rentals are available in Wolfville to help you explore the valley. One word of caution—summer weekends are busy with sightseers and people out on produce-buying trips, so exercise caution. Get off the main thoroughfares and have a super day!

After such activity you can easily justify your return to dine at Tattingstone. It should go something like this—a mussel bisque laden with garlic, or, if you are lucky, some solomon gundy, the pickled herring for which the Maritimes are famous. The Atlantic salmon is sometimes baked with cracked black pepper or merely poached and served with a dill sauce. The Bill Glovers Filet of Beef is named after a special and loyal customer whose favorite grilled tenderloin is smothered with black olives, tomatoes, onions, and garlic. The rack of lamb is baked in a seasoned crumb crust and served with a fresh mint demiglacé. Pheasant and duckling also make periodic appearances on the menu, depending on the supply available from the local Five Counties Pheasant Preserve.

Desserts range from inn-made ice creams like dark rum/eggnog to Betsy's favorite, a cassis cheesecake that is topped with a dollop of whipped cream and a candied violet. The meal ends with her homemade Swiss chocolate truffles.

The inn is fully licensed, and its wine list, although not large (about 20 wines are in stock), is chosen from the Port of Wines, the marketing arm of the Nova Scotia Liquor Commission that specializes in finer and more unusual wines.

It is a tribute to both Betsy and her inn manager, Robert Kingdon, that every Christmas they receive gifts from former guests. The atmosphere is comfortable at Tattingstone—elegant but not stiff. As Betsy says,

"We watch people mellow out here—they just relax and get happy."

***

Tattingstone Inn is located at the point where the Cornwallis River empties into the Minas Basin, about an hour via Route 1 from Halifax on the opposite side of the province.

Address: *434 Main St., Wolfville, N.S. B0P 1X0, tel. 902/542-7696, fax 902/542-4427.*
Amenities: *European Plan. Dietary requirements are no problem. Prior notification is appreciated. Meeting space limited to 20-25 people during the day in the sun porch. The dining room and its washroom are wheelchair accessible. Three bedrooms have one step up.*
Rates: *Main House double $78-$98; Carriage House double $68-$85; Toad Hall (a private cottage with sleeping loft, bath, fireplace, and queen-size bed) $125. Special rates available on request. EnRoute, MC, V.*
Restrictions: *No pets. No smoking. Closed Jan. 1, Dec. 24-26.*

A Nova Scotian Wine Tour

Sainte-Famille Wines (Falmouth, N.S. B0P 1L0, tel. 902/798–8311) is located near the inns of Wolfville, close to the community of Falmouth. A small family-owned vineyard, it sits on an original (circa 1685) Acadian village site known as La Paroisse Sainte-Famille de Pisiguit. It is a lush area leading into the most fertile growing area in the Maritimes, the Annapolis Valley.

The 15-acre property has a good variety of soils, from clay to sandy loam; one special tract is as rocky as northern France. Winemaker Nicolaas Opdam outlined the winery's philosophy when he stated flatly that they were going to stay small and produce a premium product. Already they are selling futures on certain special wines.

Owners Suzanne and Doug Corkum were particularly pleased that their wine was rejected by the Nova Scotia Liquor Commission for the general listing because it was too good. It is now being marketed through the Nova Scotia Liquor Commission's upscale shops, Port of Wines, in selected stores throughout the province.

In 1992–93, the first *"méthode champenoise"* sparkling wine ever to be produced in Nova Scotia will be released. Opdam is making a dry Riesling as well as a more expensive Chardonnay. They are also producing several red wines— Maréchal Foch and Michurinetz, a light Cabernet-like vintage with overtones of black currants.

The winery has a small gift store and welcomes visitors for tours and tastings.

* * *

On the Sunrise Trail, about midway between Amherst Shore Country Inn, the Marquis of Dufferin Seaside Inn, and Normaway, is **Jost Vineyards** (Malagash, N.S. B0K 1E0, tel. 902/257–2636).

In 1970, Hans Jost and his family emigrated from Germany, where he had owned and operated a winery/vineyard in the Rhine Valley. At their new winery, Hans and his son, Hans Christian, carry on a 300-year-old family tradition on hills protected by the warm waters of the Northumberland Strait, with Prince Edward Island floating in the mist. The long frost-free growing season allows grapes such as Riesling, Kerner, Maréchal Foch, and Vidal to flourish. Because the 1985 winter was severe, Jost made the Atlantic provinces' only German-style icewine—still for sale at the somewhat unrealistic price of $60 for 375 milliliters.

The winery is open in the summertime for tours, which commence at 3 P.M. The store does tastings, which are free of charge.

The Northwestern Coast
Amherst Shore Country Inn

This inn has the most popular dining room in the entire region. It is patronized by locals and, of course, brilliant tourists. Donna and Jim Laceby's small inn overlooks the Northumberland Strait with Prince Edward Island in the distance.

The old farmhouse was renovated, a large kitchen added, and the dining room furnished with Donna's impeccable taste. Upstairs two newly created suites and two bedrooms all have private baths and lovely ocean views. There are also two rustic seaside cottages, each with a fireplace and three bedrooms. But people don't go to Amherst to lounge in their rooms; they go to eat and explore.

If you make your dinner reservation (they are *de rigueur*) far enough in advance, you can choose from the entire menu for the dining room from Donna's handwritten master menu plan. She tests each new recipe time after time until she is sure that it will be up to her exacting standards. The choice is staggering, but because only four or five entrées are prepared each evening, guests are guaranteed absolute freshness and attention to every plate. The vegetables are mainly from the Lacebys' huge garden that rolls down the meadow toward the sea. Food at Amherst Shore is Nova Scotian country cooking at its best!

Seafood is a specialty at Amherst—from the inn-baked halibut with an onion-laced cream-cheese topping to the crab bisque splashed with white wine and spiked with fresh herbs. Donna does wonders with sole and scallops. She creates a chicken Kiev oozing with cheese. Beef and pork also appear on the menu and are particular favorites for those who can have fresh seafood every day of the week.

Many restaurants leave their guests dangling when it comes to desserts. Not so at Amherst. Donna's desserts are spectacular! She won a national prize with a creation she calls Wind and Brass, a Grand Marnier chocolate mousse that is laden with seasonal fruit and served on the most delicate of meringues. Try her Nova Scotian blueberry flan—or perhaps just a bit of her lemon-curd charlotte.

Amherst Shore's part in the thick Nova Scotian guidebook is officially called the Sunrise Trail. But the little inn makes a perfect base from which to explore many other areas in the northwestern part of the province. Just outside the tiny village of Joggins (from Amherst, take Route 302, then Route 242) fossil formations in which you can see half-buried trees and plant material. There is a privately operated fossil museum (tel. 902/251-2727); tours are available daily throughout the summer depending on the tides. Fossil collecting is acceptable; the one rule is that only those easily carried by hand may be removed.

It follows that there are major coal deposits in the area as well. At Springhill, the deepest mine shaft in Canada (4,000 feet [1,220 m]) was worked until 1958, when 76 lives were lost in what was the worst mine disaster in the country's history. The Springhill Miners' Museum (tel. 902/597–3449) has underground tours and exhibits open to the public. It is dedicated to those community members who were killed in the accident.

Springhill is also the birthplace of recording star Anne Murray, and the town is justifiably proud of her remarkable career, which has propelled her onto the world stage from her beginnings as a schoolteacher who loved to sing. The Anne Murray Centre (tel. 902/597–8614) is open seasonally.

Along the Sunrise Trail about 15 miles (24 km) or so is the village of Pugwash, whose most famous son was Cyrus Eaton, the Cleveland financier and founder of the Pugwash Conference, an international "thinkers convention." Its purpose today, as it was in 1951 when the first conference was held, is to attract world dignitaries for the purpose of promoting better understanding among nations in the quest for world peace.

From Amherst Shore, you are within easy striking range of the Cape Tormentine Ferry to Prince Edward Island and the vast wetlands of the Tantatmar Marsh in New Brunswick. It's a lovely day's drive from either Nova Scotian coast and a perfect place to stay before driving onward to Cape Breton Island.

Amherst Shore Country Inn is at Lorneville, 20 miles (32 km) from Amherst on Route 366.

Address: *R.R. 2, Amherst, N.S. B4H 3X9, tel. 902/667–4800.*
Amenities: *European Plan. Special diets can be accommodated if advance notice is given. Limited meeting facilities.*
Rates: *double $69–$79; cottage double $95, with $7 per person supplement. Three-day cancellation policy on rooms: one month on cottages. MC, V.*
Restrictions: *No pets. Smoking is restricted to certain areas of the inn. Dining room is wheelchair accessible but rooms are not. Closed Canadian Thanksgiving (early Oct.)–Apr.*

***

Prince Edward Island

Prince Edward Island

Prince Edward Island is a tiny slit of sand and red soil (it's the iron oxide) that is as lush as Ireland. Purple wild thyme flowers take over when the lupins stop blooming, brown-eyed Susans wink beside the sunlit roadsides, and the soft summer evenings have a fragrance like potpourri.

As Nova Scotia's Cape Breton is to the Scots, this island is to the Irish. Verdant fields full of potato plants stretch for miles; the serrated coastline matches that of the Emerald Isle; Prince Edward Island even has its own brand of shamrock—the oxalis. At least one-third of Islanders have Irish somewhere in their family trees. Names like O'Halloran Road, Fitzgerald Station, and O'Keefe's Lake dot the countryside, and Irish moss (carrageen) is harvested on much of the rural shoreline.

By the time Canada's Fathers of Confederation met at Charlottetown in early September 1864, the island had already been visited by countless travelers and immigrants. The first settlers were, of course, the Micmac Indians, who named it Abegweit, which means "land cradled on the waves." Legend has it that Saint Brendon the Navigator and his crew of Irish Monks sailed these waters as early as A.D. 544. But officially, it was Jacques Cartier in 1534 who sighted "the fairest land 'tis possible to see." Following him were two waves of French immigration: The first was in 1719, to their new homeland called Île St-Jean. Later, when the British government expelled the Acadians from eastern Canada after the fall of Louisbourg in 1758, some fled and settled on the south shore of the island, where they live to this day. An Acadian pioneer village (circa 1800–1810) at Mont-Carmel has been reconstructed. An excellent dining room, L'Étoile de Mer, serves delicious renditions of the old dishes like fricot au poulet *(hearty chicken stew) and* pâté à la rapure *(chicken-and-potato pie). Many homes and businesses fly the tricolor French flag with the gold star of the Virgin, patroness of the Acadians, emblazoned on its blue stripe.*

The Irish influence was strong, but in 1803 the Selkirk Settlers, a troop of 800 hardy Scottish Highlanders, arrived.

Because so many immigrants filtered through the province, many North Americans have island roots. To unearth your roots, you can use the extensive genealogical services provided by the Museum and Heritage Foundation (Beaconsfield, 2 Kent St., Charlottetown, P.E.I. CIA 1M6, tel. 902/892–9127). It could make your holiday much more complete.

Nowadays, agriculture is this pretty province's number-one industry. Virtually all the key ingredients for the island's tables are grown in the fertile soil. Fishery is the third-ranked industry, with the inshore cultivation of plump ebony-shelled mussels high on the list. Lobster pounds dot the island, where you can sometimes purchase freshly steamed lobsters for a beach picnic. In Malpeque Bay, the famed oysters are cultivated. More than 10 million seven-year-old oysters are harvested annually from their salty estuaries and shipped all over the world for gourmets to relish their sharp, clean taste.

If oysters are the princes of P.E.I. shellfish, lobsters are without question the kings. Between May and October, thousands of lobster suppers are served in churches like St. Anns in Queen's County. These give visitors and natives alike a chance to really dig right up to their drawn-butter-covered elbows into the culinary traditions of the island. All-inclusive dinners are usually well under $20 and are served by local women who supervise the cooking.

Prince Edward Island was the home of Lucy Maud Montgomery, author of Anne of Green Gables, *which is now staged every summer at the Charlottetown Festival. Few Islanders are as passionate in their praise of the island as*

*Montgomery was. "Compressed by the inviolate sea, it
floats on the waves of the blue gulf, a green seclusion and
haunt of ancient peace." She eloquently describes her
feelings for the island in the following passage:*

> *Peace! You never know what peace is until you walk on
> the shores or in the fields or along the winding red roads
> of Abegweit on a summer twilight when the dew is falling
> and the old, old stars are peeping out and the sea keeps
> its nightly tryst with the little land it loves. You find
> your soul then. You realize that youth is not a vanished
> thing but something that dwells forever in the heart. And
> you look around on the dimming landscape of haunted
> hills and long white sand beaches and murmuring ocean,
> on homestead lights and the old fields tilled by dead and
> gone generations who lived then . . . even if you are not
> Abegweit born, you will say, 'Why . . . I have come home.'*

*L. M. Montgomery now rests in Cavendish Cemetery,
overlooking the dunes, the pond, the shore, and the harbor
on the island she loved and that still adores her.*

* * *

*For further information about the island or ferry
schedules, write or call* **Visitors Services,** *Box 940,
Charlottetown, P.E.I. C1A 7M5, tel. 800/565-0267.*

*For tickets and information about the Charlottetown
Festival, contact* **Festival Ticketworks,** *Box 848,
Charlottetown, P.E.I. C1A 7L9, tel. 902/566-1267.*

The Eastern Coast
The Inn at Bay Fortune

Even the name "Inn at Bay Fortune" is enticing; once you are there, the holiday, however brief, will be unforgettable. As the little brochure says, "The secret to getting ahead is knowing where to get away."

In the early 1900s, playwright Elmer Harris, who wrote the broadway hit *Johnny Belinda*, built this rambling, wonderful house. His love of company is legendary and his good humor lives on. After his death, the estate had a brief sojourn as an artists' colony before the late actress Colleen Dewhurst bought it. Ms. Dewhurst, although born a Canadian, spent much of her time on the U.S. stage and was once called "the Matriarch of Broadway" by *Time* magazine for her portrayals of powerful women. After she had appeared in a number of "Anne of Green Gables" television dramas, her connection with P.E.I. was firmly established.

Her house on the hill overlooking Bay Fortune was in disrepair. When she finally sold it to David Wilmer she stipulated that it had to be restored. Wilmer and his family, though from Connecticut, had summered on the island on a nearby farm since 1968. There was no way that he would have ripped the old place down, and his loving restoration shows that.

The outside was covered with cedar shakes, the structure was reinforced (there was no foundation under the main house), fireplaces were added, bathrooms were constructed, and a great commercial kitchen was created (the floor had fallen in) to attract an excellent chef to only seasonal employment. They poured the cement in the winter during a "relative heat wave of 39°F" (3.8°C). The whole project was so massive that Wilmer, who has a degree in business and a real estate license, swears that often he felt "like I was doing it by the seat of my pants." With the help of his wife, Paula, who remained in Connecticut to raise their young family, and coaching from his parents and brother, Bruce, the inn opened in 1989.

Now that the inn is into its fourth season, things are running smoothly. Guests are returning, and the best sign of all is that it is being supported and encouraged by the local populace.

The large guest rooms have an airy, seaside feel. Island antiques grace the inn, including some that are original to the house, such as the old sideboard that Wilmer says may have belonged to the first governor general. For the cool maritime evenings, eight of the suites have fireplaces with island stone hearths. All have at least one view of the sea.

One of your toughest problems will be which room to choose. The Rose Room, with its mixture of antiques and handmade furniture, overlooks the courtyard and the sea. The Green Room is the same, only better. You can climb spiral staircases to one of two Tower Rooms, which have windows on three sides. Or you could choose a courtyard suite and gaze over the pastures, the river, and the harbor.

However, after you have made your choice, throw your suitcases and your cares into a corner, forget the real world, and sip a fresh strawberry margarita on the lawn.

Both the chef and innkeeper insist on focusing on local ingredients and inn-prepared foods. Fresh island snails are baked in their shells with garlic; P.E.I.'s famed mussels are prepared traditionally by steaming them in white wine. Use their home-made French bread to soak up the garlicky sauces. Fresh pasta is rolled daily to complement dishes like fresh scallops and lobster marinara with local chanterelles and garden herbs.

The seafood is fresh, fresh, fresh! It changes with the season, but there is lobster all summer long. Sole, halibut, and skate show up periodically on the menu.

Grilled leg of lamb is enhanced with a rosemary-and-roasted-garlic sauce and is served with goat cheese ravioli. And since islanders love beef (they can have lobster anytime), one of the inns most popular entrées is a fillet of beef that is first seared, then roasted, before a Madeira-and-Stilton-cheese sauce is added.

With a complete liquor license, the inn has put together a small but good French wine list and a fun collection of cocktails.

But there's more to Bay Fortune than eating. Prince Edward Island is the bluefin tuna capital of the world. Deep-sea charters can be booked from Souris, North Lake, Naufrage, and Morrel, all located in King's County. In late summer and early autumn, sport fishermen are lured here by the chance of hooking a big one. Some of the world's largest tuna have been caught in these waters, and more than a thousand have been boated in a single season. The world's record bluefin (1,496 pounds/ 680 kg) was landed by a North Lake fisherman in 1979. When a tuna is hooked, the ensuing battle can last mere seconds or stretch into a marathon of endurance. The tuna belongs to the boat captain, the sore muscles

to the fisherperson. And remember, if you decide to try your luck, pack a warm jacket and your camera.

After the spring lobster season ends in June (the lobsters are kept alive in saltwater pounds), many local skippers welcome tourists with their families aboard to learn how to jig with multihooked lines that are simply tossed over the side and tugged or jigged up and down to pull in mackerel, cod, hake, and herring.

There is good scuba diving, but this sport hasn't really come of age in this region, so you will have to drive back to Charlottetown for air fills. All is not lost, though, because both Bruce and David can tell you where the best dive spots are and how to get to them.

Basin Head Fisheries Museum, northeast of Souris, recounts in a graphic way the history of the inshore commercial fishing industry— from the drying racks to an old lobster cannery. Take a picnic lunch (the chef will pack one for you if you ask nicely in advance) and swim, canoe, or hike at Red Point Provincial Park, near the museum.

The Atlantic Golf Classic is held yearly at Brudenell's 18-hole championship course, southwest of Bay Fortune. According to Wilmer, it's an excellent course.

If you plan to continue your odyssey for a few days, you might consider a magnificent side trip to the Îles de la Madeleine (Magdellan Islands) in the Gulf of St. Lawrence. The car ferry leaves Souris daily in the summer to carry you to this unspoiled island chain, which is officially in the province of Quebec (*see* p. 79). If you can, take a good touring bicycle.

***

The Inn at Bay Fortune is eight miles (13 km) west of the ferry terminal in Souris in Kings County, and 45 miles (72 km) from Charlottetown on Kings Byway 310.

Summer address: *R.R. 4, Souris, P.E.I. C0A 2B0, tel. 902/687–3745, fax 902/687–3540.* **Winter address:** *266 Foote Rd., South Glastonbury, CT 06073, tel. and fax 203/633–4930.* **Amenities:** *Full breakfast included. Meeting rooms for small groups are the dining room and observatory (Tower Room). One guest room and the dining room are wheelchair accessible. Some smoking areas are available.* **Rates:** *double $65–$115 in the shoulder season; double $90–$150 in summer. Special golf and Romantic Getaway Packages are available. MC, V.* **Restrictions:** *Closed mid-Oct.– mid-June.*

The Charlottetown Area
Dalvay by the Sea Hotel

Lordly in its presence, Dalvay oversees the sweeping dunes of Brackley Beach from its privileged position within the national park. It is unquestionably the most elegant of the Maritime inns.

But because of the sea and the forest, it hasn't taken on a stuffy "don't touch the polished furniture" attitude that it might have if it had been built in a city. Dalvay is approachable.

In 1896, Alexander MacDonald, a wealthy Cincinnati businessman and president of Standard Oil, built Dalvay as a summer residence. It is said that on a summer vacation in 1895 he discovered this magnificent setting and bought 120 acres. A wise and frugal man, he used local materials exclusively, hence the magnificent sandstone fireplace and wood interior that still glows like burnished gold. The name, Dalvay, is a tribute to his ancestral home in Scotland.

Today the inn has retained a grandeur of which MacDonald would be proud. David Thompson, the manager, strides through the hotel with the gait and smile of a veteran hotelier or of a seasoned ski instructor. He calls the island home, but during the winter, unlike most Canadians, he heads for the more frigid climate of Blackcomb Mountain in British Columbia, where he supervises an adult ski school, and Sussex, New Brunswick, where he owns a mountain.

The gardens are lush and colorful, the nearby lake seems set there by design, and as you tread on the tiny blue thyme flowers that creep on slender vines through the grass, the perfume of a Prince Edward Island summer fills the air. From the broad veranda you approach the inn through double screen doors leading to the spacious paneled lobby. It can be a bit overwhelming. A wide staircase leads your gaze upward to the gallery that encircles the entire open foyer.

The guest rooms off the gallery, for the most part, are furnished with antiques. Bathrooms are blessed with deep, clawfoot bathtubs that allow one to soak away the most frenzied life-style while birds flit and soar outside the window.

On the property are two cottages, perfect retreats for families with children or for guests who want complete privacy.

Innkeeper Thompson has preserved the civility of the Victorian era even in the activities that he has made available for guests. One can see dapper gentlemen and their ladies lawn bowling on clipped greens, playing a game of tennis, or simply relaxing in the huge, old wooden lawn chairs.

Thompson has also striven to provide his guests with excellent island foods. The dining room features local seafood and fresh produce, all prepared by cooks from the area. Although the menu changes from summer to summer, chances are you will trip through a feast that leads off with marinated island mussels or scallop seviche, continues with a wonderful chilled fruit soup or, if the day is foggy, a lobster bisque, and proceeds with any number of seafood dishes—perhaps the sole almondine will tempt your palate. For a change, the lamb baked in a peppercorn crust should jump-start the old taste buds. And then there are the desserts! You would have to stay for at least a week to sample them all and by then the pastry chef would probably have come up with a few new ones.

Both breakfast and dinner are included in the rates. Lunch is not, because it's so easy for guests to wander the island in other directions and not return till sundown.

Dalvay is an easy drive from all parts of the island. You can design your own tours—a day in Charlottetown, a day exploring the national park, a day traveling along the Cavendish shoreline (not on a weekend, if you can help it, unless you enjoy crowded roads) or a day at the deepsea fishing ports that dot the Kings County coastline. And don't forget the best option of all—just staying put.

***

Dalvay by the Sea Hotel can be reached from either ferry by taking the Trans-Canada Highway (Route 1) to Charlottetown before turning north on Route 2 for six miles (10 km). Make a left onto Route 6, and proceed past Grand Tracadie to Dalvay.

Address: *Box 8, Little York, P.E.I. C0A 1P0, tel. 902/672-2048 (summer), 902/672-3315 (winter).*
Amenities: *Modified American Plan for all 26 rooms and the two cottages. Special diets can be accommodated but prior notification would be appreciated. Meetings are encouraged only at the beginning and end of the season. Space for small- to medium-size groups.*
Rates: *In June and September low rates are $90–$115 for a single, $130–$200 per couple, and $230 for the Alexander Suite. In July and August, rates increase to $110–$125 for a single, $150–$220 per couple, and $260 for the suite. Lake Cottage is $180 (low season) to $220 (summer) per couple. Governor General's Cottage is $200–$240 per couple. Special rates available for children and additional occupants of the two cottages. Minimum stay two nights in high season. For full reservations details, contact the hotel. AE, EnRoute, MC, V.*
Restrictions: *No pets allowed. Smoking is restricted in the dining room and certain other areas of the inn. Three rooms on the main floor are wheelchair accessible, as is the dining room. Closed early Sept.–mid-June.*

Shaw's Hotel and Cottages

It all begin in 1860. Neil Shaw had a rambling island home, and his friend's daughter was very ill. The doctor prescribed a sojourn in the clean seaside air, and she came to mend in one of Shaw's bedrooms. From that time, the Shaws have been welcoming guests with unmistakable Maritime hospitality. Shaw's is the oldest family-run hotel in Canada. Their guest book dates back to when steamers brought well-heeled tourists from New York City and Boston.

Great-grandson Robbie Shaw now has taken over the operation, and like his ancestors, he provides a welcome that is hard to beat. It is little wonder that family reunions bring people from as far afield as Florida, Washington State, Chicago, and Toronto. You can kick off your shoes, forget the telephone (there aren't any in the rooms), pore over that novel you've wanted to read for the past year (there aren't any TVs either), and, horrors, forget the diet.

Shaw's has been blessed with a superb location. The 75 acre property has its own freshwater lake for sailboarding and canoeing. It is adjacent to Prince Edward Island National Park, "just a sand dune away." In July and August, the water temperature of the ocean rolling in on 12 mile (19 km) long Brackley Beach is in the low 70s—perfect for swimming. In September, there is a hiatus when a privileged few who are actually able to holiday without

worrying about children can soak in the sun, walk the then deserted beaches, collect shells or Irish moss, and be at peace.

The food at Shaw's is country fresh. There probably isn't another more authentic lobster dinner on the island unless it's at a fisherman's kitchen table. They are steamed in sea water the same day they are harvested—no holding tanks for these spiny critters. Twice a week they're on the menu, surrounded by new potatoes, vegetables from "just down the road," a healthy serving of drawn butter, and inn-made bread. Try a bottle of Nova Scotian wine with your feast.

Blueberries are a favorite at Shaw's. They are served with cream, spooned onto fresh blueberry cheesecake, or put in Robbie's favorite—fresh blueberry pie. Island strawberries show up in shortcakes, pies, and jam. No doubt you've figured out that one of the specialties is baking.

But the hotel also excels in chowders. Even if you normally don't eat clam chowder, try Shaw's. Salmon and scallops are delivered daily from the fishermen; the mussels are cultured in Brackley Bay.

Robbie and his wife, Pam, are slowly renovating the older rooms of the hotel. It is not a luxury resort; it's a comfortable one. They recently built 18 hideaway cottages around the rim of the lake, with kitchen facilities and hot tubs that overlook the water. Guests are able to eat at the hotel if they choose, or cook their own meals.

If you have time to explore, take the interpretative hikes on the miles of boardwalk woven throughout the park. You'll guide yourself through the forests, past a bubbling pond, by reeds and rushes. Have the kitchen pack a lunch, and picnic in some hidden corner or in a "blowout" in the sand dunes.

Visit the P.E.I. Preserve Company in New Glasgow. Owner and founder Bruce MacNaughton will most likely be flying around somewhere in his kilt. He specializes in island-grown fruit preserves but also has a great little tearoom with delicious German pastries and breads.

You also will be close to the hubbub that is *Anne of Green Gables.* Head into Charlottetown to see the play, or buy one of Lucy Maud Montgomery's classics, relax on Brackley Beach, and set your imagination free.

If you do tear yourself away long enough to explore the province's capital, you might consider a visit to the Confederation Centre Art Gallery and Museum. The largest permanent collection of the works of Robert Harris is on display, and there's always a touring exhibition from somewhere else in Canada.

If you've chosen to cook some of your own meals in the cottages, visit the Charlottetown Farmers' Market on a Saturday morning. It's not the largest in Canada, but with over 40 independent vendors, it is one of the best. During the summer season, it's also open on Tuesdays and Thursdays from 9 A.M. to 2 P.M.

"Our future is guaranteed by happy customers," stated Robbie last year.

There is little doubt that the second- and third-generation travelers who now book regularly at Shaw's would agree wholeheartedly.

***

Shaw's Hotel and Cottages is located on Route 15, 12 miles (20 km) from Charlottetown, just before the entrance to the national park at Brackley Beach.

Address: *Brackley Beach, P.E.I. C0A 2H0, tel. 902/672-2022.*
Amenities: *Cottages open year-round for cross-country skiing. Modified American Plan. Rates include breakfast and dinner. Dietary requests can be handled according to the individual's needs. Meeting facilities for small groups (15–40) available. Smoking is allowed.*
Rates: *$65–$115 per person. AE, MC, V.*
Restrictions: *Pets allowed in cottages. Not wheelchair accessible. Restaurant closed Oct.–May.*

Strathgartney Country Inn

Strathgartney Country Inn has had a long and difficult history. It was built in 1863 by Robert Bruce Stewart of Perthshire, Scotland, and became the home of many generations of the Stewart family, one of the richest on the island. At one time their landholdings of 67,000 acres were second only to their island rivals, the shipbuilding Cunard family. Over the years the estate was whittled away, and when Martha and Gerry Gabriel bought it, only 30 acres remained of the old Stewart empire. An old stone gateway was crumbling at the end of the lane and a group of "investors" had stripped the house of most of its wonderful wood trim. The Gabriels bought a memory and a dream.

Now six pretty guest rooms in the main inn overlook the Northumberland Strait. My favorite is the Royal Stewart Suite with its fireplace, whirlpool, and four-poster mahogany bed. The Coach House has recently been restored and features the warmth of the hand-hewn beams. Scatter rugs spot the tongue-and-groove flooring. White wicker furniture and brass beds decorate the four rooms.

Martha teaches sixth grade in Charlottetown and is a skilled musician. Several years ago she received a grant to collect original Prince Edward Island folk songs from the old men and women who could still sing them. Music is a large part of rural culture in eastern Canada. With her trusty tape recorder, she gathered many of those old pieces, wrote the scores, and preserved a valuable bit of Canada's national heritage.

Life slows in the colder months, and on P.E.I. the winter is a time for having a *ceilidh*, or Highland-style party. Friends gather to sing, tell stories, and recite poems. This rapidly disappearing side of life is reflected in the dining room of Strathgartney Country Inn, where folk songs fill the room between courses.

The food at the inn is upscale country. Because of the proximity to the sea, fish and shellfish are specialties of the inn—fresh scallops, tender sole, rich salmon, and, of course, fat Island Blue mussels and oysters from the briny deep. Martha brings feathery-light rolls, piping hot, to each guest's dinner table. Praline cheesecake is a favorite dessert.

Both the Gabriels are committed educators, and it is because of this that they have instituted retreats that deal with specific subjects. Their connection to the educational community has allowed them to tap into expertise that would otherwise be reserved for island students. Dr. Sandy Ives of the University of Maine, author, songwriter, and a specialist in collecting oral history, offered a course in folklore and folk music. The Institute of Island Studies was a cosponsor.

Al Ledgerwood, "the best salmon fisherman on the island," teaches the basics of wet and dry fly-fishing at his own set of secret fishing holes around the province. Students are walked up island rivers or ferried by boat to spring-fed pools. Because of concerted conservation projects, the West River, just down the hill from Strathgartney, will be, according to Gerry, the best salmon river in P.E.I. within the next two to three years.

In late summer and early autumn, Dr. Katherine Clough, a plant pathologist with the provincial government, offers mushroom workshops. Field mushrooms are collected for lunch in an early morning tramp through the island meadows and forests. Chanterelles are everywhere in the Maritimes.

Henry Purdy, director of the Holland School of Visual Arts, offers a personal workshop for artists in the autumn called "Capture the Light." Throughout the summer, local and international artists hold five-day weeks of painting: watercolors, pastels, and oils.

Strathgartney Country Inn is located in Queen's County, the central part of the island. It's 30 minutes from the huge north-shore beaches of Cavendish. The theater is a 20-minute drive from Charlottetown, where you can have a lobster-stuffed croissant or bowl of homemade soup at a second Gabriel venture, the Strawberry Patch Tea Room on Water Street. In North Rustico, Irish moss is still gathered after summer storms by teams of horses pulling rakes. If you're feeling a little famished after watching all that work, you *must* stop by the Blue Winds Tea Room, on Route 6 between Kensington and Cavendish, where you will be served fresh fruit ice cream, a strawberry tart with generous amounts of cream, or a curiosity called a hot potato tart, which blends the Islanders' love of potatoes with a traditional Oriental recipe.

***

Strathgartney Country Inn is located on Route 1, about 30 minutes from the eastern ferry terminal at Borden and 20 minutes from the international airport at Charlottetown. Air Canada flies directly into the airport, where vehicle rentals may be arranged.

Address: *R.R. 3, Bonshaw, P.E.I. C0A 1C0, tel. 902/675-4711, fax 902/675-2626.*
Amenities: *"Continental plus" breakfast. Special diets can be accommodated with advance notice.*

Meeting facilities are small, but groups of 5–15 can meet during the day in the dining room or sun porch.
Rates: *The Royal Stewart Suite with fireplace and whirlpool, $110 for two; double with private bath, $75–$95; with bath "down the hall but private," $60. Modified American Plan also available. AE, MC, V.*
Restrictions: *Not suitable for pets. Not wheelchair accessible. Smoking is allowed in spacious veranda but not in guest rooms. Dinner served June–Oct.*

The Western Coast
West Point Lighthouse

In Prince Edward Island, all but three stations are automated. In 1963 the West Point lighthouse was demanned, a nice way of saying the keeper was pensioned off. But that was just the beginning of the story. The West Prince Region, a community of 132 people, was not in great shape economically. There was little local industry, and employment was sparse for women. Most kids had to leave to achieve any sort of success. The community decided that enough was enough. They needed a make-work project, and the lighthouse was it. Funds were raised to built a small community center, and then, with that completed, a contract was drawn up with Transport Canada and the actual task of restoration began.

Under the leadership of Carol Livingstone, granddaughter of the last lightkeeper, bedrooms were constructed within the old wooden building, and a museum of sorts was made out of the memorabilia that were part of the structure. A small gift and craft store was added, managed and supplied by the West Point Craft Guild. A family-style restaurant was opened that used recipes from the mothers of the region. Looking about, they realized that the government was not maintaining the nearby Cedar Dunes Provincial Park; however, after the group's intensive lobbying, it was cleaned up.

The lighthouse sits behind the grassy dunes, facing the Northumberland Strait, on a long beautiful, sometimes windy, beach. There are nine rustic rooms that are furnished with antiques; in addition, there is the Tower Suite, with a super whirlpool. A complimentary champagne breakfast is provided in the Tower Suite on your first morning. The old lighthouse can be very warm in the summer months, but it's not often that one gets to sleep in such a unique setting. The dining room is usually busy with tourists and locals who've come over for a bowl of excellent chowder or some chunky lobster stew. The food isn't exotic—it can even be a little mundane. With that in mind, you'll have a good chance of grasping what rural island life is about. These people had a belief in the future and weren't afraid to go after it.

West Point is about as far away from the bustle of the Charlottetown-Cavendish corridor as you can get. Because it's so laid-back, the onus falls on the visitor to create the day's activities. Besides hiking, lying about on the beach, building sand castles, and swimming, you can get quite involved in day-to-day island life. If there's been a storm, farmers and fishermen along the north shore of the island gather on the beaches to harvest Irish moss. The dark, purplish seaweed is uprooted by wind and waves before harvesters rake it from the surf or pick it up by hand from the sand. Loaded into horse-drawn carts, it's taken to drying plants to make the colloid carrageen, which acts as a natural emulsifier in ice cream, milkshakes, toothpaste, and cosmetic products. Almost half the world's supply comes from the shores of this island.

The silver-fox industry made many Islanders very wealthy. A breeding pair of these elegant foxes was worth as much as $15,000 at the peak of the trade in 1911. The industry was started in Alberton, just down the road from West Point, where there is a museum that illustrates the fox-pelt trade. This same town hops in midsummer when the Prince County Exhibition opens. You'll find a small midway, displays of farm produce, and competitions in home cooking, fiddling, step dancing, and square dancing.

Prince County grows more than half of the island's spuds on more than 30,000 acres. Thirty-two varieties flourish, from the russet Burbank to the Sebago. At O'Leary, the Potato Blossom Festival celebrates this crop in late July.

If you are a golfer, one of Canada's top 10 courses, the Mill River Provincial Golf Course, Resort and Fun Park, is within 10 minutes of the lighthouse.

Not too far away, at Bloomfield Corner, is MacAusland's Woollen Mills. Atlantic Canada needed good wool to survive the bitter winters of old, and these folks provided the yarn. At MacAusland's you can see local wool being carded, spun, and woven.

On Route 14 the way north skirts a coast of curving red cliffs. Stop at the Miminegash for a picnic and visit the marine plant experimental station where scientists are researching Irish moss, queen crab, and the scal-

lop industry. Before returning, continue up to Cape North, where an international laboratory has been set up to test and evaluate wind generators.

***

West Point Lighthouse can be reached by following Route 2 west and then branching off on Route 14 toward the island's southwestern tip.

Address: *c/o Carol Livingstone, West Point, R.R. 2, O'Leary, P.E.I. C0B 1V0, tel. 902/859-3605, winter tel. 902/859-3117.*
Amenities: *7 rooms with double bed, 1 with twin beds; luxurious Tower Room with whirlpool; Keepers Quarters, with a view of the sea and a whirlpool. Four rooms are no-smoking. European Plan. Coffee is complimentary in the evening, but rates do not include meals. Special diets can be handled if advance notice is given. The dining room is wheelchair accessible but the rooms are not. Meeting facilities are limited.*
Rates: *double $110 (excluding taxes and service) for suites (including champagne on arrival and breakfast on the first morning); double $55–$65 for other rooms. $5 per additional person. Weekly rates available.*
Restrictions: *No pets allowed. Closed Oct.–mid-May.*

New Brunswick

New Brunswick

New Brunswick, a province of unspoiled countrysides and shorelines, is a haven for the outdoor adventurer. It is a region of natural landscapes, a place where there is such a relaxed pace that one never feels the need to hurry by.

The welcome in this province is genuine, for the people are intensely proud of their heritage. New Brunswick is finally coming into its own, as urbanization swallows up other places and people seek out those virgin areas where they can still find peace.

New Brunswick, like most of Canada's other provinces, is quite regional in character. Along the coastline of the Baie des Chaleurs and out to the northern tip of the province at Miscou Island, the main language is French and the heritage is Acadian. The Saint John River drains much of the central part of the province, creating a lush, green valley in which many Loyalists and English folk settled. Small car ferries crisscross the river and bird-watchers can count hundreds of different species. By the Fundy Basin, high tides ebb and flow around dozens of small islands. This is whale-watching territory. It is here that most of the world's remaining right whale population comes to mate and be with their young. The shores of Fundy also provide some of the best hiking in the Maritimes.

***

For information and a travel guide, write or call: New Brunswick Department of Tourism, Recreation and Heritage, Box 12345, Fredericton, N.B. E3B 5C3, tel. 800/561–0123 (from Canada and the continental U.S.) or 800/442–4442 (from New Brunswick).

The province also provides specific information and self-guided maps for cycling, hiking, and sailboarding.

The Acadian Connection

The story of the Acadian people is inextricably woven into the history of the Maritime provinces. It is a tale of great courage and patriotism, for some people, by the early 1800s, had been deported six times. The French colony of Acadia was founded in 1604 at the Habitation (*see* pp. 29–30). The colonists were farmers who slowly reclaimed the tidal marshlands by an extensive system of dykes. Some of those dykes still are visible today from the roadway that hugs the western shore of the Bay of Fundy, north of Fundy National Park, near Riverside-Albert.

After the colony was ceded to England by the Treaty of Utrecht in 1713, the Acadians were to be continually caught in the crossfire between the French and English. Peaceful people, they simply wanted to be left alone. But fate would not have it. They refused to swear an oath of allegiance to the British Crown unless the oath was qualified by recognition of their freedom of religion, their neutrality in war, and their freedom to emigrate. For three decades that worked. Life went on as usual, with the addition of trade between the Acadians and the new fortress town of Louisbourg on Île Royale (Cape Breton Island).

But rising tensions made the Acadians' presence a thorn in the British side, and soon they were to be pummeled between British and French interests. In 1755 they were asked for an unqualified oath by Lieutenant Governor Charles Lawrence, who basically just wanted to be rid of them. When the delegates from various Acadian settlements refused, they were imprisoned. Villages were sacked, families were separated, and 75 percent of all the Acadians living in the Maritimes were "dispersed." From the Grand Pré area, 1,500 were shipped to Maryland, Pennsylvania, and Virginia. More than 1,600 were loaded by force at Annapolis Royal to be carried off to North and South Carolina, New York, Connecticut, and Massachusetts. From Île St-Jean (Prince Edward Island), 3,000 were deported to France. While some escaped and found refuge in the far reaches of the colonies and near Quebec City, most were not so lucky.

They were a tenacious and lively lot. They passed their culture down from one generation to the next by story, song, and dance. Like water finding its own level, however, they slowly began to trickle back to their Maritime homelands or to other regions, like Louisiana. *Cajun* became their nickname in Louisiana, and their cuisine is well known.

Their wanderings were relatively unnoticed until the 1800s, when U.S. poet Henry Wadsworth Longfellow wrote his classic poem "Evangeline." In it, two young lovers are forcibly parted, as indeed many were during those troubled decades, but finally are reunited at the end of their lives. The story brings the poignancy to life and tells the true story of the Acadians far better than any historical text.

"Dwelt in the love of God and of Man, Alike were they free from/ Fear, the reigns with the tyrant, and envy, the vice of republics."

Today the remaining Acadian regions in the Maritimes are quite visible, with their tricolor flags flapping in the ocean breezes. They are still a proud and fun-loving people. In Nova Scotia the French Shore is south of Annapolis Royal, but there are Acadian pockets in Cape Breton and at Pomquet in the north; in New Brunswick, the entire shore bordering the Northumberland

Strait is mainly Acadian; and on Prince Edward Island, two small regions carry the flag.

To enjoy the taste and feeling of early Acadian life, make a visit to:

Acadian Historical Village. Rte. 11, 6 miles (10 km) west of Caraquet, N.B., tel. 506/727–3467.

The Acadian Museum, 15 St. Pierre St., Caraquet, N.B., tel. 506/727–3269. The town of Caraquet also has an Acadian Festival in mid-August of each year.

Le Village Pionnier Acadien, Rte. 11, 1 mile (1½ km) west of Mont Carmel, P.E.I., tel. 902/854–2227.

Grand Manan Island and the St. Andrews Area
The Compass Rose

When you round by ferry the spit of land that juts into the Bay of Fundy, North Head appears—small, white clapboard houses focused on the harbor. It is what most of us imagine a Maritime fishing community should look like—picture-book perfect, with gulls sitting on old pilings, fishing boats tied up, nets in heaps on the docks, the salt sea air bracing.

The Compass Rose is close to the ferry wharf, beside the sea. All the bedrooms overlook the water, and innkeeper Cecilia Bowden has decorated them with wildflowers and calico. It is most appropriate because more than 100 species of wildflowers bloom on the island from May until the first frost. Black-eyed Susans, multicolored lupins, roses, and daisies all splash the seaside fields. The Flagg House, next door to the Compass Rose, has five bedrooms upstairs that are named after the Flagg family—Ebenezer, Josiah, Sadie, Katy, and Jack. All guest rooms share baths.

Breakfast is served to guests in the dining room overlooking the harbor. A cup of coffee on the long deck is about the best way to wake up before setting off to explore the beaches and see what wonders the receding tide has left in the shallow pools. Discover sea urchins, small fish, crayfish, and the many seaweeds. Don't forget a pair of good rubber boots for such outings—they are invaluable.

If you miss lunch (lobster stew, coquilles St. Jacques, seafood lasagne), there is always afternoon tea. Scones, hot from the oven, are graciously served with clotted cream as well as island-plum and wild-raspberry jam.

Dinners center on the freshest fish available. The recipe for their Maritime brown bread has been published many times in magazines from coast to coast. It's typical of East Coast cookery and is baked in the kitchen of the Compass Rose every day. The other specialty is dessert, especially their seasonal fruit pies. Cecilia's favorite is the one she bakes with Indian pears, a small fruit that resembles a saskatoon berry. Their wine list is inexpensive; it reflects the difficulty of obtaining top vintages in the small towns of Canada. If you want to have a special bottle with this superb seafood, you are advised to bring your own.

During any Grand Manan visit, one must include several things. First, of course, is a whale- and bird-watching expedition. You may get a small dose of this on the free ferry to White

Head Island. The best way, however, is to have Cecilia organize one for you. Because it requires phone calls to fishermen and running back and forth between houses to see who wants to join the trip, it is essential that guests make their wishes known as soon as they land. You will most likely see whales, porpoises, seals, and scores of different bird species. These full-day trips require a picnic lunch, which the inn's kitchen will pack.

The Bay of Fundy has the largest right whale population in existence. Only about 250 of the species are left; there was a massive slaughter of them in the 1800s. It is said that the right whale was named because it was "the right whale" to kill. Large, with lots of oil-rich blubber, it was an easy target for harpooners. In August and September, 40 to 50 of these whales summer near Grand Manan. Feeding on microscopic krill, they are so large that an elephant could fit inside one of their rib cages.

Dark Harbour is famous for its dulse, the purple seaweed that is a Grand Manan specialty. It is possible to pick your own. Dried dulse is available, as well as the rubber boots you will need to gather the fresh variety, at the local general store.

The island is crisscrossed by miles of hiking trails. Bring a good pair of light hiking boots and have Cecilia provide a map. Binoculars are also a nice thing to have along, as the island is on the main eastern flyway. In fact, conversation at the dinner tables in either of Grand Manan's two good inns generally focuses on what birds were seen that day, and where. The museum at Grand Harbour has the huge bird collection of ornithologist Allen Moses, the man who confirmed the island's position as a key stopover for tens of thousands of migratory birds.

There is something for most outdoor lovers on this island—geologists, photographers, cyclists, or people who want to putter down back roads or just sit by the ocean.

***

The Compass Rose is reached by ferry from Black's Harbour south of Saint John, New Brunswick. Located by the North Head harbor, it's difficult to miss. For ferry information, contact the inn or call Tourism New Brunswick's toll-free numbers, 800/561–0123 (from Canada/continental U.S.) or 800/442–4442 (from N.B.).

Address: *North Head, Grand Manan, N.B. E0G 2M0, tel. 506/662–8570 (summer) or 506/446–5906 (winter).*
Amenities: *Breakfast is included in rate. Special dietary requirements can be accommodated with advance notice.*
Rates: *$40 single, $55 double (excludes tax). V.*
Restrictions: *Only well-behaved pets are welcome. Not wheelchair accessible. No smoking in the bedrooms. One dining room is nonsmoking. No meeting facilities. Closed Nov.–Apr.*

Loon Bay Lodge

The gravel highway leading to the lodge was originally named King's Mast Road. The trees were so tall that they were harvested by the local shipbuilders. At the end of a fairly bumpy journey east of St. Stephen is Loon Bay Lodge, an unpretentious, rustic log construction with braided rugs and clothes hooks made of young saplings in the rooms.

The lodge overlooks the St. Croix River, a Canadian Heritage River and the border between Maine and New Brunswick. The area was originally populated by loggers and farmers. An old orchard sprawls down the riverbank, a perfect refuge for the woodcock that feast on the fallen apples and regularly grace the table at Loon Bay.

Innkeepers David Whittingham and Judy Ells are true outdoors people. Shirley Shannon, an exceptional home-style cook, creates hearty meals ready to satisfy anyone who has spent the day canoeing the St. Croix.

Hunting and fishing are definitely the focus for most of the operation. Land-locked salmon can be taken on two-hook streamers in nearby freshwater lakes. Their annual spring feeding frenzy occurs in May and June when spin-cast gear is used from 20 foot (6 m) laker canoes.

Guides will take guests to rivers, lakes, and head ponds that hold a variety of fish, from speckled and lake trout to chain pickerel and yellow perch. Most are taken on a catch-and-release basis, especially the now-rare wild Atlantic salmon. The feisty smallmouth bass can reach four pounds (1.8 kg). The lodge can supply rods and lures. In the thick woodlands that surround the lodge, ruffed and spruce grouse are hunted. Shirley will cook them to order for her guests. The rich flesh of a grouse is like a finer version of turkey, while woodcock has the texture of liver.

David and Judy are expert canoeists. Between them are well over 20 years of experience. Private lessons are available for all skill levels of both canoeists and kayakers. From the white water, upstream from the lodge, to the smoother less hairraising downstream areas, there is a "classroom" for everyone. The lodge supplies all the equipment, including life jackets.

Longer, more intensive trips can be taken down the St. Croix. The river on which Loon Bay guests play was named after the island of St. Croix by Pierre de Gua, Sieur de Monts. De Monts was the leader of the expedition that was to begin the French colonization of North America and that had Samuel de Champlain as its chief cartographer. It was on the tiny island of St. Croix, just downstream from the present site of Loon Bay Lodge, that the first settlers to this part of North America starved through their first winter. Now a historic site administered by the Maine government, it has no ferry service. Because all the original houses were either transported to Port Royal or burned in 1613 by a Virginian, Captain Samuel Argall, there is little to see.

Loon Bay Lodge is the only lodge in Canada that offers to their guests float tubes for bobbing down the river. Less strenuous and with far more water contact than either canoeing or kayaking, this ride is guaranteed to bring out the kid in everyone.

The lodge was built in 1935 by Richard Crooks, the singer who was known as "the voice of Firestone." When city life got the better of him, he would hop on the train from Boston, get off at McAdam, the nearest whistle-stop, and paddle down the river to his hideaway.

The immediate vicinity is full of great side trips, by land or by water. The St. Croix River empties into Passamaquoddy Bay. A small system of ferries connects Letete, New Brunswick, with Deer Island and then, in July and August, with Campobello. Deer Island has the world's largest lobster pound; at certain times of the year it holds up to one million pounds of live lobster. Cline Marine (tel. 506/529–4188) has whale-search cruises on the open waters of Fundy and a more sedate version that stays within the somewhat sheltered waters of the 50 islands that scatter the basin. These veteran mariners sail from Richardson on Deer Island, from St. Andrews, and from Head Harbour on Campobello Island.

On Campobello, Franklin Delano Roosevelt's summer home and estate is now a 2,600 acre memorial park. Administered by a joint international committee of three Canadians and three Americans, it is open, free of charge, to the public from late May until early October.

If Roald Dahl's Charlie ever had a chocolate factory, it would be one like the Ganong business in St. Stephen. In the 1870s children (and adults) discovered the joys of chocolate and candy. The Ganong brothers started experimenting and concocting their own special temptations— the first five-cent candy bar, the first heart-shaped Valentine box, and tubes of hard candy filled with bitter chocolate and named, unappetizingly, "chicken bones." Although the factory has moved to a new location outside the town, the Ganong name is still synonymous with high-quality made-in-Canada chocolate. During the first week of August, when the International Festival celebrates the friendship of St. Stephen and Calais, Maine, there is also a Chocolate Fest.

The Atlantic Salmon Centre (tel. 506/529–4581), east of St. Andrews, is on the banks of Chamcook Creek. The natural stream setting has a specially designed viewing chamber and a wooded location much like a nursery site. Open from mid-May until late August and on the Canadian Thanksgiving weekend, the center is sponsored by the Atlantic Salmon Federation, a nonprofit organization, which promotes conservation and research.

The Huntsman Aquarium Museum (tel. 506/529–4285) is also open from May until October. Its focus is the marine ecology of the Bay of Fundy, and it is professionally associated with universities across Canada.

***

Loon Bay Lodge is 1¾ hours from Saint John and 2¼ hours from Bangor, Maine. Car rentals are available at major airports and at St. Stephen and Calais. From St. Stephen, take Route 3 toward Fredericton. Follow signs to McGraw Hill Ski Park. Go past the ski hill about four miles (six km) to the end of the paved road. Take the left fork onto the dirt road and go about three miles (five km) to the lodge.

Address: *Box 101, St. Stephen, N.B. E3L 2W9, tel. 506/466–1240, fax 506/466–4213.*
Amenities: *Full American Plan. With advance notice, some dietary restrictions can be handled. Meeting facilities are good for an executive getaway for up to 20 people. No restrictions on smoking.*
Rates: *double (excluding taxes) $124.33. Modified American Plan*

and bed-and-breakfast options also available. V.

Restrictions: *House-trained dogs are allowed. Not wheelchair accessible. Closed Dec.–Apr.*

Rossmount Inn

itting in a multicolored sea of wild lupins, Rossmount Inn overlooks the green islands of Passamaquoddy Bay. St. Andrews-by-the-Sea is nearby, with the Huntsman Marine Station, world-famous Scottish-designed golf courses, and whale watching at its finest. Half the town's homes are more than a century old. In 1783 a group of disgruntled Loyalists took apart their houses in Castine, Maine, and reassembled them on a protected peninsula, St. Andrews-by-the-Sea. It was the beginning of a U.S. love affair with this beautiful part of New Brunswick. Just out in the bay is Campobello Island, the summer home of Franklin Delano Roosevelt.

Innkeeper Lynda Estes has created an inn that fits into the ambience of the area. Designed by Boston architect H. N. Black, the inn was built for the Reverend and Mrs. Henry Phipps Ross in 1902. Their taste still lingers, not only in the St. Andrews museum that bears their name, but also at their former home at the base of Chamcook Mountain. Richly carpeted, and laden with antiques and stained glass, the inn has won awards from both the AAA and the CAA.

Lynda doubles as the chef, serving Maritime country cooking in her fully licensed dining room. The meal may begin with cream of fiddlehead soup or a seafood gumbo. A wild pink dressing with the bite of radish is tossed with the salad greens.

Fundy lobster is steamed or cooked to order; salmon from the nearby aquafarms may be grilled or poached in wine and served with a sweet red-pepper sauce; snow-white scallops are sautéed in butter with fresh herbs and lemon; and haddock from the local fishery is stuffed with corn-bread, lobster, and crab meat. Chicken and beef appear in token form on the menu. Seafood is their specialty!

Their desserts are reminiscent of rural cooking—fresh berries from the garden and fruit cobblers that change with the season. First there's rhubarb, rosy-pink and tender, then strawberry/rhubarb when there aren't quite enough strawberries in the patch to make a pie. Next, blueberries and, finally, New Brunswick apples.

Rossmount Inn provides a superb base from which to explore the region. Guests can wander the 87 acre property and count the 350 species of birds (the Atlantic flyway is right overhead), pausing now and then to drink in the panorama of sea and sky. On a warm summer day, an afternoon beside or in the outdoor pool can heal all the wounds of long-distance travel.

For anyone who has the least bit of interest in aquaculture or marine biology, the Huntsman Marine Science Centre and Aquarium will hold you fascinated for hours, or even weeks if you choose to study there. Founded in 1969, the Huntsman is one of Canada's leading research facilities. The aquarium/museum complex attempts to educate its visitors about their relationship with the marine environment. Its live exhibits include harbor seals, wolffish, lumpfish, lobsters, and sea cucumbers. A hands-on "touch pool" really lets observers, young and old, get into it. In addition to the dry-land courses, the Huntsman offers marine biology for scuba divers. One word of caution—the tides of Fundy are so strong that diving should be limited to those who have advanced diver certification.

In conjunction with the Huntsman and the Atlantic Salmon Federation, St. Andrew's holds the Atlantic Aquaculture Fair in early summer of each year. Although it's a trade show for farmers of the sea, there are a number of opportunities that otherwise would not exist for the traveler. The Salmonoid Demonstration and Development Farm is opened for tours. A salmon barbecue and mussel feast completes one day, while fish cooking demonstrations occur on another. For specific times and events, contact the Chamber of Commerce, Box 89, St. Andrews-by-the-Sea, N.B. E0G 2X0 (tel. 506/529–3555).

Sunbury Shores Arts and Nature Centre (tel. 506/529–3386) offers one- and two-week intensive art classes for adults. As a recognized art gallery, it attracts instructors in every medium. In addition to the watercolor, pottery, printmaking, oil painting, and wildlife illustration classes, courses in marine ecology, mycology, and wildflowers are offered. Workshops for children age 6–12 also take place during the summer.

The area is as rich in antiques as it is in old architecture. The architect of Canadian Pacific's venerable Algonquin Hotel built himself a small cottage on a quiet street nearby. It is now a fabulous antique-store-cum-tearoom named the Pansy Patch, open only during the summertime.

Whale-watching tours leave from town. The Cline family has been fishing in this region for generations, and if you have the opportunity to tag along on one of their tours, you will be with some very knowledgeable seamen.

***

Rossmount Inn is west of Saint John off Route 1. It also may be approached from the west via St. Stephen. In either case, take Route 127 to St. Andrews-by-the-Sea. The inn is about one mile (1.6 km) east of the town.

Address: *R.R. 2, St. Andrews-by-the-Sea, N.B. E0G 2X0, tel. 506/529–3351, fax 506/529–3088.*
Amenities: *European Plan. Special dietary requests can be handled with advance notice. Meetings may be held in the dining room for larger groups and in the parlor for six to eight people.*
Rates: *All rooms include private baths (excluding taxes and service): $85 single, $95 double, $10 extra per person. MC, V.*
Restrictions: *Pets are allowed. Guest rooms on the first floor of the inn are nonsmoking; the second floor is smoking. No smoking allowed in the dining room. No rooms are wheelchair accessible, but the dining room is. Closed Oct.–May 15.*

Shorecrest Lodge

Andy and Cindy Normandeau are sixth-generation Vermonters who are now in their third summer on Grand Manan. Living on the island all year round, as they do, takes real commitment. The winters can be bleak. But Grand Mananers are a special breed, and it seems that the Normandeaus are fitting in beautifully.

Shorecrest is an inn on its way up. Don't expect glamour at Shorecrest, just genuine Maritime hospitality. They have recently renovated to add private bathrooms to all 13 bedrooms.

New gardens yield much of their fresh summer produce and what they can't grow they purchase from other Grand Mananers. They are known for their scallops, which are broiled or barbecued with a little lemon butter, thyme, and basil. A frying pan is purely decorative at Shorecrest because they are attempting to focus on healthier methods of food preparation. When the menu reads "catch of the day," that's what it means. Local fishermen provide fresh halibut, pollock, and salmon that Andy grills outdoors and serves on a tarragon/lemon salsa. Once a week, Andy's Mysterious Barbecued Chicken attracts a good local clientele. The marinade, in which the chicken is soaked for several days, is a well-guarded secret. On Saturdays fresh Fundy lobsters are boiled. Though the inn's most expensive meal, at just over $20 per person in-

cluding tax, it's one of the bargains of the island. Wild blackberries and the small wild blueberries that grow all over the island find their way into deep pies.

The Normandeaus can arrange whale- and bird-watching tours with Preston Wilcox, a man about whom Andy can't say enough good things. Wilcox, a lobster fisherman in winter, has access to Machias Seal Island, where colonies of puffins, razorbill auks, and Arctic terns nest. The inn provides the lunch and the captain provides the rest. After the two-hour voyage, you'll reach duck blinds, which allow close observation of the birds. Walking trails skirt the island.

The chances of seeing a whale on the journey to and from Machias are quite good. As a local, Wilcox knows where the endangered right whales feed and mate. Humpbacks and fin whales are the most common sightings.

***

Shorecrest Lodge is located on Grand Manan Island, a two-hour car-ferry ride from Black's Harbour, south of Saint John. The ferry docks in North Head and the inn is about ½ mile (800 m) from the terminal. For ferry information, call the inn or Tourism New Brunswick tel. 800/561–0123 (from Canada/continental U.S.) or 800/442–4442 (from N.B.).

Address: *Box 88, North Head, Grand Manan, N.B. E0G 2M0, tel. 506/662-3216.*
Amenities: *A homemade buffet breakfast is included in the rates. Special dietary requests can be handled with advance notice. Meetings and workshops for up to 20 people are regularly held at the inn.*
Rates: *$55 single, $65 double (excluding tax). Off-season rates available. The seventh night is free. V.*
Restrictions: *No pets during the summer. Pets allowed during off-season with advance notice. No smoking in dining room or guest rooms. Working on wheelchair accessibility. Call ahead to confirm. Closed Jan.–Apr.*

The Eastern Coast
Quaco Inn

Originally named Quaco, meaning "home of the hooded seal," the village of St. Martins, east of Saint John, had a huge shipbuilding industry. At the turn of the century, the stony beach had as many as 126 ships drawn up beyond the tide line in various stages of construction. But with the advent of steam and the scarcity of tall trees for masts, this style of shipbuilding vanished, leaving only memories in the minds of some very old people and some albums of yellowing photographs.

Quaco Inn was originally the home of the Skillen family, local merchants. When innkeeper Marilyn Jackson purchased it, she was delighted that the villagers brought back bits of memorabilia that had been scattered throughout the hamlet. Old pictures reappeared with neighbors who came over for a cup of tea and a few of Marilyn's ginger-spice cookies.

In thanks, she named each room of the inn after people who lived in the community. The Brown room was named for the youngest St. Martins' man to receive his captain's papers. He eventually died in Russia after a colorful career. The Carson Room is for a man who was born in Italy and traveled to Ireland, where he married well. The story has it that he then stole the family jewels, shortened his name, and came to the village without a history. The Parker room was named after "Painless" Parker, the village's first dentist. Mathias Moran changed the name of the village, then known as Quaco (pronounced quack-oh), to St. Martins in honor of his ancestral home in the Alsace region of France. Appropriately, the Skillen room has the best view. The Vaughan room, named after a family that had a fleet of sailing vessels, is the most luxurious, with a white eyelet covering the king-size bed, a fireplace and a bay window overlooking the shore. All seven have private baths.

Marilyn specializes in outdoor adventures and great country cooking. Before a day of hiking into the wilderness, adventurers tuck into a hearty breakfast of oatmeal topped with blueberries or an omelet served with smoked trout. Rum-spiked French toast is served with New Brunswick maple syrup. A bowl of dried dulse, the seaweed that is harvested around the Bay of Fundy, is always on the table. Muffins are hot from the kitchen.

After returning ravenous, day-trippers can feast on Atlantic salmon served with an old-fashioned lemon sauce. Although this is still the most popular item on the menu, a traditional roast chicken dinner with cranberries, squash, mashed potatoes, and gravy is a close second. Every Saturday night they have a lobster boil, where 1½- to 3-pounders (.7 to 1.4 kg) find their way into the pot. Served with drawn butter, the lobsters are accompanied with side salads, deviled eggs, and homemade rolls. And speaking of salads, all the lettuces are organically grown.

The inn's food is country gourmet at its best. Guests often see one of the cooks or Marilyn herself running to the garden to pick fresh rhubarb for the strawberry/rhubarb pies, to dig some potatoes, to gather fresh green beans, or to pull some carrots.

In the late summer, hikers often find chanterelles, which the inn's kitchen will cook for them as a special treat.

Desserts are as comforting as the main dishes. Banana layer cake with cream-cheese icing is delicious, and there is usually a fresh fruit crisp.

Full bar service is offered, with a selection of French wines and top-of-the-line liquor.

The other half of life at Quaco is hiking and climbing. As a partner in East Coast Expeditions, Marilyn sets up adventures that can last up to four days and challenge everyone from the beginner to the seasoned veteran who is in above-average physical condition. Some of the hikes are led by botanist Donna Crossland, while others are guided by Marilyn's partner, mountaineer Paul Fenton. There are day trips or overnighters in which the comfortable four-posters of the Quaco are exchanged for a blanket of stars. These longer hikes probe the coastal wilderness and can take you into Fundy National Park.

Both rock-climbing and ice-climbing on frozen waterfalls are taught over various weekends.

The village of St. Martins is very quiet. The two centers of activity seem to be the post office and the picturesque wharf with its covered bridge. The lighthouse is the location of the heritage garden, where members of the community have planted traditional flowers in turn-of-the-century beds. When mature, these perennials will be divided among the village gardens to help create an old-fashioned atmosphere.

A new salmon ladder has been built with an observation room inside the dam where visitors can watch salmon migrating upstream in the spring.

A little beyond the lighthouse are the sea caves formed by the tremendous Fundy tides. There, at Hutges Diner, you can sample the chowder, which is given a standing ovation by the local populace.

***

Quaco Inn is 18 miles (29 km) from the Saint John airport, 28 miles (45 km) from Sussex and 95 miles (153 km) from Calais, Maine. From Saint John take Route 111 to Whitney Corner. Turn left; proceed to St. Martins. Turn right off Main Street onto Beach Street. The inn is at the end of the street on the right.

Address: *Beach St., St. Martins, N.B. E0G 2Z0, tel. 506/833-4772, fax 506/833-2531. European Plan. A full breakfast is a nominal $5. Special diets can be handled with advance notice. Meetings may be held in the dining room or in the board room located in the Carriage House, where climbing/hiking seminars are held. Capacity is 20 people.*
Rates: *Rooms: double $55-$65; suites: double $80. Special-occasion packages available. MC, V.*
Restrictions: *No pets allowed. The property is entirely nonsmoking. Closed for two weeks at Christmas and four days at Easter. Dinner is by reservation.*

The Saint John River Valley
Shadow Lawn Country Inn

Awinding, tree-lined road that follows the course of the Saint John River leads to Shadow Lawn in Rothesay. The beautiful 19th-century mansions along the way speak of an era that is fast disappearing. However, the town is in reality a wealthy bedroom community for the city of Saint John.

Shadow Lawn is one of those stately homes, built in the 1880s by James Robertson, the founder and president of the largest department store in Saint John. This huge, then-pillared manor was built as a summer home and named Karslie, after a battle that occurred during the Crimean War and made Robertson's uncle a hero.

Although not as ornate and pompous as it must have been in Robertson's day, Shadow Lawn's architecture and interior are still quite impressive. The shaded garden has been the scene of many weddings. The rich woodwork inside glows with the patina of age.

The hospitality is gracious and professional. Seven of the clean and airy bedrooms have *en suite* baths; the eighth has its own private bath, which is a short journey down the hall. Best in the house is a beautiful suite with high windows ready to be thrown open to catch the valley's breezes, a working fireplace, and a most comfortable bed. Unfortu-

nately, the dining room cannot be recommended. But since Saint John is so close, a traveler has other options.

On June 24, 1604, Champlain arrived at the mouth of the wide river spilling into the Bay of Fundy. It was the Feast of St. John, so he named the river in honor of that revered saint. Saint John, like so many East Coast port towns, was settled by the Scots, the English, and a great number of Loyalist families.

Travelers to the city should make a special point of visiting the city center and its refurbished Market Square. Like Halifax's Historic Properties, this area has been restored to house indoor and outdoor shopping facilities, a conference center and the Old City Market, the oldest and one of the best farmers' markets in eastern Canada. At the market, held Mondays–Saturdays all year round, you will find all sorts of edible treasures. In the spring watch for fiddleheads, the tightly clenched fronds of the ostrich fern. In late March, New Brunswick maple syrup starts to appear. Cheeses, seafood, fresh blueberries, crunchy apples, jams, jellies, and homemade vinegars can be found at market in their seasons. It's the best place in the area to collect ingredients for an inexpensive, truly gourmet picnic lunch.

***

Shadow Lawn Country Inn may be reached by following Route 1 north of Saint John to Rothesay. The Saint John airport is about six miles (10 km) east of Rothesay.

Address: *3180 Rothesay Rd., Box 41, Rothesay, N.B. E0G 2W0, tel. 506/847-7539, fax 506/849-9238.*
Amenities: *European Plan, but breakfast is available. Special diets are difficult, "but we try." Meeting facilities for 20–25 people.*
Rates: *$59–$89 for suite with fireplace. MC, V.*
Restrictions: *Pets are fine with advance notice. No smoking allowed in dining room, but fine in lounge. Not wheelchair accessible. Dining room closed Sun.*

The Steamers Stop Inn

Thehe open veranda beckons boaters to dock and stay for a while at the inn. In the 1800s, steamers plied the Saint John River with passengers and cargo. Now it's pleasure cruisers that sail the wide waterway for days or weeks at a time. The depth is 10 feet (3 m) or more next to the wharf, so virtually any size of craft can tie up for the night.

The Steamers Stop Inn will be almost 90 years old this year. It stretches along the green riverbank. Its seven rooms, furnished with antiques, share three bathrooms. It is quite Victorian.

Innkeepers Vic and Pat Stewart have roots that are deep in the province's history. Their family has been "on the river" for six generations. Pat's maternal heritage goes back to the time when Indians were still hostile. The inn's dining room reflects her culinary heritage, and you will find, tucked in among the more standard offerings, dishes like scalloped tomatoes, chicken and dumplings, lobster rolls, and fiddlehead soup. Every now and then, Pat offers a buffet featuring molasses-baked beans and homemade brown bread. There is always a seafood casserole, fresh salmon from Black's Harbour, and, in fiddlehead season, the traditional accompaniment, baked shad with bread-and-butter stuffing. Real gingerbread and whipped cream are dished up for dessert. And in season there's honest-to-goodness strawber-ry shortcake, with rich, fresh biscuits split and filled with sliced berries and sweetened cream.

Local beer brewed near Moncton is about the only regional beverage on their list. New Brunswick has no commercial wineries or cideries to date.

The Saint John River was the commercial highway of New Brunswick for a century. Gagetown, originally known as Grimross ("place of settlement" in the Malaseet Indian language), is a community that time seems to have passed by. The oldest trading post on the river is now the home of the Loomcrofters, weavers of international renown and creators of both the New Brunswick and the Royal Canadian Air Force tartans. The building (circa 1761) was used for trade with the Indians. Look carefully, because names and dates have been scratched on the inner walls ever since. The studio is open daily from May through October. The rest of the year, visits can be arranged by appointment (tel. 506/488–2400).

In June, there is a superb crafts show where dozens of local artisans sell their wares. Boats may be rented in Gagetown, and fishing for trout and bass in local streams is good. The area is ripe for exploring and puttering about. Ferries crisscross the river, and every now and then a paddlewheeler, the *Pioneer*

Princess, makes the trip from Fredericton to Gagetown and back.

The quiet, traffic-free roads of this area seem to be made for cycling. At the moment, though, guests need to bring their own bikes. The inn will pack a picnic lunch, so that all the extra equipment that is needed may be a backpack.

***

The Steamers Stop Inn is 65 miles (105 km) northwest of Saint John and 32 miles (51 km) southeast of Fredericton. Take Route 102, the scenic river drive to Gagetown, and head toward the center of the village. The inn is at its heart.

Address: *Box 155, Gagetown, N.B. E0G 1V0, tel. 506/488–2903.*
Amenities: *European Plan. Some dietary restrictions can be handled with advance notice. Small meetings can be accommodated. Smoking allowed.*
Rates: *$50 single, excluding taxes, $55 double, $58 twin. $10 per extra person. Full breakfast $4.80 per person. MC, V.*
Restrictions: *No pets. Dining room and main floor have limited wheelchair accessibility; guest rooms have none. Closed Sept.–May, but open on weekends in May and Sept. and for Thanksgiving and Christmas dinners.*

The Northern Coast
Heron Country Inn

On the Baie des Chaleurs, two Acadian women, Maria Doucet and Marie Boulay, have opened an inn that reflects the lifestyle of these hardworking people. A large, painted clapboard structure, which in a former life was a United Church manse, is surrounded by an expansive lawn with Heron Island in the sometimes misty distance.

The inn itself is serviceable and clean, with polished hardwood floors and crisp linen on the tables. Up the wide staircase, the guest rooms are spotless but share common bathrooms. Meticulous housekeeping is evident everywhere. The inn is a convenient spot to stop for the night. The women make great pickled herring and substantial Acadian dishes like *chaudrée aux coques* (clam chowder) and *pâté au poulet* (chicken pie). Both Baie des Chaleur lobster and the famous Restigouche salmon are prepared in season. The warm and friendly dining room is well patronized by the locals, a sign of longstanding service and quality. A full breakfast, homemade from the jam to the bread for the toast, is included in the room rate.

Heron Island has an interesting history. It was an ancient Micmac Indian burial ground. European fishermen arrived in the area around 1500, when an unscrupulous Portuguese captured a number of Micmac

from the Gaspé and returned them to Europe as slaves. The following year, he decided to give a repeat performance at Heron Island. There, his crew was murdered and the Micmacs roped the scoundrel to a rock to let the tide slowly drown him. A search party, organized by his brother, appeared on the horizon the following year. Ambushed and burned by the Micmac, the flaming ship is said to still be seen in the eye of the fierce storms on the bay.

By 1842 there were 46 permanent settlers on Heron Island. Their main crops were potatoes and eel grass, which was used as furniture stuffing and insulation. Cruises can be taken over what was once called "the sea of fish" to the island where there are miles of secluded sandy beaches, well known for their clam-digging. It's a haven for bird-watchers, and for photographers who want to spend a day poking around the abandoned house sites and ancient rusted machinery.

Activities for the traveler in the immediate vicinity are pretty low-key, and the rooms of the inn are not particularly conducive to lying about in, although the new library is quite comfortable. Stroll down to the wharf, where kids and adults are fishing, or if you don't mind a little drive (it's about 60 miles/100 km), you can make a day visit to the excellent Village Historique Acadien outside Caraquet. This village is an authentic reproduction of French life in early New Brunswick, complete with a small restaurant and a bookstore. Try to take the road that winds along the bay. Away from the faster Route 11, you will see the beauty of "L'Acadie," its proud little painted houses with their tricolors flapping in the ocean breezes. Have a meal at Chez Paulin, in Caraquet, or La Poisonnière, at Grand Anse. Both are excellent.

In the other direction, you can enter Quebec and fish or sightsee across the Gaspé peninsula in about half a day, heading toward the glory of the inns of either the Charlevoix or the Montmagny areas.

***

Heron Country Inn in New Mills is about 40 miles (65 km) from the Quebec border at Matapédia on the southern shore of the Gaspé peninsula. It is about the same distance from Bathurst, N.B. Bathurst is 157 miles (253 km) from the capital city, Fredericton. Take Route 11 or Route 134 west of Bathurst. Just after the two highways combine, you will reach New Mills.

Address: *Site 13, Box 10, New Mills, N.B. E0B 1M0, tel. 506/237-5306 (summer) or 506/684-2816 (winter).*
Amenities: *A full breakfast is included. Special diets can be accommodated, but advance notice is appreciated.*
Rates: *1 bed/one person $34; 2 large beds/two people $55; 1 double bed/two people $50.50. Additional person $8.50. G.S.T. included but provincial taxes are not included. MC, V.*
Restrictions: *No pets. The inn is not wheelchair accessible, but if called ahead, the innkeepers will arrange to have strong arms available. No guest rooms are accessible. The enclosed balcony and one of*

the dining rooms are set aside for smoking. Closed mid-Oct.–Apr.

Quebec

Quebec

Quebec, a colorful collection of regions as varied as any in the country, brackets the mighty St. Lawrence River. Rolling farmlands, remnants of the days of the seigneuries, sweep down to the river, which is liberally dotted with pastoral islands and rural fishing villages. The granite of the Canadian Shield, the oldest geological formation in North America, lies brooding under the Laurentian Highlands.

Quebec's utter charm radiates from its people and their willingness to enjoy life. From the cosmopolitan atmosphere of Montreal, where art and sports in all their forms are queen and king, to the lively Laurentians, and from the undulating green hills and pristine lakes of the Eastern Townships to the plunging cliffs of the Charlevoix, the province is delightfully reminiscent of Europe.

Jacques Cartier landed on the Gaspé in 1534, but it wasn't until the early 1600s that the fur traders, missionaries, and explorers paddled upriver to establish settlements. Tossed back and forth between the English and the French, the region experienced many struggles for supremacy.

Quebec is Canada's only truly French province. Its culture has been passionately defended over the years. It's little wonder that even the license plates bear the slogan Je me souviens *(I remember).*

No season has affected the face of the province more than winter. When the upper classes abandoned their lands and headed back to France after British rule began in 1763, those Québécois (Quebeckers) who were left had to dig in and survive throughout this harshest of seasons. The settlers clothed themselves in furs and leather. They hunted, fished, and farmed. When the roads were clogged deep with snow, they took to the frozen rivers and lakes. The natives showed them how to use snowshoes, and as

early as 1664 they were using tobaggans to transport their
goods. It is little wonder that it was a Quebecker who
invented the snowmobile.

The foods of the province reflect the winter as well. Many of
the dishes hark back to medieval France. In Quebec they
formed the basis of a hearty cuisine, one on which
lumberjacks and fishermen could thrive. Julian Armstrong,
the food editor of the Montreal Gazette, the province's
largest English-language newspaper, has written the best
book in recent times on the foodways of her province.
Titled A Taste of Quebec, it is available throughout the
region and in many bookstores across Canada.

Quebec is known for its outdoor winter sports. The skiing
is exceptional from Mont Tremblant in the northern
Laurentians to Le Massif, the undeveloped mountain in the
Charlevoix where skiers are transported to the top by bus
to ski slopes covered with only natural snow. The province's
snowmobile trail system is the best in Canada. The wide,
well-marked tracks link small villages and towns, where
travelers can stay and eat or have their machines serviced.
Guidebooks are available for each region. Dogsledding,
cross-country skiing, and ice fishing are all enjoyed by
residents and tourists alike.

In summer there is something for everyone: from the gentle
joy of watching whales feeding in the St. Lawrence to the
more strenuous thrill of rafting on the Rouge River. There
are magnificent formal gardens and parks that stretch for
thousands of square miles into the lake-dotted wilderness.
Summer theaters, mainly performing in French, are
scattered throughout the province. And, like Nova Scotia,
there are festivals celebrating everything from blueberries
to caplan (a small fish).

***

For information call or write: **Tourisme Québec,** C.P.
200000, Quebec City, Quebec G1K 7X2, tel. 800/363-7777,
(toll-free from Canada and the U.S.).

Greater Montreal Tourism and Convention Bureau, *1555 Peel St., Suite 600, Montreal, Que. H3A 1X6, tel. 514/844-5400.*

Quebec City Region Tourism and Convention Bureau, *399, rue St-Joseph est, Quebec City, Que. G1K 8E2, tel. 418/522-3511.*

Iles de la Madeleine
Au Vieux Couvent

Jagged crescents of sand appear to float on the St. Lawrence River between the coasts of Quebec and Prince Edward Island. The Îles de la Madeleine (Magdalen Islands) are a string of 12 fragile, low islands, ruffled with dunes and red cliffs and connected by sandbars.

The population of 15,000 is mainly descended from the shipwrecked sailors and Acadians expelled from other Maritime areas in the 1700s. "Madelinots," they call themselves.

Au Vieux Couvent will send anyone who has ever attended a Roman Catholic convent school back in time. Constructed close to the beach at Havre-aux-Maisons in 1917, it has changed its habit for a dance dress. The chapel was converted into the dining room, and the classrooms were made into 10 comfortable guest rooms complete with quilts, antiques, and private baths. A light Continental breakfast of café au lait, croissant, and jam is included with the room. The mother superior's room, with its private parlor, is now a summery café, La Terrasse Rest-O-Bar, that overlooks the Gulf of St. Lawrence. The inn's other bar, Chez Gasparo, features live entertainment all summer long.

The inn's main restaurant, the one in the chapel, is called La Moulière. It's specialty is mussels—served in a variety of mouth-watering ways. They may be steamed in white wine and perfumed with orange rind and Grand Marnier, or they may be in combination with other fresh fish, straight from the ocean. For purists there is the classic *moules et frites*.

The wines, beers, and spirits are "selected religiously."

Brief mention should be made of the other restaurants on the islands. They are extraordinarily good. La Table des Roy, on Île du Cap-aux-Meules; La Saline, in La Grave; and Le P'tit Café, in Havre-aux-Maisons, are all worth a trip.

Dozens of shipwrecks surround the islands. It is a scuba diver's heaven. You can not only explore the old ships, but also swim face-to-snout with seals and fish, or look for the odd lucky lobster who has escaped the traps. Air fills, complete rentals for certified divers, classes, and tours are available at the Centre Nautique (tel. 418/937–5266) and at the Centre de Plongée (tel. 418/986–6475). Roads have few hills and even less traffic for cyclists to negotiate. Mountain bikes can be rented for $15–$20 per day at Le Pedalier at Cap-aux-Meules (tel. 418/986–2965).

Swimming is excellent; the Gulf Stream moderates the water temperature to a reasonable 65°F (18°C).

In mid-August of each year, there is a sandcastle-building contest on the Sandy Hook beach near Havre-Aubert. About 60 teams compete to create marvelous structures that are washed away on the incoming tide.

Summer is the time to fly a kite, swim to caves hidden among the shoreline cliffs, sailboard with the champions, or ride a horse on the beach in the golden sunset.

But winter is reserved for one thing—seal watching. In March the ice floes are home to hundreds of harp-seal mothers and pups. Thanks to the world-wide protests, they are now completely protected. Helicopters fly from the main towns on the islands, and guides will show you the way to reach the breathing holes of the seals. If you are careful not to get between the mother and her pup, you can hold the white fur-ball in your arms.

***

Au Vieux Couvent is on Highway 199, in Havre-aux-Maisons. The Îles de la Madeleine may be reached by car ferry from Souris, P.E.I., or by Air Canada connector flight from Montreal. For information, contact: 800/363–7777.

Address: *C.P. 497, Havre-aux-Maisons, Îles de la Madeleine, Que. G0B 1K0, tel. 418/969–2233.*
Amenities: *Breakfast is included. No meeting facilities. There are no nonsmoking regulations.*
Rates: *Double $35–$65, excluding tax. V.*
Restrictions: *No pets. Special diets may be a problem. The inn is not wheelchair accessible. Closed mid–Sept.–mid–May.*

The Charlevoix
L'Été

L'Été, which simply means "summer," is another of the small gems that consistently surface in the Charlevoix region! Madame Desgagnés has operated the homey *auberge* for 23 years. Her son, Gérald, is taking over more and more and continues the family devotion to fine food and good service. It is open only during the summer season, when the gardens are in full bloom and the long languorous evenings illuminate the dining room until the candles are lighted.

Regional, seasonal food is uppermost on the menu, but French wines show prominently on the Carte du Vin. Since the table d'hôte changes daily, it is difficult to say what specialties might be available when you arrive. Some recent dishes are *pétoncles "vapeur" fleur de courgette* (scallops steamed in a squash blossom); *lapin rôti au* Pineau des Charentes (roasted rabbit in wine sauce made with Pineau des Charentes; *steak au caribou aux bleuets et poivre* (caribou steak with the famous Charlevoix blueberries and peppercorns); and a marvelous variety of dishes based on fresh fish like salmon and flounder, and on shellfish like lobster. The dessert list is sumptuous. It may begin with their version of Quebec's best loved treat, *tarte au sucre* (sugar pie), and continue with homemade frozen fruit yogurt and *gâteau aux amandes* (almond cake). Or, it may be as simple as a bowl of just-picked blueberries with cream, or as decadent as a chocolate *genoise*.

The accompanying wine list is heavily loaded with medium-priced French vintages. An Australian Chardonnay and a Spanish Rioja are the only other foreign contributions.

The rooms are comfortable, with shared baths—fine for a night or two as a well-centered base for sightseeing.

The village of St-Joseph-de-la-Rive is the jumping-off spot for the sort-of-hourly ferry to L'Île-aux-Coudres (island of hazel trees), named by Jacques Cartier in 1535. It is the only place in the province of Quebec, and perhaps in Canada, where two mills, one powered by wind and the other by water, are side by side. They were built in the early 1800s to grind grain for the local farmers (*insulaires*). They are open to the public on a limited basis but are really worth the trip if you happen to be in the region from mid-May until mid-June or from the end of the first week in September until that same weekend in October. L'Île-aux-Coudres has perfect roads for an afternoon, or even a full day, of cycling. Rentals are available on the island at Vel-"o"-Coudres (tel. 418/438–2118).

Near l'Été, in St-Joseph-de-la-Rive, is the Papeterie Saint Gilles, where paper is made by hand and embellished with maple leaves and wildflowers, which are pressed into rustic-looking sheets.

***

L'Été may be reached by journeying east of Quebec City to Baie St-Paul. Continue along Highway 362 and, at the village called Les Éboulements, turn toward St-Joseph-de-la-Rive and Île-aux-Coudres.

Address: *589, chemin du Quai, St-Joseph-de-la-Rive, Cté Charlevoix, Que. G0A 3Y0, tel. 418/635–2873.*
Amenities: *Modified American Plan. Special diets can be arranged*

*ahead of time. Small meetings
could be held in an intimate pavil-
lon for about 10 people. No smok-
ing restrictions.*
Rates: *$85–$125 per person, depend-
ing on style of room. MC, V.*
Restrictions: *Not suitable for pets.
Not wheelchair accessible. Closed
Canadian Thanksgiving (Oct.) until
Queen Victoria Day/Fête de la
Reine (May 24 weekend).*

Auberge des Falaises

Auberge des Falaises seems almost chiseled into the hillside above Point-au-Pic. The view of the mountains is the best in the Charlevoix. The auberge was built in 1885 as the summer residence of an American, and its history is dotted with stays by well-known Quebeckers, including an ex-mayor of Quebec City. Denys Cloutier purchased the inn in 1983 and since then has renovated and added a pavilion. Each guest room has its own balcony (three of them are 40 feet (12 m) long) overlooking the river that flows below. These three deluxe suites have two bedrooms each, with a bath, a kitchen, a gracious salon with dining area, and a fireplace. It's a home away from home. The other suites, all with more than 400 square feet (3,700 square decimeters) of living area, are also quite spiffy.

The French chef, Régis Hervé, is a mycologist: When the wild mushrooms start popping up throughout the forests of the Charlevoix, it is to him that other chefs turn for their identification. He carefully harvests them to treat the taste buds of the diners at Auberge des Falaises. Little wonder that even on weeknights the dining room is often full. Régis loves the outdoors, and because he also loves to cook, his knowledge of the wild edibles that inhabit this rich region is extensive. *L'ail du bois* (wild garlic), *raisins sauvages* (wild grapes), rose petals from bushes that bloom in late August's hedgerows, and even cedar branches find their way into his kitchen.

Innkeeper Cloutier has encouraged his innovative chef by engineering, on the hillside above the inn, a little smokehouse in which fresh trout are cold-smoked over whatever wood Herve thinks suits the product.

The inn's recreation facilities include a heated pool, which is perched on the hill overseeing the area, and a badminton court. A thalassotherapy spa nearby offers four-day programs in cooperation with the inn. A special menu is in place in the dining room, and by the end of four days, the guarantee that the client will "feel like a new person" seems to have been an honest one.

* * *

Auberge des Falaises is in Pointe-au-Pic and may be reached by following Route 132 east of Quebec City on the north shore of the St. Lawrence. At Baie-St-Paul, take Route 362. At Côte Bellevue, turn left and continue to chemin des Falaises.

Address: *18, chemin des Falaises, Pointe-au-Pic, Que. G0T 1M0, tel. 418/665-3731, fax 418/665-6194*
Amenities: *Rates can include breakfast, or guests can request either a Full or Modified American Plan (MAP). Special diets can be handled with prior notice. Three meeting rooms will accommodate up to 30 people. The inn has 12 guest rooms that are wheelchair accessible. There is a nonsmoking section in the dining room.*
Rates: *$88–$125 per person, MAP. AE, EnRoute, MC, V.*
Restrictions: *No pets.*

La Maison Otis

I t's a difficult decision to make. Does one visit La Maison Otis in the warm and glorious summer? Or does one journey there to find a true Quebec winter?

Baie-St-Paul, the town in which the *auberge* is located, is abuzz from May until September with artists from all over the globe. The numerous local galleries are in full dress, and hundreds of fine-art students take part in workshops and seminars at the Canadian young painters' symposium. Baie-St-Paul has attracted great Canadian artists since the 1800s; its powerful scenery at all times of the year drew the likes of Clarence Gagnon and Jean-Paul Lemieux.

The town was built on a sheltered bay where the Gouffre River joins the St. Lawrence. A salmon stream of the first order, the bay has 50 pools registered with the ministry of fish and wildlife. A detailed map, including primary and secondary access roads, is available in Baie-St-Paul from the tourism office. The record Atlantic salmon caught was 26.4 pounds (12 kg), the record rainbow trout 8.8 pounds (4 kg).

The snows of winter begin in late September on Le Massif, a mountain unlike any other in Quebec. This past year there were three feet (1 m) by the first of November. Few know about Le Massif; it is the secret hot spot for lovers of downhill skiing. Part of the reason for its anonymity is that it has no tows. Shuttle buses take a maximum of 350 skiers up to the top of the mountain, which is covered with only natural snow. Skiing therefore is by reservation only. Patrols go with the groups, and the skiing is superb.

La Maison Otis offers transportation directly to the hill—and from it if the skiers ever want to leave. When making a reservation at the inn, ask them to call ahead to the mountain to ensure that there is space for any skiers in your party.

The inn was built between 1840 and 1850. Looking at the thick walled stone and masonry construction, you understand why it took so long. One of the oldest buildings in the town, it was scheduled for demolition when the town council decided a shopping center was needed. Jean-Baptiste Bouchard and Michel Villeneuve refused to let it happen. They purchased the old building, renovated it, and became its innkeepers almost by default.

Their restoration began with the main building, but continued with several other *pavillons,* in one of which Jean-Baptiste has created a marvelous art gallery with reasonably priced works. They built a complete health center that they have leased to Mme Gilbert-Thibeault, a woman who was awarded the Order of Canada for her work in health care. Twenty-three modern guest rooms are housed in the pavillions as are the enclosed swimming pool, the shops, and the conference room.

La Maison Otis has everything one dreams of in an inn from Quebec: wide fireplaces, an excellent dining room, a lively bistro/bar, lots of wood and stone, and a joyful ambience.

Chef Bernard Tapin is an intense, quiet young man who is dedicated to the cuisine of his province.

Breakfast must include *pain doré aux pommes gratinées:* Homemade bread is made into golden French toast. It is then topped with an apple compote and a layer of cheddar cheese, broiled until bubbling, and served with maple syrup.

One of the highlights of the year at the inn is *réveillon*, the traditional celebration before and after midnight Mass on Christmas Eve. The town is decked out in snow (one hopes) and Christmas finery. The church bells peel over the countryside to call the faithful. When the worshipers return, they are greeted by an accordionist and a buffet of the foods that Quebec was nurtured on—thick *tourtière* (the famous spicy meat pie), a rich *râgout de boulettes* (meatball stew), cured ham, and lots of salads. (The latter is a concession made to 20th-century tastes.) A *bûche de Noël* (yule log) is proudly displayed before the revelers dig into their desserts.

While everyone is at Mass, Santa Claus slides down the chimney and into each guest room with stockings full of candy, fruit, and sometimes a toy for those who have been especially good. About 2 A.M. the party winds up, and young and old troop off to bed.

***

La Maison Otis is one hour east of Quebec City on Highway 138. To find the inn, simply head into town and turn left on rue St-Jean-Baptiste.

Address: *23, rue St-Jean-Baptiste, Baie-St-Paul, Que. G0A 1B0, tel. 418/435-2255.*
Amenities: *Modified American Plan. Special diets can be handled if advance notice is provided to the chef. The inn has two meeting rooms that will accommodate up to 40 people with full audiovisual equipment. The inn has eight wheelchair-accessible rooms plus*

the dining room. There is no designated nonsmoking area.
Rates: *single $90–$165 low season, $115–$200 high season; double $140–$200 low season, $156–$220 high season. MC, V.*
Restrictions: *Well-behaved pets are allowed.*

Auberge au Petit Berger

One of the prettiest inns in the Charlevoix is "the inn of the little shepherd." In typical Quebec fashion, it has a wide, welcoming porch and a roofline that swoops to keep the snow from building up too thickly. Given the name, it follows that the specialty in the dining room is the lamb for which the Charlevoix is famous. *L'agneau* is prepared in a multitude of ways by innkeeper Marthe Lemire and her co-chef, Danielle Amyot. These two innovative women are doing a lot of experimental, light cuisine that was inspired by a visit to Michel Guérard's restaurant, Les Prés d'Eugénie, near Bordeaux. Fine cuisine does not have to be heavy and rich. Danielle is definite that food should be prepared without salt, added fat, or extra flour. She believes that it is the essence of the ingredients that should be tasted. Try their inn-smoked leg of lamb on sautéed lettuces and fresh herbs. Four varieties of lettuce, including chicory, are quickly sautéed with fresh sorrel, parsley, and celery leaves. Thin slices of the smoked lamb are arranged, fanlike, over the brightly colored greens. Their classic leg of lamb with fresh juniper berries harks back to olden days in France. Danielle and Marthe also prepare seafood with a gentle touch. Scallops, salmon, and Dover sole grace the table. It's an inspired menu.

At Petit Berger a full health spa has just been added. Jacques Lemire, Marthe's husband and partner, has engineered the development of the $4 million project, which includes the first saltwater *bassin aquatonique* in North America. This relatively shallow pool has both widely varied temperatures (40°F–105°F/4°C–40°C) and water movements that tone the skin and the muscles. Thirty minutes in the pool is sufficient to give an indescribable feeling of well-being.

Swimmers can work out against the current in the *bassin de natation sur place*. The Lemires have even created a program for those who are afraid of the water, so that the various forms of therapy will ultimately be effective.

The knotty-pine-paneled bedrooms have comfortable, duvet-covered beds and private baths. They are restful and quiet; most look out into the trees or over the bay that looms in the distance.

To regenerate and relax, the spa is a perfect place. But unlike at most spas, guests are encouraged to explore the region. It would be a sin not to take full advantage of the outdoors that is so special in the Charlevoix. Bicycles are provided for guests to ride into town or poke down the back roads. A half day can be spent whale watching or simply visiting the ecology center at Port-au-Saumon. There are myriad opportunities.

***

Auberge au Petit Berger may be reached by following Highway 132 east of Quebec City. At Baie-St-Paul, take Highway 362. Before entering Pointe-au-Pic, at the foot of the first hill, turn left and follow the signs.

Address: *C.P. 398, Pointe-au-Pic, Que. G0T 1M0, tel. 418/665-4428.*
Amenities: *Modified American Plan. Special diets pose no problem. Meeting facilities include three rooms that will accommodate up to 75 people. Nineteen rooms are wheelchair accessible. At present, smoking regulations do not exist.*
Rates: *double $160–$210 (tax not included, but service is). Spa treatments are à la carte. AE, MC, V.*
Restrictions: *No pets.*

La Pinsonnière

L a Pinsonnière is perched on a cliff overlooking a rocky beach on the St. Lawrence. Finches, for which the inn is named, dart from tree to tree on the property. Innkeepers Jean and Janine Authier have created an inn that has been on the leading edge of cuisine in Canada for years and will continue to be as long as Jean is able to lift a wineglass or taste a sauce.

Dining is a great event at La Pinsonnière. Menus change daily and seasonally. Chef Dominique Beaussier, from the Loire in France, uses the region's finest and, sometimes, most traditional ingredients. Gourganes, a flat bean that is grown only in this area in Quebec by gardeners who save their seeds from year to year, are made into soups. Charlevoix lamb is prized for its tenderness. *Les perles bleues de Charlevoix* are the tiny wild blueberries that grow in the rocky highlands and really can be likened to pearls. Wild mushrooms, maple syrup, and cheeses come from Quebec; the seafood, from the lower St. Lawrence.

The Authiers collect two things— fine wines and great art. Jean is a member of seven wine societies, and his collection of great vintages is stored in his new central wine cellar, which has a special tasting room that is in use virtually every day. The new cellar gives Jean a marvelous excuse to buy more fine wines. The cave now holds 10,000 carefully chosen bottles. It is for that reason that *The Wine Spectator* has just honored the Authier cellar with their Award of Excellence.

M. Authier and his sommelier, Jean Hudon, head to the wine cellar to lead tastings that last for two hours and are quite technical in structure. They are designed to teach partici-

pants the differences between various grapes, regions, and vintages. An added bonus is that the whole process is very enjoyable, especially when one has to "finish up the bubbles" (between 16 and 20 champagnes are on the list).

The Authiers' art collection graces every nook and cranny of the inn. In the dining room are some extremely valuable paintings by René Richard and Bruno Coté. In the foyer, others are even for sale.

The *auberge*'s 28 guest rooms reflect a peaceful elegance. Each suite is decorated individually, from *grand luxe* (with a salon in the inn's turret, a whirlpool, and a huge brass bed) to a room of delicate simplicity. Guests can light the fire that is already set up, put on their soft terry bathrobes, and turn up the music—life really can be sweet.

There are many common areas where guests can relax, including the deck beside the indoor swimming pool. The Authiers have just opened a riding academy located on a farm only three miles (five km) from the inn. It is the sole equestrian center in the area and specializes in English-style horsemanship.

Near La Pinsonnière is one of Canada's most private gardens, Les Quatre Vents. For owner Francis H. Cabot, it represents over six decades of dedication to horticulture. From spring until late autumn, it is filled with blossoms. Hundreds of multicolored crocuses bravely push up through the spring snow. The parade continues until the final leaves touch the ground in autumn. On five well-spaced days, from late spring until summer, the garden is open to the public. Guides explain the plantings, the sources of some of the plant ma-

terial, and the ongoing development
of new gardens. A very limited number of tickets are sold on a first-
come basis. Jean Authier has access
to some of those spaces and will
make them available to his guests.

La Pinsonnière is an elegant base
for the other adventures that make
the Charlevoix so exciting for travelers: whale watching on the Saguenay; golf on two courses that
overlook the St. Lawrence; nature
hikes through the wilderness of Les
Palissandes, near St-Siméon; cruises
up the Malbaie River to the Haute
Gorges, the highest cliffs east of the
Canadian Rockies; troutfishing; and
superb alpine and cross-country skiing.

***

La Pinsonnière is in Cap-à-l'Aigle,
east of Quebec City. Drive 93 miles
(150 km) east on Highway 138, past
La Malbaie. It may also be reached
by ferry from Rivière-du-Loup,
which crosses the river to St-Siméon.
Travel west on Highway 138 for
about one hour.

Address: *124, St-Raphael, Cap-à-
l'Aigle, Que. G0T 1B0, tel. 418/665–
4431, fax 418/665–7156.*
Amenities: *Modified American
Plan. Special dietary requests can
be handled. Three meeting rooms
are available for conferences.*
Rates: *MAP, including service, excluding tax: $99.75–$170 per person. Additional person $87.75.
Children under 10 are $67.75/night
if sharing room with parents. Special packages available. MC, V.*
Restrictions: *No pets. Not wheelchair accessible. No pipe or cigar
smoking is allowed in the dining
room.*

Auberge des Peupliers

No other *auberge* in the Charlevoix has the lengthy history of Peupliers. It was founded more than a century ago by the grandparents of the present innkeeper, Ferdinand Tremblay, who today shares the daily chores with his niece, Anne Rochette. It began as a *pension* (boardinghouse) in the days of the *bateaux blancs*—the white boats that brought tourists from the United States and Montreal to the Charlevoix for the summer. It was an opportunity for the residents of the region to make a little extra money. Ursule Tremblay cooked from morning until night. Her husband, Henri, and their children slept in the bar so the guests could sleep in the house. People kept coming back because of her reputation as a fine country cook. It's said that her roast chicken and homemade ice cream would tempt most city folk even today. The inn still makes orange marmalade using Mme Tremblay's recipe.

In 1973, Ferdinand returned to the *auberge* to carry on the tradition after his mother's death. He and his sister, Georgette, did everything. Ferdinand was always the last to bed and the first to rise.

In 1974, when the nearby ski hill, Mont Grands Fonds, opened, it became obvious that the inn had to be open year-round. New rooms were added, local artisans were commissioned to build furniture, and a whirlpool/sauna area was completed. A tennis court was laid out so that players could enjoy the magnificent view of the river and the hills plunging into it, even if they were losing their games. Soon it was clear not only that the dining room had to be enlarged, but also that more help was needed in the kitchen. Chef Dominque Truchon has been with Peupliers ever since. This young, locally born man has brought the menu closer to today's tastes, but many of the older ingredients are still in place. Wild rabbit and caribou are side by side with Quebec's signature dessert, *tarte au sucre* (sugar pie). Sherbets have replaced Mme Tremblay's ice creams, and *pâté de foie maison* (liver pâté) has made *cretons* (minced pork) move over.

In the Charlevoix, winter, with its huge amounts of snow, and summer, breezy and flower strewn, are equally beautiful—in fact, autumn and spring are wonderful as well. In the winter the Tremblays have provided both downhill and cross-country ski packages in cooperation with Mont Grand Fonds. This area has 88 miles (141 km) of marked, maintained, and patrolled *ski randonnée* (ski-circuit) trails for beginners and experts alike. The runs, which weave their way around lakes and forests, have small, heated huts dotting their length. Four lifts service the 13 alpine slopes, with a vertical drop of 1,000 feet (300 m). Rentals are available there.

Skate, take a sleigh ride, mush
a dog team, or hop aboard
a snowmobile to power along on
some of the best trails in Quebec.

The rest of the year—that is, when
the ice is off the river—there are
croisières baleines (whale-watching
cruises) that can be taken from the
inn. From mid-June until October,
boats of various sizes ferry guests
out into the St. Lawrence to see the
10 different species of whales that
live in the vicinity, especially the
rare and graceful white belugas.
These endangered whales were ex-
tensively hunted, and the population
that at the turn of the century was
5,000 in the St. Lawrence has shrunk
to 350. They are now under attack
not from fishermen who thought the
whales were eating their catch, but
instead from chemical dumps that
range as far upstream as Niagara
Falls, New York. The Institut
d'ecotoxicologie in Rimouski, Quebec, has launched an "adopt
a whale" campaign in an effort to
create a research fund to study and
help the St. Lawrence River belugas.

A roadside park at Pointe-Noire, east
of Cap-à-l'Aigle, overlooks the confluence of the Saguenay and St.
Lawrence rivers. In an earlier time,
fires were lit there to warn sailors of
strong currents and shoals. Today,
the Halte-cotière Pointe-Noire is
home to an exhibit on the St. Lawrence beluga. From this point visitors can see many of the resident
population, often feeding close to
shore.

***

Auberge des Peupliers is a little
east of La Malbaie, in Cap-à-l'Aigle.
From Quebec City, head to Baie-St-
Paul. Continue on Highway 138, or
check your brake linings and head
down Highway 362. Pass Pointe-au-
Pic and follow directions to Cap-à-
l'Aigle and St-Siméon. The inn is on
the north side of the roadway. Note:

The ferry that crosses the St. Lawrence from Rivière-du-Loup arrives
at St-Siméon.

Address: *381, rue St-Raphael, Cap-
à-l'Aigle, Que. G0T 1B0, tel.
418/665-4423. Modified American
Plan. Special diets can be accommodated. No meeting facilities as
such, but small groups could get
together in some of the common
areas that are in the main lodge.
Smoking is allowed throughout the
inn.*
Rates: *Modified American Plan
(dinner, breakfast, room), double
$69–$94 per person, $50 per addi-
tional person. Numerous packages
available for skiing, whale watching, long-term stays. AE, EnRoute,
MC, V.*
Restrictions: *No pets. Not wheelchair accessible. Closed Dec. 24–25
for a family Christmas party.*

Auberge des Sablons

Beside the wide St. Lawrence River, Auberge des Sablons is sheltered by the Charlevoix hills. The sparkling-white clapboard inn with sky-blue shutters was built in 1901 by Joesph Lavergne on a tract of land purchased from Sir Adolphe Basile-Routhier, who wrote the original French words to "O Canada." A close personal friend of Lavergne's, politician Sir Wilfrid Laurier, was Canada's first French-Canadian prime minister. Laurier often recouped his strength here at Sablons, finding the calm and peace that is not part of Ottawa's political reality.

In 1986, the inn was purchased by Jean-Guy and Marielle Alain. Their guests can now experience the comfortable, thoughtful ambience that was part of another era in Charlevoix history. Take summer strolls on the sand beach or simply let your cares vanish in the sun. Golf, croquet, and fishing are all nearby. In the winter there's skiing at Le Massif, an unserviced hill with natural snow—buses get skiers to the top of the marvelous runs. Or you can drive in the opposite direction to Mont Grand Fonds, near La Malbaie. After you've spent an exhilarating winter's day, the fire that crackles in your suite feels particularly wonderful—Laurier never had it so good.

Jean-Guy caused a stir when he rejected the *fourchette* (fork) rating system devised by Tourisme Québec. He awarded his establishment a *cinq cuillères* (five spoons) classification and made sure that all his media connections were aware of it. A lesser man would have failed, but Jean-Guy is straightforward in his approach. He simply doesn't think that the province's system is fair, and his kitchen is certainly attempting to prove him correct. The menu is very good and strives, at least in some measure, to rely on local ingredients. Smoked sturgeon and *éperlans* (smelt) are both served in season. Local veal, rabbit, and pork also appear. Meanwhile, in spite of the kefuffle, he has been the recipient of both the AAA three-diamond award and the Grand Prix du Tourisme Québécois.

The many-windowed dining room overlooks the river, as do 12 of the 15 bedrooms. Six bedrooms have balconies, and all have private bathrooms. The four suites have their own fireplaces and whirlpools. Another very costly but valuable addition to the inn is the newly installed elevator, which makes four rooms wheelchair accessible. It's a real plus for those who are physically challenged. The new fitness room includes both a spa and a sauna for those days when a gallop on the shore is not too appropriate.

Next door to Sablons is a summer music academy, Le Domaine Forget (tel. 418/452–8111). Concerts are held throughout the season, and musicians often find their way into the inn's dining room to accompany the evening meal. In addition to the concert program, summer master classes in music and dance are held.

Auberge des Sablons is a quiet jewel of a place in a region that is as magical as any in Canada.

***

Auberge des Sablons is about 1½ hours east of Quebec City on the north shore of the St. Lawrence. Follow Highway 138 until Baie-St-Paul, then take Highway 362 for about 40 minutes to St-Irénée. The inn is right on the shore.

Address: *223, chemin les Bains, St-Irénée, Charlevoix, Que. G0T 1V0, tel. 418/452-8116, fax 418/452-3240.*
Amenities: *Modified American Plan (MAP) and Bed-and-Breakfast (they call it European Plan) are available. Special diets are available if advance notice given. Space is available for small meetings. Wheelchair accessible. One non-smoking section in dining room.*
Rates: *Include GST and gratuities. Double MAP per person: low season $67.50–$110, high season $77.50–$115. There are also many different special events throughout the year with package rates. EnRoute, MC, V.*
Restrictions: *No pets. Closed Nov.*

Auberge des Trois Canards

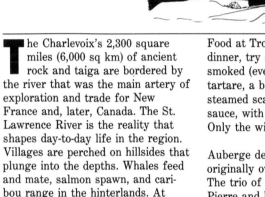

The Charlevoix's 2,300 square miles (6,000 sq km) of ancient rock and taiga are bordered by the river that was the main artery of exploration and trade for New France and, later, Canada. The St. Lawrence River is the reality that shapes day-to-day life in the region. Villages are perched on hillsides that plunge into the depths. Whales feed and mate, salmon spawn, and caribou range in the hinterlands. At Port-au-Saumon is an interpretative center that was established for public education and research. Dry-suit scuba diving is exceptional in the tiny bays and inlets around the center; surprisingly, autumn is the best time.

Autumn is also innkeeper Pierre Marchand's favorite time of the year. The hills are wildly painted in scarlet and orange. Local wild game is on the inn's Quebec-focused menu.

After the beautiful but hair-raising drive along Highway 362 to Trois Canards, a visitor will find the cozy, charming rooms complete with fireplaces a welcome relief. Many of the rooms have views of the spectacular and ever-changing St. Lawrence. Through the curtains it is often possible to see a rainbow spanning the river and touching down just beyond the inn. In the evening, the glassy and silent river provides a base for the starry skies and the coastlines that stretch to the horizon, glittering with chains of light on both sides.

Food at Trois Canards is a treat. For dinner, try a spoonful of home-smoked (everyone's doing it!) salmon tartare, a braid of trout fillet, fresh steamed scallops in a coarse tomato sauce, with Premier Cru Chablis. Only the wine is not from Quebec.

Auberge des Trois Canards was originally owned by three doctors. The trio of "docs" sold the inn to Pierre and his wife, Christiane, but the name stuck—only it became "the three ducks" or *trois canards*. On approaching the inn, travelers are welcomed by a group of jolly wooden revelers—perhaps likenesses of the original owners. The carver, Léon Émond, lives in nearby La Malbaie.

The inn has a spacious living area focused on a floor-to-ceiling fireplace. It's a perfect place for a predinner cocktail. The dining room, in which both breakfast and dinner are served, overlooks the St. Lawrence and, on most nights, is very lively. Quebeckers love a party, no matter what evening of the week.

Winter usually brings huge snow-falls—sometimes as much as 36 inches (1 m) in a week. Groomed snowmobile trails run by the inn, and if you wish they can take you all the way to Montreal, a distance of 251 miles (405 km). In La Malbaie it is possible to rent the machines and all the gear that one needs for some short touring.

In the summertime, the inn has
a pool, a tennis court, a putting
green, and shuffleboard. You can
even partake of an old-fashioned
game of croquet.

***

Auberge des Trois Canards is 1½
hours east of Quebec City via either
Highway 362 or 138. If you take the
former, the inn is on the right-hand
side just as you enter the town. If
you take the latter, you will reach
La Malbaie and then double back on
362 to Pointe-au-Pic. On the way out
of town, the inn is on the left.

Address: *C.P. 70, Pointe-au-Pic,
Que. G0T 1M0, tel. 418/665–3761,
fax 418/665–4727.*
Amenities: *Modified American
Plan. Special dietary requirements
can be handled with at least two
hours' notice. Meeting facilities include two well-equipped conference
rooms with space for up to 80 delegates. Smoking is not allowed in
one section of the dining room.*
Rates: *MAP (excluding tax): single
$95–$205 per person, double $72.50–
$135 per person. All inclusive pack-
ages are available. MC, AE,
EnRoute, V.*
Restrictions: *No pets. Guest rooms
in the inn itself are not wheelchair
accessible, but the 35 rooms of the
adjacent lodge are accessible to
wheelchairs. Closed last two weeks
in Nov.*

The Quebec City Area
Manoir des Érables

It is almost possible to trace the history of the province of Quebec in the past of this gracious old *manoir*. Jacques Cartier sailed past the region's beautiful islands and noted the magnificent surroundings. In 1636, Charles Huault, the Sieur de Montmagny, succeeded Samuel de Champlain as the second governor of New France. In 1646 the French Crown granted him a seigneury that included much of the river, the offshore islands and acres of farmland. In 1655, after the death of Huault, Louis Couillard de l'Espinay acquired the rights to the seigneury on the south shore of the river. Couillard, the son of the first colonist of Quebec City, built himself a manor house on the present site of the inn. A century later, in 1759, it was burned by the English.

At this point another prominent Quebec name entered the picture, Tashereau. Dr. Antoine Tashereau rebuilt the manor between 1812 and 1814.

From then until 1953 it was a private residence. In 1975 the Cyr family purchased it and boldly began to serve *une fine cuisine du Québec.*

Today, one is met at the entranceway by a cannon, which was found on the property and dates from the Anglo-French conflict of the mid-1700s. Gracious gardens and the heavy shade of maple trees give a feeling of tranquillity and calm for which all Relais et Châteaux strive.

The rooms are filled with antiques from various parts of Quebec. Hardwood floors gleam in the bedrooms, and the woodwork and trim that date from the early 1800s is exquisite. In one of the newer rooms (those built since the Cyr family has taken over), there is a private sauna.

The Salon Gérard Delage is named after a friend of the Cyrs who is one of the province's great philanthropists. He created a foundation that provides funds for young Québécois to study both gastronomy and wine in France. Any number of enthusiastic students, among them the Roux sisters from Le Clos Joli (*see* p. 117), have been flown in to attend classes and to fundamentally upgrade the cuisine of their province.

The dining room at Manoir des Érables is legendary. The menus change with the season. You may find small pink shrimps arranged like a tiny bouquet and served with a wild garlic-and-horseradish sauce, a tarragon vinaigrette drizzled over a warm salad of rabbit liver, or smoked trout blessed with a caviar sauce. The specialties of the region include smoked sturgeon from the St. Lawrence River and *magret d'oie* (breast of goose), thinly sliced and served with whatever sauce Chef Cyr determines will balance the rest of the menu. It may be accompanied by crab apples and a sauce made from their vinegar, or it could simply be made with five different peppers. *Têtes de violins* (fiddleheads) are harvested each May in the forests around Montmagny. There is always maple syrup, which finds its way into many dishes, with a favorite their toothsome maple sugar cake.

Like any picky chef, M. Cyr cultivates his own herbs, fruits, and vegetables for the kitchen. In the autumn, as in most typical Canadian kitchens, jams and jellies are made from the year's harvest.

The wine list is carefully chosen by the Cyr family from the principal regions of Europe with some special, and reasonably priced, vintages from Australia and Chile.

The area is renowned for the migration of the snow geese. When the first of the giant birds arrive in October, the Festival de l'Oie Blanche begins. Boats sail to the island to observe the geese in their sanctuary, and the town breaks out in celebration. Special meals featuring goose are served while singers and dancers perform. Hunting is allowed (a license is required) and a guide/outfitter can be found near the town who will arrange such an expedition. Fishing is also available in season.

In the springtime, at Cap St-Ignace, the maple harvest is the center of a sugaring-off party. March and April are the best months to enjoy the flavors of *fèves au lard* (baked beans); *pâté à la viande* (meat pies), homemade ketchup, and bread; thick pea soup; and *grillade de lard salées* (grilled salt pork).

The inn has an outdoor swimming pool and a terrace among the flowers on which guests may relax or dine. An 18-hole golf course is nearby, as are tennis courts and sailboarding. Both cycling and walking in the area are great.

***

Manoir des Érables is east of Quebec City on the south shore of the St. Lawrence River. From Levis, opposite Quebec City, take Highway 20 to Exit 376, at Montmagny.

Address: *Boulevard Taché est, Montmagny, Que. G5V 1G5, tel. 418/248-0100, fax 418/248-9507.*
Amenities: *European Plan or Modified American Plan available. Two small meeting rooms for up to 20 people. Smoking is allowed.*

Rates: *Low season (Nov–Apr.): European Plan (excluding tax), single $50–$95, double $55–95, suite $140; MAP (including dinner, room, breakfast, tax, and service), double $138–$185, suite $218. High season (May–Oct.): European Plan (excluding tax), single $55–$110, double $60–$120, suite $165; MAP (including dinner, room, breakfast, tax and service), double $150–$215, suite $255. AE, DC, MC, V.*
Restrictions: *No pets. No wheelchair accessibility.*

The Wines and Ciders of Quebec

Cider making can be traced back to the monasteries of northwest France. The techniques were brought with the Catholic fathers to the New World. Cider was also prepared on the many farms that, especially in the Eastern Townships, had prolific apple orchards.

Throughout the townships, about 20 growers and vintners are making a range of unusual products. All provide guided tours, tastings, and sales on site. Both dry and sweet honey mead, the oldest of alcoholic drinks, is made by several mead producers located throughout the townships, including Bée Bec at Stanstead and Rucher les Saules at Granby.

The wine industry still depends on French hybrids rather than vinifera. Seyval Blanc, Maréchal Foch, and Chancellor are the most widely planted grapes. It will take time and money before Quebec takes its place among the top wine-producing provinces.

Several wineries are near Auberge Georgeville and the three Massawippi inns: Hovey, Hatley, and Ripplecove. Vignoble le Cep Argent is at Rural Route 5, in Magog. They vinify Seyval Blanc and Maréchal Foch. Vignoble des Cantons is located at Waterloo and produces strawberry, raspberry, and blueberry apéritifs.

The Cidrerie Artisanale Michel Jodoin, in Rougemont, and the monastery at St-Benoît-du-Lac both bottle hard cider.

For more information, contact: **Association Touristique de l'Estrie**, 2883, rue King ouest, Sherbrooke, Que. J1L 1C6, tel. 819/820–2020.

The Eastern Townships
Auberge Georgeville

L'Estrie (the Eastern Townships), in south-central Quebec, is a rambling, hilly part of this many-regioned province. Sheep graze in the meadows, and maple syrup is at its golden best. Farmers who are lucky enough to have a maple bush on their property are much like vintners. They are aware of soil types, exposure, and the mixture of trees that populate their particular stand. Consequently, they make the finest syrup in Canada.

The area was predominately English; indeed, its first name was Buckinghamshire. After the American Revolution, Loyalists settled here and were granted land by the Crown. It became known as the "eastern townships," as opposed to the "western townships" that were to become Upper Canada (later, the province of Ontario). Throughout the 1800s, a flood of French settlement occurred, and now Anglophones represent only 10 percent of the population.

In 1890 a lovely Victorian mansion was constructed on Channel Hill Road, overlooking Lake Mephremagog. Named the Ellabank Hotel, it was a stop on the Boston–Stanstead–Montreal stagecoach line. The municipality of Copp's Ferry was renamed Georgeville in 1822, in honor of the first child born in the settlement, George Fitch Copp. The ferry, for indeed there was one that plied the lake, was propelled by manpower until 1860, when it became steam powered.

More than a century later, in 1986, when Jacques and Monique Morissette purchased the huge old house, it had just gone through a few years of life as a commune.

They set to work opening their inn. Jacques, who had decided that city life no longer agreed with him, became the construction expert, while Monique became the interior decorator and chef.

A wide, graceful porch, so typical of French Canada, opens into the dining room. The dramatic colors of the exterior give way to lace, warm pine, and field flowers. Instantly, a gentle mood washes over those who enter.

The inn has 12 charming bedrooms, with shared baths on each floor.

Monique is an excellent French-Canadian-style cook. From homemade baked beans to *galette de sarassin* (buckwheat pancakes), she reflects the ancient heritage that harks back to the shores of France. In the morning, breakfast consists of crepes or French toast and the marvelous maple syrup of the region. Inn-made bread is toasted and served with another French specialty, *tête du fromage* (headcheese), or *cretons*, a particularly delicious coarse pâté. For the less adventurous, Monique always has an assortment of her homemade jams, jellies, and marmalades on hand.

Monique sincerely specializes in regional cuisine. She shops for her ingredients as close to the inn as possible. An organic farmer grows 11 kinds of lettuce for her, while others produce her beets, mushrooms, carrots, onions, and peppers. Lac Brome is famous for its plump duckling; she serves it with garlic and pears or with black cherries. Her salads are often dressed with a vinaigrette made with a local honey vinegar made in Stanstead. Apples and apple cider from the

monastery at St-Benoît-du-Lac form
a sauce for tender young rabbit.

The same apples are used in
a velvety ginger-and-apple ice cream.
Monique soaks her *baba* in maple
syrup, and her fresh fruit *clafoutis*
have a warm honey sauce.

The wine list is moderately priced,
and the Morissettes try to make as
many half bottles available as possible. The inn is in the center of the
young winemaking industry that has
just begun in earnest in this part of
the province.

Auberge Georgeville has no real recreation facilities, but there is a tremendous amount to do in the area.
Besides antiquing and exploring the
pretty towns of the townships, there
is virtually every activity, from golf
and bird-watching to sailboarding
and parasailing. In the winter the
skiing, both alpine and cross-country,
is superb. Miles of groomed trails,
with some track set, spread from
town to town. Alpine skiing centers
include Mont Orford, near Magog;
Owl's Head, at Mansionville; and
Mont Sutton. For music, there's
opera in Mansionville or Gregorian
chants at the monastery known as
St-Benoît-du-Lac.

Take your pick!

***

Auberge Georgeville may be reached
off Highway 10 by taking Exit 18.
Proceed toward Magog and then
straight to the Georgeville General
Store. Turn left and drive ⅕ mile (³⁄₁₀
km). The entrance is on your right.

Address: *C.P. 17, Georgeville, Que.
J0B 1T0, tel. 819/843-8683.*
Amenities: *Bed-and-Breakfast or
Modified American Plan available.
Special dietary requirements (food
allergies, hypoglycemia) can be ac-
commodated. Meeting facilities for
groups up to eight.*

Rates: *(excluding tax and service)
Bed-and-Breakfast $54 single, $86
double; MAP $79 single, $136 double. Reduced rates for longer stays.
MC, V.*
Restrictions: *No pets. No wheelchair access. Smoking is permitted
in dining room and living room,
not in guest rooms. Closed Nov.–
mid-Dec.*

La Girandole

Dieu a fait l'aliment, le diable l'assaisonnement.
God makes the food; the devil, the seasonings.

***

La table et le lit sont les seules endroits ou l'on ne s'ennuie jamais.
The table and the bed are the only places where one is never bored.

L a Girandole (the chandelier) is down one of the hundreds of backroads in L'Estrie. Located in Bolton Centre, which takes a blink to miss, the small *auberge* has six guest rooms that allow diners who have overindulged to stay for the night. It *is* easy to overindulge.

There are few places in Canada where the rain seems so soft as in L'Estrie. The Girandole sparkles in a summer downpour, but in the winter, plunked halfway between Mont Orford and Owl's Head, it really glows. Mounds of clean snow lie on the spruce trees while Paulette Lepage cooks up a storm of her own inside. She is the daughter of a hotelier and learned to love the business "by osmosis." She became a language teacher. In her spare time Paulette had a catering company in Montreal, but she was drawn back into the hotel business when she met Marcel Breton.

They converted their century-old farmhouse into an auberge with six charming bedrooms in 1987. Marcel's grandfather's bed is in one, his mother's great-aunt's spinning wheel in another. White lace curtains cover the windows, and cinnamon-scented sachets perfume the closets. The wide pine floors are covered with scatter rugs.

The menu changes daily, taking advantage of as many of the fresh and local ingredients as possible. Paulette has a generous hand with spicing, giving her dishes an extra zip. Thin slivers of smoked salmon were tossed into hot fettucini with lots of black pepper, red onion bits, and lemon zest before they were given the blessing of a gurgle of heavy cream. Properly peeled fresh asparagus was steamed, laid in a bed of puff pastry, and finished with the local blue cheese made by the Benedictine monks not two miles (three km) away. The rich *pâté auberge* was garnished with big chive blossoms and onion "jam." Paulette sometimes does a parchment-baked veal, which she serves with a wine sauce and tiny vegetables. She finishes her scallops with hard cider, again made by the neighborhood monks.

After they've had dinner, a lighted path allows guests to stroll the small yard at night. "It keeps them off the road—people down here drive like hell," says Marcel honestly.

On warm summer mornings breakfast is served on the terrace, with an audience of friendly cows chewing along with you. Homemade jams, stewed rhubarb, juices, mild cheddar, and muffins or croissants start the day on the right note.

For a special treat, try the inn's famous Saint Valentine's Day dinner, which is composed completely of aphrodisiacs. Paulette and Marcel sacrifice hours, indeed days, to research, develop, and test (!) the recipes for their once-a-year frolic. Lovers come from far and near to succumb to the siren song and partake in their *souper d'un diable amoureux*.

No visit to the Eastern Townships is complete without a tour of St-Benoît-du-Lac, the Benedictine monastery named after Saint Benedict, who died 14 centuries ago, in A.D. 547. The spires rise through the forests, beside the lake where silence reigns. The industrious monks have supplemented their income by making and selling chocolate, various high-quality cheeses, aged cider, and religious memorabilia.

***

La Girandole is one hour from Montreal and 30 minutes from the U.S. border in Vermont. From North Troy, Vermont, head toward Mansonville, then take Highway 243 to South Bolton. Take Highway 245 to Bolton Centre. From Montreal, take Highway 10 to the Eastman/Bolton Centre exit.

Address: *Rte. 245, Bolton Centre, Que. J0E 1E0, tel. 514/292-5070.*
Amenities: *Modified American Plan. Vegetarian diets can be handled. Small meetings for up to 12 may be held in the new living area. One room on the ground floor is wheelchair accessible. No nonsmoking regulations.*
Rates: *MAP $65-$80 per person. MC, V.*
Restrictions: *No pets. Closed Nov.–mid-Dec.*

Auberge Hatley

The words "The Art of Hospitality" appear on Auberge Hatley's brochure. This description fits perfectly. As the Canadian president of the French-based Relais et Châteaux, Robert Gagnon, with his partner and wife, Liliane, have created an inn that lives up to that organization's philosophy, which embraces both refinement and charm. (Indeed, Auberge Hatley's guests are pampered and spoiled.)

Robert and Liliane are native-born Québécois, and when one speaks to them, it is very clear how much they love their province. Robert becomes animated when describing the marvels of L'Estrie—his hands move in time with his words. He advises guests that the Jeannine Blais Gallery has the best collection of primitive art in the province, where the best buys in antiques can often be had, what special ingredients his kitchen uses, etc. He's enthusiastic and genuine.

In 1990 the *auberge* opened a hydroponic greenhouse that is now the winter source for lettuces like mache and oakleaf. Twenty-five other fine herbs are being grown so that, even deep in winter, fresh greens are available. Guests who are interested can arrange to have lunch at the greenhouse/farm. Other picnics include one on a little island in Lake Mephremagog.

Dinner is an event at Auberge Hatley! The dining room, which has won many awards, is set with fine crystal and lighted by candles. The tables are draped with linen. The menu is planned around the freshest ingredients available, so one might start with sweetbreads in a warm vinaigrette on a bed of salad greens, or a colorful appetizer of marinated scallops and salmon. Without a pause, waiters appear, bearing huge silver *cloches*. With perfect timing, and a bit of a flourish, they are placed in front of each diner. The waiters glide back and forth. Then, as if on cue, they lift the silver bells to reveal the main dishes. The fragrance of fresh herbs and cream explodes from the plates. The wine cellar, which is Liliane's territory, is one of the finest in Quebec.

Pray that the maple mousse, piped into an almond *cigare* and set gingerly on a pool of raspberry *coulis* and cream, is on the dessert menu. The finale is a plateful of sensuous chocolate truffles and other small pastries, rich coffee, and a snifter of Armagnac brandy.

There's nothing more comforting than to climb the stairs after feasting and to drop off to sleep with a fire glowing softly in the irongrated fireplace. It's the kind of night that should never end.

Auberge Hatley has 25 spotless, individually decorated guest rooms, some with a fireplace, whirlpool, and balcony, all with thick braided rugs. A swimming pool is embedded in the

hillside garden below the inn. There
is cycling, horseback riding, golf,
and live summer theater, almost all
within walking distance.

The village of North Hatley is
blessed with a gentle local climate.
Sheltered on all sides, the flora and
fauna are unique to the region. In
1922, the Village Improvement Society, North America's first association
to protect the environment, was
founded. Because it still exists
today, there are no condos in North
Hatley. The ambience of the town is
well-suited to Auberge Hatley—
clean, courteous, and a cut above the
rest.

***

Auberge Hatley can be reached off
Highway 10 from Montreal by tak-
ing Exit 121. From Boston and New
York City, follow U.S. 91 to Quebec
Highway 55. Proceed north toward
Magog and take Exit 29.

Address: *C.P. 330, North Hatley,
Que. J0B 2C0, tel. 819/842-2451, fax
819/842-2907, Relais et Châteaux
toll-free from North America
800/67-RELAIS.*
Amenities: *Modified American Plan
includes dinner, breakfast, tax, and
service. Dietary restrictions are no
problem. Two conference rooms
will accommodate 6–30 in great
style.*
Rates: *double (excluding tax) but
including room, dinner, breakfast,
and service) $200–$230 per person.
Weekend and three- to five-night
rates are available. Rates change in
mid-June. MC, V.*
Restrictions: *No pets. No cigar or
pipe smoking is allowed in the dining room. Two rooms on the first
floor are wheelchair accessible, as
is the dining room.*

Hovey Manor

Winter drifts onto the Eastern Townships like a fluffy duvet, light and comforting. After a day on the ski trails, Hovey Manor, in North Hatley, glows in the darkness. Inside, fine dining and vintage wines await. This is winter as we dream of it—soft and deep.

North Hatley is a town founded by Loyalists after the War of Independence. After the Civil War, however, another wave of malcontents traveled northward to escape the southern summer's heat. These folk, from below the Mason-Dixon Line, drew the shades on their private railway cars as they passed through New England. They brought their customs and their servants with them. Among the newcomers was Henry Atkinson, owner of Georgia Power in Atlanta. He built the most fabulous summer mansion of all, a direct copy of George Washington's home at Mount Vernon, complete with broad verandas and solid white pillars. Such is the birthright of Hovey Manor, now operated by two dynamic and committed innkeepers, Kathyrn and Stephen Stafford.

Lace-canopied beds and fireplaces in many of the 35 individually styled bedrooms wrap the Staffords' guests in warmth. The manor's steep lawn is buried thickly in winter white. Trees are snowbound, and the view from the upper balconies defines the word *panoramic*. The lake is crisscrossed with ski tracks that on sunny, windless days allow the hardy to skim the entire nine mile (15 km) length. Ice-fishing holes dot the expanse, as do a few shoveled skating rinks.

According to Kathryn, Stephen had another flight of fancy when he decided to build an ice-fishing hut that was a replica of the manor. It was duly constructed, without the pillars (because they made it too cumbersome), late one November down on the beach in front of the inn. Guests are able to fish under the tutelege of fisherman-chef "Flo" Hébert, who cooks the catch, generally perch or trout, on a wood stove. The fishing gear is all supplied, as well as freshly made salads, ratatouille, wine, beer, and cognac—all elegantly served.

Flo has an interesting past. As a child, he was so crazy about fishing that his guardians made him go to a psychiatrist to rid him of the obsession. It didn't work. He continues to be a fishing guide in every spare moment when he isn't working as a gardener or a chef.

In the summer Hovey sits in the midst of elaborate English gardens that cascade lakeward. Every year Kathryn Stafford digs up more lawn and plants all the "new" flowers that she has discovered since the previous year. Edible blossoms and unusual greens are her latest kick, much to the delight of many diners.

A sunny summer's day at Hovey is magical. The inn is a unique blend of fully equipped resort and private hideway hotel. There is 1,800 feet (545 m) of lake frontage, with two good beaches. Canoes, paddleboats, and kayaks are ready to go at the dock. For those more accustomed to speed, there's sailing, sailboarding, and water-skiing. A heated swimming pool and an outdoor bar have just been christened on the slope down to the water. Light summer lunches are served there for those who really don't want to lose a minute in the sun. Guests can play tennis under the lights or head inside for a game of darts.

The Tap Room, with its 10,000-brick fireplace, is the best place to relax indoors. Guests quaff the locally brewed, somewhat nutty Massawippi ale and lager. In the wintertime, sous-chef Martin Gagné grills salmon and lamb over the fire.

In the dining room, an authentic Eastern Townships menu is the highlight. Executive chef Roland Menard has based it on ingredients available in the immediate area, and few areas are as rich. Smoked and fresh trout, tender lamb, apples and their cider, maple syrup, wildflower honey, and, of course, all the wonderful cheeses from Abbey St-Benoît-du-Lac.

The main menu, which changes with the season, could list such elegant creations as *Le coffret de caille farcie au ris de veau et à l'estragon* (quail stuffed with calf's sweetbreads in a tarragon cream sauce), *La sole de Douvres et crevettes au beurre de betteraves* (Dover sole and shrimp in a beet butter sauce), *Le panache de laitues et fruits du noyer à l'essence de menthe* (a variety of greens and nuts with a fresh mint vinaigrette), and *Le mignon de boeuf à la fine champagne et pleurotes* (filet mignon in a champagne and wild-mushroom sauce). The trick,

of course, is to live up to the advance billing that any well-written menu gives the kitchen. At Hovey the chef does not disappoint. Desserts are equally magnificent. Try the maple mousse in a walnut crust.

Five or six times every year, the Staffords and their chefs host "a private dinner party." The menu is not disclosed even to folks who beseech them on bended knee. On the preordained Friday night, guests assemble for a drink in the library of the inn. They are, en masse, ushered into the dining room with classical marches, and the feast begins, with wines matched to the seven-course menu. Only 60 places are set, and the chefs really let loose.

If you decide to explore the surrounding area, you'll find a wealth of things to do. In the immediate vicinity there are 10 golf courses; horseback riding, including an indoor equestrian arena; summer stock theater in both English and French; and great little antique shops and art galleries.

***

Hovey Manor is 70 minutes from Montreal and 20 minutes from Vermont. From Boston, take Highway 93 to 91. Head northward into Canada onto Highway 55. At Exit 29 follow the signs toward North Hatley.

Address: *C.P. 60, North Hatley, Que. J0B 2C0, tel. 819/842-2421, fax 819/842-2248.*
Amenities: *Modified American Plan including breakfast, dinner, room, and service, plus use of recreational facilities. Other options available for longer stays. Special diets can be accommodated with prior notice. Two large, well-appointed meeting rooms are available with capacity for up to 140 delegates in the largest. The dining room has a nonsmoking area. Two rooms are completely wheelchair accessible, as*

*is the dining room and virtually
all other main-floor areas of the
inn.*

Rates: *double (including service)
$95–$140 per person, depending on
style of room. Many packages
available. AE, DC, MC, V.*
Restrictions: *No pets.*

Ripplecove Inn

I n 1945, Jeffrey and Stephen (*see* Hovey Manor, p. 105) Stafford's parents moved to Ayer's Cliff, on the shore of Lake Massawippi, and built a summer resort. It was completely wild territory, save for the village a mile or so away. There was no electricity and no running water. To reach the inn the first guests had to open a fence gate and follow a trail that crossed a cow pasture. Being urbanites, they often didn't close the gate, and it was a common site to see the Stafford cows wandering the streets of Ayer's Cliff.

In those days, guests were mainly Americans who came to catch the huge, 35 pound (15 kg) lake trout that claimed Massawippi as their home. Those whoppers are long gone, but in their place are healthy perch, pike, and trout populations.

Ripplecove is the oldest of the three inns that are on the lake. It is where Jeff Stafford grew up. It's little wonder that he and his wife, Debra, are so in love with the place. Since 1987, hundreds of thousands have been spent on the renovation and restoration of the inn. Twenty-one guest rooms, beautifully decorated and stenciled by Debra, were remodeled or actually constructed. It's the small touches that Debra has added that give the inn such a personal feeling. Many rooms have wood-burning fireplaces and whirlpools. There are several one- and two-bedroom suites.

The Staffords are justifiably proud of the solid oak and gleaming brass bar that is the center of an English pub that has 35 brands of beer in the cooler. Look for the names Massawippi, Lions Pride and St-Ambroise—they are all brewed in Quebec.

A towering 60 foot (18 m) fieldstone fireplace, rich carpeting, canopy beds, well-chosen antiques, and polished hardwood floors definitely lend the inn an upscale ambience. It suits a resort that in many ways is like a northern version of Club Med. Once you are registered, all of the activities are free of charge.

In the summer, a full-time instructor coaches guests on the mysteries of sailboarding. After you have accomplished that feat, try either the laser sailboat or a mistral, which sports two sails. Kayaks are docked next to the rowboats. After everyone is skilled enough not to drown, races are held and the winner is treated to a bottle of chilled champagne.

All-terrain bicycles can be borrowed to explore the area. Cycling in this area, the heart of the Eastern Townships, is very, very good. A flat plain, perfect for novices, is surrounded by old mountains, which provide a challenge even for experts. Stone and rail fences divide the fields where cattle graze. There are even a few round barns left.

When the first snows fall and the lake freezes, another set of adventures await the Staffords' guests. In addition to Skiwippi (p. 110), a path to the lake is shoveled and an ice hut is installed in the middle of the bay. This is ice fishing as it should be—cushioned seats, wood already piled to refuel the stove as needed, and equipment and bait waiting. And if the fish are biting, a frying pan is beside the stove with a chunk of butter ready to cook the catch. Or, for the guests who need real pampering, the inn's chef will take over.

A team of Belgian horses bring a sleigh to the inn every Wednesday after dinner for an old-fashioned sleigh ride.

The candlelit dinners linger through the evening. Recording artist Alyn Harris plays both classical music and her own compositions on piano, and often her husband joins her on his guitar. After a few hours of fine dining with the strains of classical music in the background, you'll find the muscles that were strained and tense from skiing or sailing relax. Course after artful course arrives to coax the palate into submission. Escargots are tucked into a bed of puff pastry in a cumin-flavored sauce; scallops are sautéed lightly and served with French Brie cheese. A tender filet of lamb is served in a grainy mustard sauce. Wild rabbit, farm-raised trout, Brome Lake duckling, pheasant, and St-Benoit cheeses form the foundation for a Menu Estrienne. The inn's herb and flower gardens provide the garnishes. Seventy-five labels, basically French, have been stocked in the cellar—it's a very good wine list.

Since more and more people seem to be developing food sensitivies, the chef has taken it upon himself to write all the ingredients for each dish on a master list that is available another sign of how small inns cater to their guests.

For alpine ski enthusiasts, Jeffrey Stafford recommends Mont Orford. It is the closest alpine center to the inn, located 15 minutes away in a provincial park. The Canadian Ski Instructors Alliance–approved ski school offers lessons that can be arranged through the inn. Over the past two years more than $14 million has been pumped into the area on upgrading, including the installation of snowmaking equipment right to the top of the 1,800 foot (545 m) vertical mountain. Ski equipment, both alpine and cross-country, can be rented in Orford at Lalonde Sports (tel. 819/847-1263).

***

Ripplecove Inn is 20 minutes from Vermont. Take Highway 55 north and exit to Ayer's Cliff, south of Magog, at Exit 21. From Montreal, it will take about 75 minutes. Take Highway 10 and then travel south at Exit 121. Past Magog, head east at Exit 21. Follow the signs once you reach Ayer's Cliff.

Address: *C.P. 246, 700 Ripplecove Rd., Ayer's Cliff, Que. J0B 1C0, tel. 819/838-4296, fax 819/838-5541.*
Amenities: *Modified American Plan including dinner, breakfast, service, but not tax. Special diets are fine, although advance notice is appreciated. Two conference rooms for up to 50 guests. Complete audiovisual equipment is available.*
Rates: *double, per person (including breakfast, dinner, service but excluding taxes), summer season $99–$160, other seasons $92–$140. A number of other packages are available. AE, MC, V.*
Restrictions: *No pets are allowed. Smoking is restricted to one area of the dining room. Five rooms in the new wing are wheelchair acces-*

sible. Getting to the dining room can be a problem because there are   *several steps; however, the person can enter from the outside.*

Skiwippi and the Moveable Feast

Skiing in Quebec's Eastern Townships has always meant negotiating, at screaming speed, one mogul after another through the famous forested glades. But now there's Skiwippi, a gentle cross-country skiing experience that links the three finest four-fork, five-fleurs-de-lis inns that the region has—Auberge Hatley, Hovey Manor, and Ripplecove Inn. Skiwippi's start rotates among the three inns. Innkeepers chauffeur luggage (and tired skiers, if necessary) from one auberge to the next. The 20 mile (35 km) trail winds through maple farms, spans creeks full of ice-coated rocks, slides through *une cédraie* (cedar forest), and climbs to a plateau where the lake spreads out below. Wild rabbits, partridges, and raccoons shyly haunt the stands of white birch along the trail.

Although the trail is designed for intermediate skiers, novices can still take part in most lengths of the course. The Kateville Loup, behind Hovey Manor, is an easy beginners' run that can be combined with a picnic. Trail-maintenance personnel turn on the heat in the little huts to provide shelter and warmth. It's a comfortable run for those just getting their ski legs.

The Skiwippi trail has been upgraded to International Touring Standards. Signed with fluorescent blue symbols, the hills are 15 feet (5 m) wide, the flat surfaces 9 feet (3 m) wide, and the whole system is double-tracked. Grooming equipment keeps them in near-perfect condition.

At least one lunch on the trail should be spent in the hand-hewn, barnlike Le Refuge les Sommets. Vermont is visible in the south. Mme Juliette Deland, who operates Le Refuge, is dressed in white chef's hat and starched apron and serves old-fashioned Quebec cooking—from ragout with tiny meatballs to flaky crusted *tourtière*. According to Jeffrey Stafford, owner of the Ripplecove Inn, she also ladles out "the best pea soup you've ever tasted."

The same three inns collaborate on a gourmet extravaganza they have named "The Moveable Feast." Guests stay one or two nights at each inn and savor six-course gastronomic dinners and fabulous breakfasts at each. There's nothing quite like it in Canada. Local ingredients and chefs who are at the top of the field make it an unforgettable dining experience.

***

For more information, call or write any of the inns involved: Auberge Hatley (p. 103), Hovey Manor (p. 105) or Ripplecove Inn (p. 108). Tourisme Québec can also provide information at their toll-free number: 800/363-7777.

The Montreal Area
Auberge des Gallants

The Gallants, Linda and Gérard, have an incredible 400 acres of wilderness a mere 45 minutes from the city of Montreal. A beaver family lives in the wide pond a few hundred feet from the inn, and members of their resident herd of sixty deer nonchalantly stroll by, grazing or just investigating. More than 237 species of birds have been identified flitting about during the past fourteen years. Many winter here in the hills, having retreated from the cold farther north.

In 1973, Gérard Gallant sold his restaurant in Montreal to move to the country and began renovating the old farmhouse that stood on the acreage. An album that catalogs the following decade full of building is a testament to the fortitude and dreams of this young couple. In 1988 a wing of 30 additional rooms was added, with whirlpools, balconies, and fireplaces. Five small conference rooms were built, and a new dining room, overlooking the terrace and swimming pool, was completed. A very special feature is the air-purification system that has been installed throughout the entire inn. Because one of the Gallants' children has asthma, guests who also suffer from allergies benefit from the ultraclean environment. On December 1, 1989, the government of Quebec honored the couple with the Grand Prix du Tourisme Québécois

for their small enterprise. It was deserved.

Meals are generous and well prepared. It takes courage to put venison on the menu with all the doe-eyed darlings watching, but it was there, served with pears and cranberries. Gérard is from the coastal Acadian region of Quebec, so try his seafood dishes. The marinated salmon is wonderful, as are the scallops.

Near the inn are walking trails that wind their way through the property. A putting green allows guests to warm up for a game of golf at one of the four nearby courses. The Gallants have just built a tennis court and have a workout room near the sauna. River cruises are available at Ste-Anne-de-Bellevue. The Montreal Polo Club has matches every Tuesday, Thursday, and Sunday throughout the summer at Ste-Marthe. At Windedge Farms the North American dressage championships are held, while at St-Lazare the Audi Classic, the Eastern Provincial jumping events, are held.

The summertime also brings the sound-and-light spectacle at the Sanctuaire Notre-Dame-de-Lourdes, a typically rural Quebec church that is built on Rigaud Mountain. The sanctuary itself is open from May 1 until the end of September and receives over 100,000 visitors annually.

In the wintertime, besides deer and bird-watching, guests are encouraged to visit La Sucerie de la Montagne for sleigh rides and an old-fashioned Québécois meal. Ice fishing is available on a number of bodies of water. Cross-country ski on the Gallants' property or drive 2 miles (3 km) to some moderately good slopes for alpine skiing.

One must remember, too, that the inn is very close to Montreal, with all its museums, art galleries, farmers' markets, great theater, and incredible dining.

***

Auberge des Gallants is located between Montreal and Ottawa, just inside the Quebec/Ontario border. From Montreal take Highway 40 northward and at Exit 17 turn southeast on Highway 201, which is also known as Monte Lavigne. Proceed for 2 miles (3 km) and turn right on chemin St-Henri and drive for an additional 3½ miles (6 km).

Address: *1171, chemin St-Henri, Ste-Marthe, Vaudreuil, Que. J0P 1W0, tel. 514/459–4241 or 514/451–4961, fax 514/459–4667.*
Amenities: *European Plan, but MAP packages that include meals are available. Special diets are available with advance notice. The inn has five meeting rooms that will accommodate up to 125. The inn is wheelchair accessible. No nonsmoking restrictions because the inn has been completely fitted with an air-purification system. No pipe or cigar smoking is allowed in the dining room.*
Rates: *double without meals $55–$125 (excluding taxes), double with breakfast and dinner (including taxes and service) $165–$275. AE, EnRoute, MC, V.*
Restrictions: *No pets.*

Auberge les Trois Tilleuls

L es Trois Tilleuls (the three lin-
den trees) is on the bank of the
Richelieu River, one of the main
routes of early colonization. Samuel
de Champlain sailed along it in 1608.
The wide waterway, named after
Cardinal Richelieu, was of strategic
military importance and had numerous forts along its 80 mile (130 km)
length, which stretches from Lake
Champlain to Montreal. This area,
known as the Monteregie, is south of
Montreal and has rich farmland that
provides much of the province's finest fruits and vegetables. Bordering
on the Eastern Townships, it is the
cradle of the infant Quebec wine industry.

Les Trois Tilleuls is as much an art
gallery as an *auberge.* Innkeeper
Michel Aubriot is a serious art deal-
er whose collection hangs in every
nook and cranny that can be filled.
The works of Henri Masson, Marc-
Aurèle Fortin, Goodridge Roberts,
and Stanley Cosgrove are all here. It
is fine Quebec art at some of the
best prices around.

The 23-room *auberge* is a member of
the Relais et Châteaux and has met
its exacting standards with flair.
Character, charm, courtesy, calm,
and fine cuisine are the building
blocks upon which every member in
the world stands. Les Trois Tilleuls
is firmly on that foundation. Its
rooms are furnished with pieces
handcrafted exclusively by Le Bahu-
tier and Meubles d'Antan. The balconies all overlook the river, which

flows powerfully beyond the terraced
gardens. The dining room is the finest in the area. It serves French cuisine based on fresh ingredients, and
it boasts a cellar of more than
16,000 bottles of 600 appellations, including most Grand Crus, such as
Lafite, Mouton Rothschild, and Ro-
manaee Conti; pre-1900 port; and
various Armagnacs and cognacs.

It seems appropriate that the house
cocktail is a bubbly blend of fruity
raspberry liqueur from Rougemont,
Quebec; rich French Armagnac; and
a splash of sparkling wine—the best
of the region and the best of France
in one crystal flute.

If it is offered, have a piping hot
bowl of their carmelized onion soup.
It's far better than the usual cheese-
and-bread-laden version. The salmon
scallop with *sauce Smitane* is another favorite—rich in cream and perfectly cooked. It is unlikely that
anything on Les Trois Tilleuls' menu
will be disappointing. The service is
relaxed but attentive. It's fine and
elegant dining at its best.

The river is the focus of each day at
the inn. The marina allows boaters
to dock for dinner. Hour-long cruises
up the river to St-Marc or around
the island in front of the auberge
are available during the summer. October is a marvelous month in the
Monteregie—golden and still summer. The private game preserve on
the island is opened, and the tall,

sometimes boisterous innkeeper takes his guests pheasant hunting.

The inn has its own nine-hole putting green, two tennis courts, and a heated swimming pool that overlooks the river. Hiking at Mont-St-Hilaire's Centre de Conservation de la Nature is superb. The mountain is the tallest in the area and is covered with mature forest. Bird-watching, photography, snowshoeing, and cross-country skiing can all be enjoyed there. French country theater flourishes throughout the region in the summer, and if that isn't enough, try Montreal. A holiday could stretch into a lifetime.

***

Auberge les Trois Tilleuls is located 30 minutes south of Montreal, near St-Marc-sur-Richelieu just off Highway 20.

Address: *290, rue Richelieu, St-Marc-sur-Richelieu, Que. J0L 2E0, tel. 514/584-2231, fax 514/584-3146, Relais et Châteaux toll-free from North America 800/67-RELAIS.*
Amenities: *European Plan, Modified American Plan, or Full American Plan available. Special diets are easily accommodated. Five meeting rooms are very well organized with audiovisual equipment and space for up to 37. Some areas are wheelchair accessible. No nonsmoking restrictions.*
Rates: *FAP (excluding taxes) $144–$198 single, $230–$291 double. Suites $273 (single) to $371 (double). Royal Suite $521 double. MAP $127–$181 single, $196–$257 double. Suites $256 (single) to $337 (double). Royal Suite $487 double. European Plan $71–$125 single, $84–$145 double. Suites $200 (low season) to $225 (high season). Royal Suite $375 double. AE, CB, DC, EnRoute, MC, V.*
Restrictions: *No pets.*

The Laurentians
Auberge des Cèdres

Quebeckers will drive a great distance for excellent food, and it is an added plus when their destination is also a nice place to stay. Auberge des Cèdres is on the edge of Lac L'Achigan (Bass Lake) and serves classic French cuisine. Jean and Thérèse Duval came from Normandy. Jean manages the inn while Thérèse and her assistant, André Shott, create the meals, rich in cream and blessed with fresh butter. Their foie gras alone is worth the journey.

Diners relax with an apéritif in the parlor, and order. When their dinner is ready the waiter or M. Duval shows the guests to their table. The art of eating is close to its best here. Service is excellent, but Mme Duval and M. Shott are the real stars.

To begin with, they make their own foie gras, tucking a small piece of black truffle into the center of each velvety slice. One word of caution: Like the magnificent foie gras from France's Périgord, this appetizer is expensive. Another outstanding dish is the charlotte of raw salmon in a cucumber sauce. The salmon is spiked with green peppercorns, capers, and fresh lemon juice before being enclosed in a little palisade of thinly sliced zucchini. The cucumber sauce, seasoned with Dijon and red wine vinegar, is so good you try to hide while you wipe your plate clean with a crusty roll.

Auberge des Cèdres is one of the few inns that serve veal sweetbreads, and Mme Duval usually prepares them with truffles. Her membership in the Ordre des Canardiers is a guarantee of excellent duck dishes. Their salads, at least the two that came to our table, are laced with garlic. There's a more delicate warm smoked-trout salad, and another in which quail eggs are combined with chilled cooked shrimp.

Desserts are in the same league as the entrées. Wonderful! There are inn-made fruit sherbets—black currant, strawberry, peach; the fresh strawberries sometimes bathed in *crème anglaise* (vanilla custard sauce), or spiked with Pernod and Grand Marnier, dusted with pepper, and served with rich cream. Because the Duvals are from Normandy, it would be completely inappropriate for them not to have the classic *tarte tatin* on their dessert list. They do. But for the real gourmets, and the fearless, there is an assortment of the inn's specialties that really demands a brisk walk afterward.

M. Duval has a well-stocked wine cellar. Like most French, and many North Americans, he has a love of good wine and it shows in his selection.

The activities that are *de rigueur* after such meals are generally of the make-your-own sort. Swimming in the lake, sailboarding, and paddle-boating should wear off some of your sins. In the winter it's easier, with snowshoeing and cross-country and alpine skiing nearby.

All six guest rooms have private showers but are not up to the standard of the dining room. The accommodation, though comfortable, is dated and well-worn. Thankfully, the Duvals have focused most of their energy on their food, so it is easy to overlook any minor shortcomings.

***

Auberge des Cèdres is 50 minutes from Montreal and 30 minutes from Mirabel, Montreal's international airport. Take Exit 45 off the Laurentian Autoroute north and proceed past Lesage, Shawbridge, Mont Rolland until you reach St-Hippolyte.

Address: *26, 305th Ave., Lac L'Achigan, St-Hippolyte, Que. J0R 1P0, 514/563-2083.*
Amenities: *Modified American Plan. Special diets are available if requested in advance. Two meeting rooms for up to about 20 people. No nonsmoking regulations.*
Rates: *double $170, breakfast and dinner included. AE, DC, EnRoute, MC, V.*
Restrictions: *No pets. Only the dining room is wheelchair accessible.*

Le Clos Joli

In France, where restaurants and inns are born and die with the rating system, it is safe to say that those establishments that have only one or two stars work extra hard to achieve that coveted next level. Often these are the very best places to patronize. The same sometimes holds true in the province of Quebec. The province's *fourchette* (fork) and fleur-de-lis system is taken very seriously among innkeepers and clients alike.

Down a narrow lane and behind a big, screened porch is Le Clos Joli. A huge bouquet of sunflowers, scarlet highbush cranberries, and rust-colored maple leaves grace the entranceway. It's a comfortable country place. Although the tiny inn has just received its third *fourchette* (the highest is four), the Roux family is continuously striving for that extra level of excellence. In fact, they have applied to have the "R" regional designation, indicating above-average use of local ingredients and dishes. If successful, Le Clos Joli will be the first three-*fourchette* inn to obtain it.

The no-nonsense accommodation is very clean, with miniblinds covering the windows, private tiled bathrooms, and serviceable furniture. But it's the food and the ambience that make the inn one of the real finds in the Laurentians. They are indeed *"l'étoile montant de la gastronomie"* (the rising star of great food).

Dr. Jean-Pierre Roux, his wife, Francine, and their three daughters, Marie Josée, Claudine, and Élisabeth, own and operate the inn. Marie Josée is the chef, leaving the kitchen only to purchase ingredients or to go for advanced training in France. Claudine, who is the sommelier, also journeys to Europe to study gastronomy and regional wines.

Francine is the gardener. The inn was once an old farmhouse, and the soil around is very rich. A profusion of 150 different flowers, vegetables, and herbs surround you as you sit by the pool.

The feast begins in the morning with flaky homemade croissants, thick black-currant jam or perhaps some rosy apple jelly that Marie Josée has preserved the previous summer, a fresh fruit compote, and a stack of pancakes or any style of eggs with bacon. It sets the day off to a great start.

From the inn, during the wonderful Laurentian winters, you can ski for miles. Stop in time to return for dinner.

The dining room is informal, and casual dress is fine.

Marie Josée takes culinary ingredients that are older than Quebec itself and melds them with her own upscale ideas. She may serve you a warm salad of grilled chicken breast dressed with a yogurt-mayonnaise cream into which she has added *herbes salées*, the salt-preserved herbs from ancient recipes that migrated from western France with the *colons* (settlers). Ermite, the tangy blue cheese from the Eastern Townships, is on the cheese tray along with a selection from France. Local goat cheese finds its way into warm phyllo tarts sparked with thyme and served with a honey-port sauce. Veal sweetbreads and seasonal vegetables are encased in crisp strudel pastry, their flavors enlivened with a warm pear vinaigrette. The lamb, pheasant, quail, and rabbit are all from the province, and the fresh vegetables are from the lower Laurentians, near Mirabel. All the herbs, violets, and nasturtiums are from Francine's garden. Paper-thin almond wafers (*tuiles*) are layered with fresh fruits and crème Chantilly. The *marquise au chocolat* is basically a big truffle that is served, thinly sliced, with fruit on an English custard sauce. Tarts, cakes, sherbets, puff pastries—they are all here at various times, and they are all made at the inn.

The area is rich in outdoor activities. Mountain bikes can be rented and taken up the chairlift; you then bump your way down mountainside trails that double as ski runs in the winter. Golf, tennis, and a full gym are nearby. The Laurentian Ski Museum is located in Morin Heights, a tribute to all those pioneers who built the alpine and cross-country ski tradition over the past eight decades. Winter in these ancient mountains is the way it should be, snowy and white. You can ski at Mont Tremblant, 45 minutes away, or skate at the Morin Heights rink, a mere three-minute walk.

***

Le Clos Joli, in Morin Heights, may be reached by taking Exit 60 off the Laurentian Autoroute 15 onto Highway 364. It is 30 minutes north of Mirabel International Airport in Montreal and about 40 minutes from the city itself.

Address: *19, chemin Watchorn, Morin Heights, Que. J0R 1H0, tel. 514/226-5401.*
Amenities: *Modified American Plan includes a four-course "gastronomic dinner" and a full breakfast. Continental Plan includes full breakfast. Vegetarian meals can be provided. The newly constructed solarium can serve as a small meeting room for up to ten people.*
Rates: *(exclude taxes and service) MAP: single $105, double $155. Deluxe room with whirlpool bath and queen-size bed, double $165. European Plan: single $71, double $87. Special rates for weekday stays of five nights. Special discounts can be arranged for skiing at Morin Heights. MC, V.*
Restrictions: *No pets. Not wheelchair accessible. No pipe or cigar smoking in dining room. Closed Nov. and last two weeks in Apr.*

L'Eau à la Bouche

Snuggled into a snow-draped Laurentian hillside near Ste-Adèle, its windows flickering with candles, is a small perfect French-Canadian inn called L'Eau à la Bouche. With more that 200 years of Québécois tradition behind its food, the inn (whose name means "mouth-watering") is breaking new ground by serving cuisine that's a glorious blend of classic French and old-style Québécois.

L'Eau à la Bouche is quite simply the finest inn in the Laurentians. Indeed, it is one of the very best in all of eastern Canada. The inn is operated by Pierre Audette and Anne Desjardins, who are committed to bringing as fine a dining and lodging experience to their guests as they know how. Never content to merely coast, Anne travels frequently, taking and teaching food and wine courses in France. Her credentials include a term at both the Lenôtre school of *pâtisserie* and the Hôtel Le Crillon in Paris. She lectures at the Institut de l'Hôtellerie des Laurentides in Ste-Adèle and yet manages to remain in charge, and at the stoves, in her restaurant. Pierre's courses have centered on wine-tasting in various regions of France. He oversees and does much of the hands-on operation of their restaurant; makes sure that the inn is running smoothly; and still finds time to be a great daddy to their two children, Emmanuel and Félix.

L'eau à la Bouche began life as an intimate restaurant, and the inn was built several years after their clientele began to grow and to come from rather long distances. The 26-room inn sits with its back to the hillside, slightly apart from the restaurant, and overlooks Chantecler Ski Centre, famous for its excellent night skiing. The guest rooms are furnished with pieces that have been crafted in the area, some stained with the traditional blueberry mixture that lends the wood a dusty hue. The auberge is truly country French in atmosphere—rustic but totally elegant. You will be comfortable in casual clothes or high fashion.

A woman in Ste-Adèle makes creamy truffles that are placed strategically on each guest's desk before arrival: *"Bon séjour . . . Bonne vacances,"* the note reads. (Have a good stay . . . happy holiday.)

Breakfast is served in the *auberge* itself. With a huge fire licking at the giant logs in the hearth, you will begin to understand what the food of the *colons* (settlers) was like. These dishes hark back to medieval France. You will certainly have slices of *cretons*, a lightly spiced ground-meat terrine. Every grandmother in the province supposedly has the best recipe for this ancient dish. *Fèves au lard* (beans that have been slowly baked with molasses and salt pork or bacon), *galettes* (pancakes), and *pain doré* (golden French toast) with maple syrup are prepared hot from the kitchen. As a counterpoint, or perhaps in homage to the '90s, there is always a plate heaped with freshly baked muffins or croissants, seasonal fruits, inn-made granola, and lots of steaming coffee. It's the type of breakfast that cries for a long hike in the Laurentian air, either before or after.

The day's activities can be as active or as passive as a person desires. Of course, in the wintertime there is fabulous skiing, both alpine and cross-country, at Chantecler or on snowy trails through the forests of trembling aspen and pine. In the summer the Laurentians are the playground for Montreal, so virtually every type of outdoor activity is available, from ballooning to sailboarding. At the inn, you might simply decide to settle into a chair beside the pool or book a game of golf. The old Canadian Pacific Railway line has been ripped up, and a "linear park" has been created from St-Jérôme right up to the region's capital, Mont Laurier. Mountain bikers or cross-country skiers can pick up that route in Ste-Adèle and trek for a hundred miles if they so choose.

For wine lovers and serious oenophiles, the most interesting jaunt in Quebec is to Dr. Champlain Charest's Le Bistro Champlain, in Ste-Marguerite-de-Lac-Masson. Originally an old general store built in 1865, it became Le Bistro in 1987. Jean-Paul Riopelle, one of Canada's greatest living artists, made the window displays. His paintings, owned by his good friend Dr. Charest, hang in the restaurant. In 1988, Le Bistro won the Wine Spectator's Grand Award, for having one of the best wine cellars in the world. No one else in Canada has been found worthy of that honor.

Dr. Charest must be considered a philanthropist, because he has opened up his cellar of 32,000 bottles of rare wines to the public. The restaurant was an afterthought, but a fine young chef is now at the stoves and great food is being served to complement the magnificent wines.

Dr. Charest is a very close friend of Pierre and Anne's, and hence the inn and Le Bistro often collaborate on wine-tastings and meals.

Dining is the ultimate experience at L'Eau à la Bouche. And in reality, that is why most guests journey to the inn. As soon as you arrive, make your dinner reservation for later in the evening in order to allow yourself the luxury of lingering. As night falls, the atmosphere changes. Here, as in a few other special French Canadian inns, you will experience the intense enjoyment that Quebeckers have for each other's company, great food, wine, and music. It's a joy to be part of it.

Order from either the à la carte or *dégustation* menus. The latter is a thoughtful selection made by Chef Desjardins from the main menu; it will lead you through a balanced and delicious range of that day's dishes. If you are dining at the inn for the first time and have been smart enough to work up an appetite, the latter is the wisest choice.

The selection of regional and seasonal ingredients is of utmost importance. Anne uses the western part of the province as her source of supply. She purchases *cochonnet*, the tender young pig that is raised on the shores of the St. Lawrence and is allowed to reach only 50 pounds (23 kg). She uses goat's-milk cheese from the lower Laurentians and a strain of wild rabbit (*lièvre*) that is raised locally for the restaurant, as are small quails and ducklings.

Hearty dishes with robust flavors appear in the wintertime, but the vegetables are steamed to perfection and the sauces rely on stock reductions rather than on heavy cream. In the summer, with the gardens bursting forth, the meals rejoice in the harvest.

Seafood is handled with great care. *Pétoncles unilatéraux* are tender small scallops that have been grilled on one side only, then placed, golden side up, on a pool of light mayonnaise seasoned with black pepper and finely minced cucumber and tomato. Her scampi soup, a *potage* of peppery velvet, steams with the fragrance of the sea.

It would be a great pity not to partake of Anne's desserts, even if it's only a small scoop of passionfruit sorbet. Try the devilish chocolate-ice-cream parfait, which is unmolded onto a plateful of strong coffee sauce with minuscule cream hearts floating all over its surface.

A plate of French cheeses and nut bread ends the meal; it's perfect with one of Pierre's fine collection of dessert wines.

For day visitors, L'eau à la Bouche is now serving three-course luncheons that are well under $20 per person. Again, the season dictates what is being served, but you have a choice of appetizer, main dish, and dessert or Quebec cheeses.

L'Eau à la Bouche is the perfect romantic hideaway for a lost weekend, those few days that we all need—to escape, to reflect, and to soar.

***

L'Eau à la Bouche is 45 minutes from downtown Montreal and 20 minutes from Mirabel International Airport. Take the Laurentian Auto-route 15 and exit at Ste-Adèle. The inn is on Highway 117, also called boulevard Ste-Adèle.

Address: *3003, boul. Ste-Adèle, Ste-Adèle, Que. J0R 1L0, tel. 514/229–2991 or 800/363-2582 (toll-free within Quebec), fax 514/229-7573.*
Amenities: *Breakfast is included in the room rate. Special dietary requirements pose no problem, although the inn would appreciate advance notice. The inn has three meeting rooms. Two are luxury boardrooms with complete audiovisual equipment, the third is a meeting room for up to 40. Five rooms at the inn are wheelchair accessible, as is the dining room. No smoking restrictions are in place.*
Rates: *Excluding tax but including service: breakfast only, double $95–$220; Modified American Plan, double $232–$357. Group discounted rates, with three meals, coffee breaks, service, room rental: $155. AE, MC, V.*
Restrictions: *No pets.*

Auberge Escapade

Mont Tremblant and alpine skiing have been synonymous since the 1930s, when the Wheeler brothers from Gray Rocks Inn strapped skins onto their long skis and scaled the mountain with Lowell Thomas and eccentric millionaire Joe Ryan. Ryan was rich, very rich! When he stood atop the mountain he decided to claim it on behalf of his dream, a European-style ski resort. Because of the superb ski teaching of Gray Rocks Inn and the challenge of Mont Tremblant, the whole region has flourished. Tremblant Station was the jumping-off point for the ski train that chugged its way north from Montreal. Around this station, the village grew and prospered.

Auberge Escapade is a small casual inn with a hostelike atmosphere. The bedrooms have bunks and the bathrooms are clean and shared. Because the hill is several miles away, most alpine skiers leave for the day. But cross-country skiing is also very important here, perhaps more than in any other area in the Laurentians. This is the place Herman "Jackrabbit" Johannsen called home, and his daughter, who still lives on the mountainside, has worked hard to help develop a massive, groomed trail system that runs for 56 miles (90 km). Novice and expert alike can enjoy the network, spending a day or a few hours sliding along from inn to inn—fueling up at a café, then heading off again.

Near the village and part of the trail system is Domaine St-Bernard, a large tract of land that has been set aside for retired priests (the average age is 82). Birds are pets here, and when you are cross-country skiing through the sanctuary, it is not unusual for one to land on your hat. Take some birdseed, because both squirrels and birds can be fed by hand.

Auberge Escapade specializes in hearty French-Canadian food (Suzanne is *Québécoise*) and true English dishes (David is from Great Britain). In their pub-style dining room you can find delicious French-Canadian pea soup and the best beer-battered fish and chunky chips in the area. *Pouding chômeur,* a butterscotch pudding with a cakelike crust, is side by side with date-studded Queen Elizabeth cake.

The inn is on the shores of Moore Lake, one of the small freshwater bodies of water that sparkle throughout the Laurentians. David has a love of sailing that he uses to enhance many a guest's holiday. He'll provide individual instruction or simply take you on a cruise in his 22 foot (7 m) Tanzer.

Summertime is also time for mountain biking and hiking through Mont Tremblant Park, a huge preserve that encompasses hundreds of acres of forests and lakes. The canoeing is superb, and the inn can be used as a staging place from which to mount a longer trek into the wilderness. For those who crave more excitement (terror?), there is white-water rafting on the Rouge River.

Autumn is spectacular in the Laurentians. It's also the time of year when mycologists from as far away as New York City journey to Tremblant to tramp through the woods. Before the first snows fall in late October, hundreds of pounds of wild mushrooms have been collected.

No trip is complete without a short visit to St-Jovite, the largest village in the area. There you can find antiques, handicrafts, and excellent val-

ues on ski wear or French fashion at
Louise Charette's. Gourmet picnic
supplies, *à la Française,* can be
found at Petite Europe, a great little
charcuterie-pâtisserie. Across the
road is the Société d'Alcools de Québec (the liquor/wine store).

***

Auberge Escapade is on the chemin
Principal (Main Street) of Village
Mont Tremblant. It is about 1½
hours north of Montreal via Highway 15.

Address: *Box 393, Village Mont
Tremblant, Que. J0T 1Z0, 819/425-
7311.*
Amenities: *Bed-and-Breakfast or
Modified American Plan. Vegetarian meals available. Meeting-room
facilities for 20–45 people.*
Rates: *double (excluding taxes) Bed-
and-Breakfast: summer $25 per
person, winter $35 per person. Spe-
cial packages available, such as
double $127–$177 per person, includes two nights accommodation,
two lift tickets, breakfast and dinner. Sailing charter rates for five
people: two hours, $60; half day,
$100; full day, $150. Lessons are $10
per hour. MC, V.*
Restrictions: *No pets. Dining room
is nonsmoking. Restaurant and
pub are wheelchair accessible,
rooms are not. Closed Nov. and
Apr.–early June.*

Auberge St-Denis

Any innkeeper who names his rooms after varieties of vinifera grapes is in my good books. He has to know something about the finer things and he certainly has a sense of humor. Richard Desjardins is one such innkeeper, Auberge St-Denis, his inn. Grenache, Zinfandel, Cabernet, Muscat—they are all there.

Auberge St-Denis is a wonderful oasis in the middle of the overdevelopment that once was the gorgeous Laurentian town of St-Sauveur. One thing is certain: If you choose to, there is a tremendous amount to do. Shopping undoubtedly heads the list, next comes great alpine skiing, and last but not least, there is the fine dining. The summertime brings another dimension, a complete aquatic park, one so good that the folks from the Disney corporation came up for a look.

Auberge St-Denis is located away from much of the hoopla but within a good walk of the better shops (Richard recommends Avant Garde for clothing, the art gallery Michel Bigue, gifts from Boutique Anita Barière, and the sweet shop called La Bonbonnière). Auberge St-Denis is located on lovely, shaded property. Its guest rooms are larger than most other inns, and each oversize suite has a fireplace, living room area, whirlpool, and minibar. A brand-new health spa is the latest addition. The latter was designed not for the therapeutic benefits as much as to add to the exercise and health programs that many people are already involved in. "It's really for sports-oriented people." says Desjardins.

Lace and flowers and flute music set the stage in the dining room. Chef Martin Alarie grew with the inn. He absolutely adores working with food and it shows. An amazing light fluff of foie gras floated on a citrus butter sauce—a peppery nasturtium flower setting it off. Thin slices of marinated lamb nestled in a whorl of arugula leaves. As with most of Canada's best chefs, young Alarie is using no butter, cream, or flour in his sauces. He relies heavily on fresh herbs—a sprig of rosemary here, a few lemon-balm leaves there—and the natural flavor of his ingredients.

The wine list at the *auberge* is very good. A number of half bottles are available for those who want to match wine with each course. Each of the vintages has a brief description after it, a huge, if exceedingly pleasant, task for any sommelier—or perhaps it was M. Desjardins who took over this onerous task.

The inn staff are very professional in these parts. In the Laurentians there is an institute where people who wish to work in the restaurant or hotel business can study both the basics and the frills, and their dedication to perfection shows.

Auberge St-Denis is a casual place, and guests are encouraged to really unwind. Throw on the old jeans, grab a mountain bike, and cycle through the hills. From mid-December until mid-March, try out any of the half-dozen alpine ski centers. With a family as your excuse, a visit to the Cascades d'Eau, the mammoth waterslide park, will, according to Desjardins, be "the thrill of the day."

***

Auberge St-Denis is 45 minutes north of Montreal, just off the Laurentian Autoroute 15.

Address: *61, rue St-Denis, St-Sauveur-des-Monts, Que. J0R 1R4, tel. 514/227-4602, 514/227-4766, or 800/361-5724, fax 514/227-8504.*
Amenities: *Full breakfast is included in the rate, or Modified American Plan is available. With advance notice the kitchen can handle "most reasonable dietary requests." The inn has six fully equipped meeting rooms. Wheelchair accessible. No restrictions regarding smoking.*
Rates: *Breakfast only, excluding taxes. Single: room $89, suite $99; double: room $99, suite $109. AE, DC, EnRoute, MC, V.*
Restrictions: *No pets.*

Auberge du Vieux Foyer

The Laurentian Highlands is part of the oldest geological formation on earth—the Canadian Shield, 1.8 million square acres (4.6 million sq km) of granite in which Canada's history is solidly rooted. The woods were rich in fur-bearing animals; the forest yielded her trees for a huge lumber industry; the rushing young rivers propelled the logs, many of them to be masts for the British navy, to ports on the St. Lawrence and Ottawa rivers; gold, silver, cobalt, and nickel lay beneath the earth awaiting the miners; and thousands of lakes, formed when the last great glaciers retreated, were filled with trout, pickerel, perch, bass, and pike.

The deep valleys and worn old mountains were little good to the farmers who attempted to settle them in the late 1800s. But for tourists, the Laurentians have been a playground for a century. Le Petit Train du Nord reached Ste-Agathe in 1893, and the flow of visitors began. The region first was a summer haven, away from the smoky cities of the Northeast. By the 1920s tourists realized that in the Laurentians, winter was as it should be—deep and snowy. The brand-new sport of skiing started in Canada on these old mountains.

Auberge du Vieux Foyer (inn of the old hearth) is just on the outskirts of the village of Val David. The inn looks as if it has been transplanted from Switzerland, and it is as clean.

Indeed, the innkeeper Michel Giroux does have Swiss roots, but the hospitality is definitely *Québécois* and the food is French. Magnificent stained-glass renditions of all the outdoor sports that guests may partake of are hung carefully so that the light plays on them. It's an inn with all the modern amenities but also with the warm feeling that only knotty pine and a glowing fire can engender.

Auberge du Vieux Foyer has no "best season." Rock climbing is just down the road at a rock slit that provides firm holds for the climber's pitons. Lac des Salles at Ste-Agathe is great for canoeing and sailboarding. Hikers can wander down country roads lined with birch and aspen or on the trail network that sprawls through the surrounding hills. Mountain biking could conceivably take you from one Laurentian inn to the next. The *auberge* has tennis, badminton, a heated pool, and paddleboats. Across the road is the Val David golf course. There is summer theater nearby as well as reasonably decent fishing. The best fishing is now in the northern Laurentian lakes.

In the winter the *auberge* is central to a dozen alpine ski centers, some of which have discounted lift tickets for inn guests. But it's the cross-country skiing that is without doubt the best. Trails radiate right from the auberge's door. Some are gentle, scenic runs that flow for miles through the hills; others are challenging. One such run heads to the top of a local mountain; another is a serious long-distance wilderness trek known only as Gillespie. The village of Val David, with its tiny cafés, forms the hub of the cross-country wheel, where skiers traditionally warm up with café au lait or a mug of hot cocoa.

Chef Jean-Louis Martin is as shy as he is talented. His credentials are excellent, and his menu, which changes daily, is as good. You may be able to begin with a duck *pâté à l'orange* on a mango *coulis*, or simply a plate of melon with Bayonne ham and a creamy Brie. There is always a choice of three soups; it may be a clear beef consommé with sweet peppers or a Pernod-splashed fish soup with mussels. Six or seven entrées are available, ranging from salmon and scallops to veal, Charolais beef, lamb, and rabbit. Desserts can be light, like the wild raspberry mousse, or rich, decadent, and loaded with chocolate. French wines predominate on the wine list. If you are not staying at the *auberge*, you need to make reservations for meals.

Auberge du Vieux Foyer has been granted three *fourchettes* from the tourism authorities, like Le Clos Joli at Morin Heights. It seems that young inns, with that fire of youthful optimism, seem to work a little harder than some who are already established and content to rest on their laurels. This inn is worth a visit.

***

Auberge du Vieux Foyer may be reached by driving north of Montreal on Laurentian Autoroute 15. Take Exit 76 to Val David. The inn is 2 miles (3 km) from the village, near Mont Plante.

Address: *3165, chemin Doncaster, Val David, Que. J0T 2N0, tel. 819/322-2686 or 800/567-8327 (from the province of Quebec), fax 819/322-2687.*
Amenities: *Modified American Plan or European Plan available. Some special diets can be accommodated but advance notice is appreciated. Several meeting rooms are available. No restrictions for smokers.*
Rates: *Per person, breakfast and dinner included, tax excluded: $62 for room with running water, shared bath; $84 for room with bath; $115 for chalet with bath, per person, up to two people (each person after that is $70). Weekly and seasonal rates are available. $20 less per person for European Plan. Children $24 extra if sharing room with parents. MC, V.*
Restrictions: *No pets. Accessibility for wheelchairs is limited.*

Festival du Vin des Laurentides

In mid-August the restaurants of the Laurentians, including the distinguished Bistro de Champlain, kick off a weekend festival of wine. Sommeliers and oenophiles come from all over the province of Quebec and, indeed, the rest of Canada. Foods are prepared to complement the wines, and representatives from all over the world are at various locations promoting their own particular vintages. Seminars are organized: Some discuss winemaking; others, the pairing of wine with certain foods. The best sommelier of Quebec is chosen at a competition organized by the Canadian Association of Sommeliers. All proceeds are donated to the Laurentian School for Hotel and Restaurant Studies in Ste-Adèle.

For information and a complete program, contact: **Le Festival du Vin des Laurentides.** Box 420, St-Adolphe-d'Howard, Que. J0T 2B0, tel. 819/327–3450.

Ontario

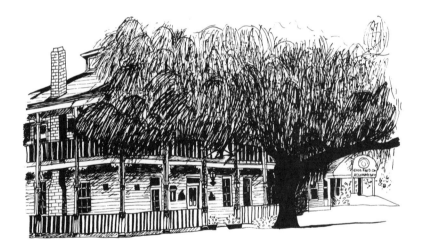

Ontario

Ontario was originally known as Upper Canada. Many of the first European settlers arrived from Scotland, England, and Ireland. This British connection was later strengthened by the United Empire Loyalists who fled from the United States. The country grew quickly. Canals were dug, stagecoach lines were established, and, little by little, the forests gave way to the teams of horses that cleared the land. Dirt and corduroy roads were the only thoroughfares, and they usually followed the paths that the first peoples had made. Wolves and deer roamed at will.

Ontario, now home to dozens of different nationalities, has emerged as the second-largest province in Canada. Traditionally it also has been the wealthiest. Toronto, the provincial capital, is only recently being challenged in its decision-making role by cities such as Vancouver, Calgary, and Montreal. Up to now, it has been the city that made things happen across the country. The financial district is very powerful. Throughout Canada, this perception of control has made Ontario the province all others love to hate.

Outside the city, and this indeed is where most Ontarians live, it is a very different story. Southern Ontario is a region of rich farmlands where the Puritan work ethic is still very much alive. Corn, grain, tender fruits, including wine grapes, vegetables, and a huge dairy industry have fed the people of the province and still have had lots left to export.

South-central Ontario has a profusion of farm markets from Windsor to Waterloo. Some of the lesser-known ones are Stratford, Simcoe, Woodstock, and Hagersville. Especially from July until October, visitors can enjoy the fruits of the summer's labors. This is where typical local foodstuffs may be found.

It is also a region of lakes and rivers. A Great Lakes commercial fishery nets splake, lake trout, pickerel, smelt, perch, and some of the recently introduced salmon. The streams, especially in the more outlying regions, regularly give up rainbow and speckled trout to skilled anglers and fly-fishermen.

Lake Huron's beaches are superb—without tides or seaweed. Summer communities abound. Farther north, toward Parry Sound and eastward, are the thousands of lakes that make up the Muskokas, the Haliburton Highlands, and the Kawarthas. Although they are crowded (in Canadian terms) in the summer, all the other seasons are free of traffic and very, very peaceful. Autumn is magical; winter is pristine and white.

Spring brings the theater season. The Stratford Shakespearean Festival began it all in 1953. Soon after followed the Shaw Festival in Niagara-on-the-Lake and numerous other small theaters from Grand Bend on Lake Huron to Gravenhurst in the Muskokas. Summer stock is lively and many Canadian plays are staged, especially at the smaller venues.

Northern Ontario is wild, and it's dotted with even more lakes than its southerly cousin. Primary industries rule. Poorly planned logging, as destructive as any in British Columbia, has caused large swatches of wilderness and first-growth forests to be destroyed. Fortunately, many of the earlier practices are being discontinued and more responsible voices on both sides of the fence are being heard.

This area is also very rich in minerals. The world's largest deposits of nickel and copper lay buried in the ancient rock of the Canadian Shield.

The far north is mostly inaccessible by car. Float planes and boats are often the only means of transportation. On the remote northern lakes, fishing and canoeing are magnificent.

Ontario is truly a land for all seasons.

***

For more information on traveling in Ontario:

Ontario Travel *counselors are available daily from mid-May to Labor Day, weekdays the rest of the year. Hours are from 8 A.M. till 6 P.M:*

From Canada and the Continental U.S. except the Yukon, Northwest Territories and Alaska: *tel. 800/ONTARIO (668-2746).*

From Canada, except the Yukon and Northwest Territories: *Information in French tel. 800/268-3736.*

From the Toronto calling area, the Yukon, Northwest Territories, and Alaska: *English tel. 416/965-4008; French tel. 416/965-3448.*

Telecommunications Device for the Deaf *(TDD) tel. 416/965-6027 (or call collect).*

Or write: **The Ministry of Tourism and Recreation,** *Province of Ontario, Queen's Park, Toronto, Ont. M7A 2E5.*

Eastern Ontario
Gallagher House Lakeside Country Inn

Gallagher House is an ornate Victorian-style building that sits on a hill overlooking Big Rideau Lake, a link in the chain of lakes and channels that form the Rideau Canal. This 123 mile (198 km) waterway was built as a defense link between the Ottawa River and Kingston, on Lake Ontario. It is said by many to be an extraordinary feat of 19th-century engineering. As the War of 1812 drew to a close, colonists in Upper Canada realized that military transport had to be more streamlined. In 1826 work began under the direction of Colonel John By. It took only five summer seasons for the Irish laborers, many of whom died of malaria, to complete the canal, which cut through virgin forest. The 47 locks still stand today as a testament to their hardships. The system is one of Canada's heritage canals and is solely used for pleasure boating nowadays, but it was once an important trade route. In Ottawa, originally known as Bytown, the canal freezes into the world's longest skating rink, and in late January the city celebrates Winterlude.

Because Al Gallagher, builder of Gallagher House, was a lumberman, the interior trim of the inn is exquisite. No paint here—just rich, polished wood. Each of the rooms is named after one of the luxurious old steamers that sailed out of Clayton, New York, and then on up the sys-

tem to Ottawa. Passengers slept on board, ate splendid meals, and enjoyed "rest and sport among the Rideau Lakes."

The Delta King room is the best room in the old inn, with an intricate iron bedstead and a balcony overlooking all the action at the government wharf. The original fireplace has a glass curio cabinet built into the mantel. The fire, built of maple logs, smokes just a bit and gives off a welcoming fragrance.

Innkeepers Patrick and Eleanor Dickey work very hard to create a comfortable atmosphere for their guests. Patrick regularly writes historical columns for the local newspaper, relating unusual happenings from the past. When they first bought the inn, they realized that they "needed the practice," so they remained open all winter long. Now, winters in this part of the country are not exactly crawling with tourists and boaters. But the locals loved to have what seemed to them to be their own personal restaurant. Even during a snowstorm, guests arrived to eat Eleanor's beefy Wexford Soup or have a slice of her tart sour-cream lemon pie.

Leeds County was once famous for its cheese makers. Now there is only one small cooperative, Forfar Dairy. They take great pride in the length of time that they age their cheddars;

a trip to the plant, southeast of Portland, will allow you to see first-hand how Ontario's handful of small cheese manufacturers now operates. Their product is superb, and you will find it somewhere on the Gallagher House menu.

In 1987, the Dickeys also completed the restoration of a second historic property next to their inn. Peter Bresee House was built in 1844 by the gentleman who owned and operated the Scovil general store—the same store that is now a summer crafts gallery called the Landing. It has a large two-bedroom suite on the second level. The renovated Bresee property has several large suites that are wheelchair accessible. Finally there is the Carriage House, a combination exercise/sauna/weight room overlooking the water. On the upper floor is a cedar-paneled conference room, a little on the rustic side but with a good number of audiovisual facilities.

The area is rich in things to do— from a tour of the Hershey's Chocolate Factory at Smiths Falls to boat cruises of the Thousand Islands, near Kingston. There are lake tours nearby and a canoe to paddle from the government dock. The fishing is good for largemouth and smallmouth bass, yellow perch, northern pike, and lake trout.

It takes about one hour to drive to Ottawa, where the list of sights to see is endless. Visit the Byward Market; take a tour of Parliament Hill; or spend a day in the National Gallery, and another in the Museum of Civilization.

In the winter, skate on the Rideau canal before eating one of Canada's great contributions to the culinary world, a "beaver tail," the crispy confection that is good when spread with raspberry jam and dusted with powdered sugar.

Staying in this area of Canada brings you as close to the history of the country as stopping by Annapolis Royal, Nova Scotia, or the Richelieu, south of Montreal. If you can manage a visit to Gallagher House, do allow yourself enough time to talk to Patrick and let him bend your ear with his wonderful stories of the olden days on the Rideau.

***

Gallagher House Lakeside Country Inn may be reached via Highway 15. It is about one hour north of Kingston and 20 minutes from Smiths Falls.

Address: *Box 99, W. Water St., Portland-on-the-Rideau, Ont. K0G 1V0, tel. 613/272-2895*
Amenities: *Breakfast included. Special diets accommodated with adequate prior arrangements. Meeting facilities for up to 20 in the Carriage House.*
Rates: *Gallagher House double $65–$90; Peter Bresee House double $50–$105; Graham Suite for 4 guests (minimum stay 2 nights) $175. AE, DC, EnRoute, MC, V.*
Restrictions: *No pets. Two suites in the Bresee House are wheelchair accessible.*

Hotel Kenney

A visit to this old inn is like returning to the 1950s—complete with elderly aunts and uncles. A warm and unpretentious innkeeper, Joe Kenney wrote the book on hospitality.

It all began in 1877 at Jones Falls on the Rideau Canal. Four generations of the Kenney family have operated this seasonal inn, which is certainly close to a record in Canada. Today, guests return after years of holidays at the hotel. One is a feisty lady from Ottawa, Lydia Philip, who always spends a month at the inn and recently celebrated her 104th birthday there.

The accommodations are simple; some include a refrigerator, and many have private baths or showers. Separate chalets and cottages sit by the waterway where square-stern boats and motors can be rented. Fishing guides can be hired who know the best spots for trout, bluegills, perch, and pickerel. There are 25 to 30 lakes within 15 miles (24 km) of the hotel.

The food is honest and old-fashioned. Mrs. Elsie Burtch has been "doing the desserts" for almost 40 years. Try her bread pudding with vanilla sauce. The kitchen packs shore lunches for fisherpeople, but otherwise guests eat all three meals in the dining room.

It's the sort of place where you can sit on the screened-in veranda, or by the pool, and watch the cruisers go by on the Rideau.

***

Hotel Kenney is located in Jones Falls, north of Gananoque and Kingston. From Highway 401 take either Highway 15 or Highway 32 north to Jones Falls. There are signs from there.

Address: *Jones Falls, Ont. K0G 1H0, tel. 613/359–5500.*
Amenities: *Full American Plan. Special diets can be handled with prior notice. One meeting room for up to 50 people is available in May, June, September, and October. Limited wheelchair accessibility, but help is always available. Nonsmoking areas are available.*
Rates: *$62–$75 per person, taxes not included. MC.*
Restrictions: *No pets. Closed Nov.– Apr.*

North-central Ontario
Arowhon Pines

Loons dive into the water with barely a ripple around the early morning mists that drift across Little Joe Lake. As dawn breaks, their calls echo from shore to forest-lined shore and smoke begins to curl from the lodge's huge stone chimney. A small motorboat slices through the watery mirror. Innkeepers Helen and Eugene Kates are arriving for the day from their hideaway on an adjoining lake. They probably won't return until late at night.

Arowhon Pines is located in the south-central part of Ontario's largest provincial park, Algonquin. In the 1930s Lillian Kates, Eugene's mother, had opened a children's camp and needed accommodation for their parents. She was agonizing over the design when one of those parents, architect Charles Coleman of Cleveland, grabbed a piece of brown paper and began to sketch. His magnificent hexagonal log lodge was hewn from the lakeside forest with hand tools before being planted firmly on the granite of the Canadian Shield by a winch and a team of incredibly strong horses.

In those early days there were no roads to the inn. Guests were picked up by motor launch from Joe Lake. They stayed at Tanglewood and dined in part of the kitchen while the familiar present dining room took shape.

To truly experience Arowhon, one should visit the National Gallery in Ottawa or the McMichael Canadian

Collection in Kleinburg, Ontario. There you will find the spirit of Canada made manifest in a picture. Tom Thomson lived and sketched in Algonquin, capturing her raw, wild beauty on canvas. A skilled outdoorsman, he mysteriously drowned on Canoe Lake (two lakes away from Little Joe) in 1917. Thomson's spirit still seems to inhabit many of the park's secret places.

Arowhon Pines has weathered elegantly under Eugene and Helen's guidance. Situated in the center of 3,000 square miles (7,770 sq km) of wilderness, it has tranquillity and style, from its cabins linked by walking bridges to its vaulted dining room, which encircles the ever-glowing fireplace. Arowhon Pines literally forces you to listen to Canada's north. There is one telephone (in the lodge) and no televisions or radios. Newspapers are delivered daily, but that's it for contact with the real world. The loons on the lake provide your wake-up call.

After negotiating the winding, 5 mile (8 km) long, gravel road that leads into the Algonquin bush from Highway 60, you'll be greeted by friendly staff who zip around the property on golf carts. They will take you to your shared or private cabin. Though the inn has no liquor license, you are welcome to bring your own and leave it with the dining-room manager for safe-keeping. Change into your casual clothes (the order for every Arowhon day), lace up your hiking boots, and head for the bush to work up an appetite.

All the food at Arowhon is made from scratch without preservatives (is rum a preservative?) and with as little salt as possible. Helen keeps a book listing all the ingredients of every dish (no mean task on a menu that changes daily) so that people with food allergies can eat comfortably. She sends a rather large taxi 3½ hours (on a good day) to Toronto's fabulous St. Lawrence Market for the finest ingredients. In sunny places, scattered randomly about the wooded property, Helen grows herbs like French sorrel, mint, and bushels of chives—there's even an old canoe full of tarragon and oregano.

"I never eat three meals a day" seemed to be the slogan of every guest table as they reloaded their plates from the mammoth breakfast buffet, the lunchtime spread, and, above all, from pastry chef Terry McKelvie's groaning dessert table at dinner. His lemon meringue pie is at least six inches (15 cm) high, his banana bread pudding is liberally laced with rum, his rice pudding is thick and creamy, and his breads are exquisite.

For those guests who are hikers or canoeists, the dining-room staff will organize a shoreside picnic or cookout for areas still so pristine that the water is drinkable.

Black flies can be a problem in May, but the Kateses have compensated for that by offering lower, "dress rehearsal" rates. A bottle of Muskol is a small price to pay for the privilege of testing *all* the summer menu items. It's a foody's heaven.

Algonquin Provincial Park is interlaced with hundreds of miles of canoe routes that range from placid lily-pad-strewn bays to roiling white water. Park activities are listed at the West and East gates and the Park Museum. Trained naturalists are on staff, and most activities are

free of charge. Arowhon has a complete complement of canoes, sailboards, sailboats, and maps. When we were there in late May, the water was still too cool for sailboarding without a neoprene suit, so we went for a quick swim off the dock and dried off in the spring sunshine. Bring your own fishing gear, and you can either canoe or rent a little motorboat to find a bass honey hole.

And don't, under any circumstances, forget your camera!

***

Arowhon Pines is located 175 miles (280 km) north of Toronto, 410 miles (660 km) from Detroit, and 300 miles (485 km) from Montreal. The nearest airport is Toronto's Pearson International, where small planes can be chartered or car/bus rental may be arranged.

Summer address: *Algonquin Park, Ont. P0A 1B0, tel. 705/633-5661, fax 705/633-5795.*
Winter address: *297 Balliol St., Toronto, Ont. M4S 1C7, tel. 416/483-4393, fax 416/483-4429.*
Amenities: *Full American Plan. Vegetarian or allergic diets available. Call ahead if you want to discuss specific dietary needs. A 1,150 square foot (107 sq m) fully equipped conference room is available for meetings. Wheelchair accessible. Accommodation for smokers provided.*
Rates: *(based on double occupancy) $150 (cabin with shared lounge, fireplace); $220 (private cabin with fireplace and sitting room). Weekly rates are available. 25% discount mid-May–mid-June (except weekends); 10% discount early Sept.– Oct. (except weekends); 10% surcharge mid-July–mid-Aug. All meals and facilities are included in the price. Motorboat rental is*

extra. There is a 15% service charge in lieu of tipping. No credit cards. **Restrictions:** *No pets. Closed Nov.– Apr.*

Domain of Killien

I n 1927 Dr. Louis Carroll built the lodge that was to become Domain of Killien. The lodge, his flight into tranquillity, was purchased in 1982 by the French Count and Countess de Moustier. It was adjacent to the 5,000 acres of forest and lakes they already owned. When their sons Dante and Jean-Edouard Larcade joined them, they named their new venture the Domain of Killien after the family *seigneurie* of Quillien in Brittany. For the past decade they have labored to make the inn a place where they can share with their guests *"un certain art de vivre."* The countess sewed the curtains; Dante, a fully qualified chef, took over the kitchen; and Jean-Edouard became the manager.

Domain of Killien is informal. Although it is requested that guests dress up a bit for dinner, the word *elegant* only applies to the food, the wine, and the innkeepers. Guests are encouraged to be themselves. There are no radios or televisions, and even the clocks are hard to find.

The first thing that strikes visitors when they enter the rustic log lodge is that it smells so good. The aroma of pine logs, a wood fire, and stocks simmering in the kitchen is indescribable. Mismatched, overstuffed furniture clusters about a chessboard in front of a fireplace that Jean-Edouard is constantly stoking. French and English magazines are scattered about. After dinner, this is the place to take coffee and liqueurs.

The Domain has a number (a fairly large number) of cozy cottages, away from the main lodge—all bearing the names of French women. The Count de Moustier decided that if he was going to be in the middle of the woods, he wanted to be surrounded, even if in name only, by beautiful women. The nicest rooms are upstairs, right in the lodge, closer to the dining room. In one bathroom, unglazed tiles cover the floor next to the whirlpool. The smallish windows open onto the lake or the forest, and at night you can hear the gentle lapping of the water before falling off to sleep. Dante and Jean-Edouard leave the birds' nests in place under the eaves, so at the crack of dawn choruses of birds can be heard.

Before breakfast, while the lake is glassy, it's fun to take the old rowboat for a spin. The smooth surface is a perfect place to learn to row.

Breakfast is a buffet of fruits and homemade croissants, coffee, hot chocolate with grated nutmeg, and several morning specials. It's easy to linger too long in the comfort of the dining room.

For those who are still hungry, or who have skipped breakfast to stay in bed or go in circles in the rowboat, lunch is also served. Picnic backpacks are filled for hikers, but dinner at the Domain is a meal no one wants to miss.

Dante creates a new menu daily and, in the tradition of great chefs the world over, cooks seasonally. He liberally uses fresh vegetables, herbs, and wild mushrooms. The peppery gazpacho is full of tomato chunks, and wild mushrooms are lightly sautéed and piled on puff pastries. He has a master's hand when preparing lamb to pink perfection. There are delicious desserts, such as a small bowlful of white-chocolate ice cream.

The Domain offers several unique programs. There are Degustation Weekends in which wine importer John Sainsbury does a "tour de France" using some of the country's older vintages—he sometimes broadens his scope to include a few fine cognacs.

Jean-Eduoard and Dante have lured naturalist R. D. Lawrence away from his two wolves and his puma to lead a series of "bush walks." Having written 21 books on Canadian wildlife, including the mammoth *Natural History of Canada*, Lawrence is eminently qualified to take guests on meanderings through the large estate. Spaces for these walks are limited, so it is essential that they be booked early.

For canoeists or cross-country skiers, Ophlie Cabin on the far shore of Delphis Lake is insulated and makes a perfect destination for the day or even for overnight. With two fireplaces, it should be warm.

Only fly-fishing is allowed on the Domain's private, stocked lakes. A tennis court is on the property. There are sailboards, canoes, and the aforementioned rowboat, all free of charge to guests. An extra charge applies to the CL-16 sailboat, fly-fishing equipment, and greens fees at the nearby Pinestone Golf Course.

The winter brings miles and miles of cross-country skiing and snowshoe-ing. The "skating rink" is getting a bit better, and as the innkeepers become atuned to Canadian technology (and skates), one year it may be perfect.

***

Domain of Killien is 2½ hours north of Toronto. Follow Highway 404 north of Toronto to Highway 48. Take that road to Coboconk and then head toward Minden. At Minden switch to Highway 121 to the village of Haliburton. In Haliburton, Highway 121 jogs at the Canadian Imperial Bank of Commerce. Instead of making the turn, head straight through the lights, go over a bridge, and turn left on Pine Avenue to Harburn Road. Follow the signs about 9 miles (15 km) to the Domain.

Address: *Box 810, Haliburton, Ont. K0M 1S0, tel. 705/457–1556.*
Amenities: *Modified American Plan, including breakfast and dinner. Special diets can be accommodated but prior notice would be appreciated. Meeting facilities for small business retreats for up to 12 people. The whole dining room is nonsmoking. The dining room and chalets are wheelchair accessible.*
Rates: *daily $112–$168 per person (excluding taxes and 15% service charge); 8% discount on stays longer than a week. AE, MC, V.*
Restrictions: *No pets, but winterized boarding facilities are nearby.*

The Inn and Tennis Club at Manitou

Every great inn makes a mark of its own on the pages of Canadian hospitality. The Inn and Tennis Club at Manitou is a luxurious spa and a superb tennis resort. Farther north and into the wilds than any other fine Ontario inn, this one offers quality far superior to what might be expected. For any establishment, it's a great honor to be asked to join the Relais et Châteaux. The Inn and Tennis Club not only has joined but has brought one of the organization's top awards, the Gold Shield, to Canada. Only two other members in the Western Hemisphere have been so honored, testifying to the dedication and the style of innkeepers Sheila and Ben Wise.

The Wises don't do anything by halves. They saw the need for an exclusive tennis club away from the city, so they built one: They imported a personable and highly skilled French chef, John Pierre Challett; a sommelier from the Hôtel Crillon in Paris; and a top-flight tennis director. Then they built an international-caliber fitness and health spa—again a first in Canada.

When they decided to offer harvest-cooking classes in mid-autumn, they collaborated with Bonnie Stern, one of Canada's best-known instructors in the culinary arts. For four hours daily, Bonnie good-naturedly leads guests through the foundations of Italian *cucina rustica* or French country cooking.

The Grand Masters Tennis Weekend has a famous guest—opera star Jan Rubes, who also happens to hold Ontario doubles titles in tennis for folks over 60, 65, and 70.

Jazz, a particular favorite of the Wises, has its own weekend, too. But it's not a small local band that's playing; it's Rob McConnell and the Boss Brass. Jazz concerts and jam sessions fill the nights.

***

To find the inn, one must drive down the narrow but paved back roads north of Parry Sound and through a forest that in June is carpeted with trilliums and other wildflowers. More modern in appearance than the other Canadian Relais et Châteaux, it nevertheless fits into the natural background of valleys and trees.

Guests share their lakeside villas with dozens of bird condos, well populated by purple martins. The warbling continues all day long.

The guest rooms are spectacular, and private balconies provide wonderful views of Lake Manitouwabing. A small ice bucket holding a split of champagne, fresh fruit, and mineral water welcomes guests in their rooms. The bathroom held more superb amenities—soft robes and a private sauna.

At night, duvets are fluffed onto each bed. More mineral water and herbal lozenges are placed on each pillow. The marble fireplace is laid with wood and kindling.

In the morning, a pot of freshly brewed coffee, fruit, and juices are brought with a wake-up knock—no horrid buzzers or bells, just Villeroy and Boch china and steaming coffee.

It comes as no surprise to find that the Inn and Tennis Club has also won "the best welcome award" from the Relais et Châteaux.

Chef Jean-Pierre ("J.P.") Challet offers two styles of menu—casual French bistro food and fine, well-sauced classical cuisine. A fricassee of *escargots* is accompanied by new red potatoes and coriander pesto. You may dine on a bowl of steamed mussels *marinière* with braised fennel and tomatoes in aniseed sauce, fresh fish, or *coq au vin* with herb croutons. Poultry sausages are layered in puff pastry, and the traditional salad "from Lyons" is a tangy mix of curly endive and bacon. Desserts are equally homespun—*tarte tatin, crème brûlée* and *Paris-Brest.*

The six-course "epicurean" menu is, as one would surmise, more formal and gracious. Great food and wine, soft music, and the glow of candlelight end any day with flair. Each day chef Challet's offerings change—no mean feat in any restaurant, let alone one in the wilds of Ontario. The velvety lobster bisque is sparked with fresh ginger and served under a puff pastry crust. The excellent leek, pear, and blue-cheese soup has slivers of sautéed leek as a garnish. Georgian Bay trout is baked in parchment with fresh peaches, a shot of brandy, and a bunch of thyme from the herb garden. J.P.'s ingredients are both regional and international—goat cheese from France and blueberries from Parry Sound. For guests who have come for a spa week, he creates

light dishes and gives calorie counts for them on all menus.

The Wises devote two weekends each season to display their young chef's talents. "For Gourmands" is just that. J.P. is given free rein and, with his brigade of 10, executes a seven-course dinner with five matching wines.

The wine list is one of the best, if not the best, north of Toronto. Developed by the Wises and Christophe Le Chatton, the current vice president of the Canadian sommeliers association, it features some of the finest French vintages, among them Château Petrus and a few specially ordered Ontario wines like the apricot-honeyed Inniskillin Icewine.

All season long, individually designed spa experiences and tennis clinics are offered in three to seven-day packages. One-day "spa samplers" acquaint day-guests with the wonders of a sea-kelp wrap or a shiatsu massage.

***

The Inn and Tennis Club at Manitou is near the village of McKellar, northeast of Parry Sound, about 2½ hours north of Toronto. Drive north on Highway 400 to north of Barrie. Take Highway 69 to Parry Sound and then follow Highway 124 to McKellar. At McKellar, take Centre Road south toward Lake Manitouwabing. The Camp Road leads directly to the inn.

Limo service is available from Toronto's Pearson International Airport, and float planes land at the inn's dock.

Summer address: *McKellar, Ont. P0G 1C0, tel. 705/389-3852, fax 705/389-3818.*
Winter address: *251 Davenport Rd., Toronto, Ont. M5R 1J9, tel. 416/967-3466. Relais et Châteaux*

*toll-free from North America
800/67-RELAIS.*

Amenities: *Modified American Plan
includes full breakfast and huge
buffet lunch daily, free use of all
watersports, tennis courts, and
mountain bikes. Dinner is not included. Special diets can be accommodated. Nonsmoking areas have
been designated in the dining
room. Meeting facilities are among
the best. Two fully equipped board
rooms have a capacity of up to 60
people. Special packages offered,
such as "Plan a friendly takeover."*
Rates: *per person (excluding tax
and 15% service charge): standard
$120–$143; deluxe $161–$199; luxury
suite $194–$239. EnRoute, MC, V.*
Restrictions: *No pets. Not wheelchair accessible. Closed late Oct.–
mid-May.*

The Moore Lake Inn

Take one Irishman, add a ghost in Room 1 and a sense of humor, and you have Derek Lowry. His inn, on the river that joins Moore and Gull lakes, is in the Haliburton Highlands with all its great fishing, antiquing, and canoeing.

The house was originally a tavern, owned by a man named O'Leary, that was a stopping place for the stagecoach and the Royal Mail. Loggers who worked shunting the timber booms downstream stopped here because of the falls.

The modest inn has six chintz-decorated rooms, all with private shower or bath. They make a reasonably priced base for exploring the area. You may rent canoes next door at the marina or, if you prefer to be a bystander, watch kayak and canoe competitions throughout the summer at the Minden White Water Preserve. The Kanawa International Museum of Canoes, Kayaks and Rowing Craft is on the Kandalore-Kanawa Road 30, roughly 18 miles (29 km) north of Minden.

The dinner menu is straightforward and fresh. Like the inn, it is unpretentious and satisfying. In the summer a chunky gazpacho heralds the arrival of fresh tomatoes, while in autumn a favorite is smoky pumpkin soup. A particular favorite is baby beef liver sautéed in shallots and red wine. Other entrées include a daily pasta special. A delicious chocolate cake is always available for dessert. Coffee and liqueurs can be enjoyed in the lounge.

The area is rich in outdoor activities, from snowmobiling and skiing, both alpine and cross-country, in the wintertime to antique-hunting, cycling, and hiking in the summer.

***

The Moore Lake Inn is located on Highway 35 at Moore's Falls, about two hours north of Toronto. Take Highway 401 to 48 North, then 48 to Highway 35. The inn is 4 miles (6 km) north of Norland.

Address: *R.R. 1, Norland, Ont. K0M 2L0, tel. 705/454-1753 (call collect).*
Amenities: *A full breakfast is available, as is a Modified American Plan. Vegetarian requests are fine; the inn's kitchen will try to accommodate others. Small casual meetings may be held in the living area for up to 12 in board-room style.*
Rates: *per person (taxes not included): bed-and-breakfast $35–$49; MAP $49–$69. EnRoute, MC, V.*
Restrictions: *No pets. No wheelchair accessibility. No nonsmoking policy, but they are attempting to discourage smoking.*

Sherwood Inn

In earlier times Muskoka was Ontario's favorite summer playground for well-heeled Victorian ladies and gentlemen. Before the days of speedy four-lane highways, they would head 250 miles (400 km) northward on the train from Toronto. On arriving at the Muskoka wharf early the next morning, they would board a small steamer that would transport them and a summer's worth of baggage to their particular island or someplace farther up the lake system. Every day the tough old boat would sail, picking up parcels, delivering supplies, or ferrying vacationers back to the train.

This restful ambience has only recently begun to fade. But at Sherwood Inn, you can find it all. This CAA/AAA Four Diamond Award–winning inn provides seclusion, service, elegance, and the outdoors. Summer and winter the inn caters to those who have discriminating taste.

During those days of steamer stops and good manners, a hostelry named Edgewood was built on Lake Joseph, on the edge of towering woods. It was not refined! Cornhusk mattresses were upstairs, a broken-down couch was in the living room corner, a ramshackle veranda encircled the place, and a moth-eaten hammock hung outdoors. Still, when they weren't in France or England, the regulars returned—doctors from Buffalo, a professor from New York. When Edgewood burned down in the 1930s, several lifetimes of memories were lost.

It was on the site of Edgewood that the gracious Sherwood Inn was born. This inn's guests still come back, but the decor has certainly changed.

Innkeeper John Heineck grew up in Germany. After graduating with a degree in hotel management from Heidelberg, he decided to improve his language skills. The years that followed saw him journeying and working from West Africa to Spain. In 1964 he decided to come to Canada to improve his English. He has never left. He and his wife, Eva, purchased Sherwood in 1979 and moved in.

The startling white clapboard inn is nestled among the trees, and flags wave proudly over the entrance. Flowers line the manicured lawns. Near the water, wonderful old painted lawn chairs beckon the tired traveler to sit and meditate.

Nine private cottages provide the most luxurious accommodations. Several have their own docks, and all have fireplaces, electric heat, private baths, and refrigerators. In the winter the lodge is the place to be. Many of its rooms overlook the lake, and most have private baths or whirlpools.

The Heinecks have made provision for all types of meal plans, but the most commonly used is the Modified American, whereby guests can travel and sightsee for the day or simply have a large late breakfast and skip lunch.

Dining at Sherwood tends toward more formal European fare—good if a little predictable. All the food is inn-made. When the menu says "chicken Cordon Bleu" it means that the tender chicken rolls have been fashioned by the chef, not taken from a box. Local maple syrup, trout, and blueberries all find their way into the kitchen in season. The wine list is excellent, and many of the international vintages are more reasonably priced than in most restaurants.

Sherwood is totally self-contained, with dozens of winter and summer activities for guests. They could be as simple as a snowshoe hike through the forest, a refreshing swim from the beach, or a challenging game of billiards or broom ball.

Muskoka is a vacationers' heaven. There's fine summer stock—don't forget that this is expensive cottage country for Torontonians who all winter long enjoy fabulous live theater. The Muskoka Festival Theatre (tel. 705/687–2762 from late May) is located in Gravenhurst, Huntsville, and Port Carling. The company stages plays from late June until Labor Day weekend in September.

The last of the coal-burning steamers, the R.M.S. *Segwun*, takes passengers on pleasure cruises from mid-June until mid-October. The ship sails by Millionaires Row, a series of fabulous shoreline summer houses on Lake Muskoka, or goes through the lift locks for a day on sparkling Lake Rosseau. Lunches and dinners are served on specific sailings in the wood-paneled lounge. The crew of the *Segwun* advises advance bookings (tel. 705/687–6667), especially in the months of July and August.

The Muskoka Autumn Studio Tour has been held yearly in the third week of September for more than a decade. Dozens of fine artists and craftspeople make the region the permanent home for their galleries. However, some only welcome visitors by appointment. The studio tour provides tourists and locals with a chance to view and perhaps purchase. Metal sculptures and hand-carved croquet mallets, blown and sculptured glass, silk weaving, and carved burl bowls—the range of designs and mediums is fantastic. For information, send a self-addressed, stamped envelope to Muskoka Autumn Studio Tour (Jamie Sherman, R.R. 1, Bracebridge, Ont. P0B 1C0).

A self-guided tour can be taken anytime among the area's 10 antique dealers. They all seem to have their own specialty—from Canadian folk art and English porcelain to maple furniture and pressed glass. The inn has copies of the brochure that outlines the route.

***

Sherwood Inn is two hours north of Toronto via Highway 69 north to Foot's Bay. Turn right to Highway 169 south and travel south to Sherwood Road, about 6 miles (10 km). Turn right just before the junction with Highway 118.

Address: *Box 400, Port Carling, Ont. P0B 1J0, tel. 705/765–3131 or 800/461–4233, fax 705/765–6668.*
Amenities: *All plans available. Special diets can be accommodated but prior notification would be appreciated. Meeting facilities are excellent. Six function rooms can hold up to 120 people for a reception. Secretarial services are available. Audiovisual equipment is provided.*
Rates: *per person double occupancy (excluding tax and 15% service charge): Modified American Plan, (breakfast, dinner, and room) $134–$196; cottages with MAP $120–$222. Numerous other combinations can be arranged. AE, DC, EnRoute, MC, V.*
Restrictions: *No pets. No pipes or cigars are allowed in the dining room. No rooms that are truly wheelchair accessible. The cottages and the dining room have several steps to reach them.*

Sir Sam's Inn

Sir Sam's is a stately inn with a wide screened porch stretching across its front. Flowering plants hang from the rafters, tended lovingly by innkeeper James Orr. Sir Sam's was built in 1917 by Sam Hughes, a prominent parliamentarian and the minister of the militia during World War I. He was granted thousands of forested acres in the north and chose to build his summer mansion on Eagle Lake. It is a lovely location. After Hughes's death it became a fishing lodge, and later it was simply deserted.

In 1979, just after he had graduated from college, James Orr set in motion his plan for Sir Sam's. He interviewed all the successful restaurant owner/entrepreneurs in Toronto, gathering information that would assist him. He bought the inn and since then has developed a full-service resort without sacrificing the charm of the older buildings. In his newest addition, Northwoods, 12 luxury suites, most with fireplaces and whirlpools, are discreetly set aside from the older buildings. Little by little he has renovated the original guest rooms, a never-ending task.

In the summer a waterfront director leads guests through the day's activities. They are encouraged to help themselves to sailboards, canoes, rowboats, paddleboats, and sailboats. The swimming is excellent from the sandy beach, water-skiing is available, and for the daring there is cliff-jumping into the deep waters of Moose Lake. Near the waterfront are two tennis courts, and rackets can be borrowed from the front desk.

In the winter Sir Sam's has its own small ski hill with double chairs, a T-bar and poma lift. There is always heaps of snow from December until March. A cross-country trail system runs for 170 miles (275 km) through the forests and across the lakes near the inn.

Year-round facilities include a sauna, an exercise room, a movie room, and an outdoor whirlpool.

The dining-room menu holds few surprises. Changed daily because many guests stay longer than one night, it has a variety of well-prepared dishes—cognac pâté, escargots in puff pastry, fresh green salads, and entrées that range from steak to seafood. The wine list is good, and reasonably priced, featuring mainly imported vintages.

The village of Haliburton is 20 minutes away. There, one can find antiques, gifts, and groceries. Three golf courses are also within 20 minutes.

The main reason people come to Haliburton is to enjoy a summer holiday by a lake or to ski the deep snow that is virtually guaranteed in the winter. But late September and October is a spectacular time, when the leaves are a riot of color and the nights are cool but the lakes still hold the heat of summer. These days of Indian summer seem all the more precious because they are an unexpected gift before the long Canadian winter sets in.

***

Sir Sam's Inn may be reached by taking Highway 400 north to Highway 11. Follow Highway 11 north to Highway 118, which you will follow east to West Guilford. Take County Road 6 to Sir Sam's Road.

Address: *Eagle Lake, Ont. K0M 1M0, tel. 705/754-2188, fax 705/754-4262.*
Amenities: *European Plan or Modified American Plan available. Special diets can be accommodated with prior notice. Excellent meeting facilities in four rooms for up to 72, with full audiovisual equipment and office services provided.*
Rates: *per person (includes sports facilities and service charges): no meals $45–$79; with two meals spring/fall/winter $98–$125, summer $125–$155. Special weekend, honeymoon, and conference packages available. AE, DC, EnRoute, MC, V.*
Restrictions: *No pets. Limited wheelchair accessibility.*

South-central Ontario
Breadalbane Inn

For almost two decades the Breadalbane Inn has had the most consistently good dining room in the Fergus-Elora area. Their menu has remained much the same for that length of time for one reason: The guests simply won't let Phil and Jean Cardinal change it. They specialize in steak, and when the menu says "tender and juicy," it is. Phil, who has been dealing with the same butcher for 16 years, scoffs at restaurateurs who constantly check prices and shop around. Business people, friends, neighbors, and visitors keep coming back for their own personal favorites. The back spareribs are cooked to order and take 25 minutes of constant turning on the grill. Within seconds after cooking they are in front of the diner, basted with a secret maple-and-honey sauce. No heat lamps and steam tables in the kitchen of this inn. Dinners are prepared *à la minute*.

Their rack of lamb has brought rave reviews, and a table of four got up and walked out when the scallops were taken off the menu—they are now back on.

Phil's hot-fudge cake is a must. Ladles of the decadent sauce are poured over fresh chocolate cake and ice cream. For a chocoholic, it's a bit of heaven.

When you run such an inn, you have to understand who your clientele is—or who you want it to be. The Cardinals have chosen to be friends with their own community. They have kept their prices low, their food fresh, and their wine list about as reasonably priced as it can be. The people have responded. It is impossible to walk in for dinner without a reservation on any night toward the end of the week. Lunches are much the same, busy with people from town having meetings or just exchanging news.

The Breadalbane was once called Mapleshade, the home built by the cofounder of Fergus, Adam Fergusson, for one of his sons. Its two foot thick (⅔m) walls, ironwork from Naples, and high ceilings have caused one Scottish historian to call it "the gem of Fergus architecture." The stairways, banisters, and newel posts are made of solid walnut, as are the doors and huge bay windows. Originally there were five working fireplaces, and it is said that it took two men cutting wood all winter long to keep enough on hand to heat the place. The terraced lot has now been enclosed to create a private garden for the inn's guests, who can sit in the shade of maples that were planted before the turn of the century.

When the Cardinals bought the inn in 1975, they changed the name in deference to the first Earl of Breadalbane, Adam Fergusson's uncle.

Their renovations have included the addition of seven guest rooms, all but one with private washrooms.

The town of Fergus was founded in the early 1800s by Fergusson and James Webster, two thrifty and far-sighted Scots. Fergusson, a member of the Highland Society of Scotland, was the man appointed to visit North America to obtain "such information regarding those countries as may prove beneficial to rural economy and the useful arts at home." In other words, they wanted to know how to go about sending settlers. In February 1831, Fergusson left Edinburgh and made his way into Canada via New York, the Erie Canal, and Lake Champlain. On this trip he reached the end of known civilization, Guelph, Ontario. The treatise that he published on his return to Scotland not only sold many others on the idea of immigration to Canada, but he also sold himself. He enticed a number of "other gentlemen of property" to journey with him. After a long search for the appropriate site, he found a place where the earth was good and "a fine falls on the river, which is clear as crystal, flowing over a limestone bed, full of delicious trout, and the forest abounds in a variety of game." He purchased a block of 7,000 acres where Fergus now stands. At that time there were no real roads, and in 1833 the first log house was raised.

The Scots who came to Fergus from Perthshire were not poor crofters. They were men and women of substance. Both the town's architecture and its Scottish heritage reflect those roots. Today, the Fergus Highland Games are the premier event of its kind in North America. For three days in mid-August, the town decks itself in its finery and welcomes visitors and competitors from all over the globe. Both the International and the North American Scottish Heavy Events are held here yearly. The

skirling of the massed bands quickens the heart of anyone with even half a drop of Scottish blood in their veins. Hundreds of dancers compete, and huge men dig in their heels for the North American Tug-of-War competition. There is always a Scottish concert with preference shown to Canadian talent. Cape Breton musicians are often found here. Last year, a Welsh Choir from Cardiff was in the spotlight; the year before, it was the rousing strains of the Cape Breton Symphony.

Piobaireachd, the classical music of the Highland bagpipe, are the ambitious pieces that are at the very least 200 years old. This is the music of the competition. The piper begins with the theme or ground, followed by variations that become increasingly more complex for the performer. The finale, called *crunluath*, is nothing short of spectacular, especially if you have ever tried to choak a note from an unwilling bagpipe.

Information on the games can be obtained from the Fergus Highland Games, Box 3, Fergus, Ont. N1M 2W7. It is essential to book accommodation at least a year in advance at either the Breadalbane or the Elora Mill Inn (*see* p. 154).

***

Breadalbane Inn is 20 minutes north of Guelph, Ontario, on Highway 6. It is 1¼ hours west of Toronto, four hours from Detroit.

Address: *486 St. Andrews St. W, Fergus, Ont. N1M 1P2, tel. 519/843-4770, fax 519/843-7600.*
Amenities: *Continental breakfast included. Special diets can be handled with advance notice. A meeting room accommodates up to 15.*
Rates: *Sun.–Thurs. $60 per room; Fri.–Sat. $70–$90 per room. Taxes are extra. MC, V.*
Restrictions: *No pets. The inn has one step for a wheelchair to negoti-*

ate, but no room is set up for the physically challenged. Although there is no nonsmoking policy, smoking is not encouraged. Dining room closed Mon.

The Cataract Inn

The Niagara Escarpment is the backbone of Ontario. It begins in the fruit and bench lands near Niagara-on-the-Lake and rises northward, across the countryside, and finally dives into Lake Huron at Tobermory. Thick forests cluster along its wild ridges, dappled with wildflowers in the spring, a cool haven for deer in the summer and a photographer's paradise in the autumn. Out of cracks and crevices, streams tumble. Through its valleys, rivers flow.

The Bruce Trail, a 400 mile (720 km) footpath, leads thousands into a fuller understanding of Ontario. Generous landowners have allowed hikers to cross and even camp. A few bed-and-breakfasts have sprung up along its length, but only one inn—the Cataract. The Bruce Trail Association has published a guidebook, which is available in many bookstores for around $20 or through the association's offices (*see below*).

The village of Cataract was founded around 1818 by would-be millionaires who came following a rumor of a gold strike. Although the story proved to be false, the pseudo-prospectors discovered a beautiful, rocky area, quite unlike the encircling meadows and woods. The wild river, later to be named the Credit, surged and plummeted over a 60 foot (18 m) fall. In the ensuing years, mills were built and the village of Cataract prospered.

The Cataract Inn was built in 1855 as a tavern. A graceful building with pulled brick down its corners and highlighting the many-paned windows, the hotel has had many faces and once was named the Dewdrop Inn. Today, innkeepers Rodney and Jennifer Hough have restored the inn without destroying its casually comfortable ambience. The five second-floor guest rooms share two bathrooms. Clothes can be hung on pegs or folded into the antique dressers. Fat, cushy sofas make the common room a private, away-from-it-all spot to relax. The most charming room is #6, with its old spindle bed and valley view.

The Cataract Inn is close enough to Toronto that it has become a favorite weekday retreat for business people. On the weekends the three small dining rooms are patronized by many of those same city folk who this time are wearing their other hats as gentlemen farmers.

The fare is as good as it sounds. Diners can begin with *escargots* with garlic and roasted almonds in a pastry shell, smoked salmon dill mousse, sushi beef, or all three. The most popular salad is their Caesar, but for those who want a change, try the romaine and spinach tossed with roasted garlic, mushrooms, and drizzled with sun-dried tomato vinaigrette. New York strip loin is rolled with cracked black peppercorns and served with sautéed oyster mushrooms. Rainbow trout and grilled scallops are blessed with saffron/cilantro butter.

The dessert menu is equally strong. Try the warm chocolate pecan pie with chantilly cream. A New York–style cheesecake is sliced and served on a pool of cappuccino *crème anglaise* studded with white-chocolate-covered almonds. Although they don't freeze their own ices, they purchase the very best that Toronto has, from Italian gelato maker Gelato Fresco.

The proximity of the city has helped the Houghs establish and maintain the inn's successful catering company. As an offshoot of that enterprise, a Shop at the Inn was created last year where guests, picnickers, or passers-by can purchase the inn's own breads, pastas, salsas, pâtés, and terrines.

The Forks of the Credit Provincial Park is just across the road. It's 650 acres with miles of hiking and cross-country trails link up with the Bruce Trail, and even if guests decide not to hike the Bruce, they can stroll for hours. In the park along the river there are many ruins, including the old Deagle Power Plant. The cataract itself may be reached by going down recently mended wooden steps.

The inn also arranges hot-air ballooning during the summer—right from the back lawn. Or if guests prefer to simply wander down back roads and explore, the inn's kitchen will pack a picnic hamper.

This area is known for its good trout streams, but when the season opens each May 1, it's obvious that this is close-by urban Canada.

The cross-country skiing is excellent, and the Caledon Ski Club has a small downhill facility. Check for snow conditions, though. Some winters there's a lot of it, while during others one almost has to cut the grass.

***

The Cataract Inn may be reached from Toronto by taking Highway 10 north past Brampton to the town of Caledon. Turn west (left) on Highway 24 and continue to the 3rd Line. Head south toward Cataract and watch for the inn as you round the first corner.

Address: *R.R. 2, Alton, Ont. L0N 1A0, tel. 519/927–3033, fax 519/927–5779*
Amenities: *Breakfast included in rates. With prior notice most dietary restrictions can be handled. The dining room and patio are wheelchair accessible; no rooms are. Designated areas for smoking.*
Rates: *double (excluding taxes) $60. Special packages available. AE, MC, V.*
Restrictions: *No pets and no facilities for children. Closed Dec. 24–27.*

For information on or membership in the Bruce Trail Association, write or call: **The Bruce Trail Association,** Box 857, Hamilton, Ont. L8N 3N9, tel. 416/529–6821.
Membership is about $30 and includes regular newsletters, etc.

The Elora
Mill Inn

Elora—few other small Ontario hamlets have so much to offer in terms of ambience, natural beauty, raw artistic talent, theater, and, especially, music.

Elora was founded by Captain William Gilkison, who bought 14,000 acres in 1832 at the confluence of the wide Grand River and Irvine Creek. These waterways run through a deep limestone gorge that is so inaccessible and treacherous that it was the hiding place for the Neutral Indians during various native wars. Caves line the chasm, and when Gilkison saw them he named the future settlement after his brother's ship, which in turn had been named after the hand-hewn Ellora caves near Bombay.

Captain Gilkison could be considered one of the first architects of life in Upper New York State. In 1797, he was making a regular supply run to the Northwest Company outpost in Detroit and returning the furs to Buffalo, then a thriving metropolis of five residents. It was on Gilkison's advice that John Galt, another thrifty Scot, realized the land named Ontario might hold promise and came to found the cities of Guelph and Cambridge.

Like Fergus, the area was originally settled by industrious and reasonably wealthy Scots. The buildings in Elora are a living testament to their labors and skill as stonemasons. The local Liquor Store, originally the Ar-

moury Hall, was built in 1865 by the village council in direct opposition to the wishes of many of the ratepayers (little has changed). The first farm market took place in that parking lot, and if you look closely, you'll see the likeness of a rooster cockily carved into the stone above the doorway. Probably the most elegant and impressive of all the local stonework is the Elora Mill Inn, rising 100 feet (30 m) above a treacherous part of the river. The spring breakup booms so loudly with water and chunks of ice that it can be heard all over the village.

The Elora Mill Inn was most recently a gristmill owned by the Drimmie family, who have lived here for generations. Pigeons and feed trucks once populated Mill Street, now lined with upscale shops. In the mid-1970s, several sharp-witted and farsighted women opened the Nightingale Tea Shoppe, a craft and gift store called the Green Owl, and an antique store in the dilapidated buildings on the short street leading to the Mill. The only other occupants were the Wellington County Museum and a cold-storage facility. It was a true *bas ville.*

By 1975, the old, somewhat dusty mill and its outbuildings were in the midst of restoration, a project that has just lately been completed. When it was first renovated, 32 comfortable guest rooms filled the structure. The present mill-keepers, Tim and Kathy Taylor, and Tim's father,

Crozier, installed a working 148-kilowatt generator that harnesses the power of the Grand River. It provides so much electricity that even the village purchases it periodically. The Penstock Lounge boasts a beautiful glass-enclosed balcony overlooking the river rushing around Islet Rock. You can sip imported or local beers (Sleeman's/Upper Canada/Brick), and a plethora of wild and wonderful cocktails including hot "teas" that would warm the toes of any frostbitten cross-country skier.

The food of the Mill, like that in many such inns, has had its less-than-great moments over the years, but is now on solid ground and constantly improving. Their Bermuda chowder is wonderful, with a hot dash of peppered sherry. Tender Muscovy duck is raised just down the road. Waterloo County maple syrup is splashed into a number of sauces, and, shades of the 1950s, many dishes are being prepared, even flamed, at table side. The wine list features some of the very best Ontario wines.

As winter approaches, its hoped with snow falling outside, the whole inn is decked out as beautifully as Charles Dickens would have wished. The Elora Mill's Christmas Feast follows those wonderful old traditions. For three days in early December, Highland pipers and choristers evoke the spirit of Christmas. Reservations for this five-course banquet and wassail are absolutely essential—several months in advance.

Like most innkeepers, the Taylors are full-fledged community workers. Their specialty is the Elora Festival, a multiweek celebration that William Littler of the *Toronto Star* called "the gem of summer music festivals." The Mill itself hosts several cabarets and has sponsored a number of top-flight events over the years. Tim is currently serving as the festival chairperson. This unique summer festival is quite intimate in nature, because most of concerts are held in small churches where the audience has personal contact with the performers. Many of the events center on the resident 24-member professional choir and the resident chamber orchestra. Although the event focuses mainly on Canadian talent, international musical stars have also made appearances. Baritone Christopher Trakas of New York City, gospel singer Laura English-Robinson from Atlanta, flutist William Bennett, and classical guitarist Simon Wynberg have all appeared.

If music isn't your interest, a studio tour is held on the weekend before Canadian Thanksgiving. Artists, many of whom are seasoned veterans of Toronto's One-Of-A-Kind Show, all open their workrooms to display their creations. Huge pieces of stained glass in fanciful designs can be found at Boney Fingers. Whimsical pottery fish plates can be seen at Geoff Steven's Elora Pottery. Fabulously intricate batiks of Monet's garden and Canadian country scenes by Linda Risacher Copp are on display. And there are the consummately earthy wares at Peter and Nancy's, a shop run by two villagers who were pottery pioneers in the early '70s.

If you feel like a picnic, you can purchase supplies at Wellington Fare (try their butter tarts) or the Elora Farm Market. And no trip to the area is complete without a totally homemade breakfast at Marge's Kitchen in Alma, where, if you can get in the door despite the usual line, you'll rub elbows with truck drivers, radio personalities, farmers, and writers.

The Gorge Cinema, a small, eclectic theater, is just down the street from the Elora Mill Inn. But if you really want a thrill, don your bathing suit, buy an old inner tube, and go tubing in the gorge. Swimming is excellent in the pure water of the quarry from which most of Fergus and Elora was built.

If you run out of ideas, the final suggestion is to buy a local paper and find a bake sale, a community dinner, (October is good for that), or perhaps a craft fair.

***

The Elora Mill Inn is located about 20 minutes north of Guelph and about 1¼ hours drive west of Toronto. Nearest major airport is Pearson International where car rental may be arranged. Amtrak periodically services Guelph enroute from Chicago to Toronto.

Address: *77 Mill St. W, Elora, Ont. N0B 1S0, tel. 519/846-5356, fax 519/846-9180.*
Accommodations: *32 with private bath including rooms in the Mill Cottage, the Ross House, and the Granary.*
Amenities: *Continental breakfast included. Vegetarian and allergy-sensitive diets are available with prior notice to the kitchen. Meeting facilities: three well-appointed meeting rooms with capacity to 150. Wheelchair accessible. Accommodation for nonsmokers provided.*
Rates: *double $90–$170. AE, MC, V.*
Restrictions: *No pets.*

Gate House Inn

The lush Niagara region grows the bulk of Canada's fine wine grapes. Its winemakers celebrate at the Gate House.

The town of Niagara-on-the-Lake has North America's only theater season devoted to the staging of works by George Bernard Shaw. Its luminaries dine at the Gate House.

The Gate House Inn's Ristorante Giardino, with its cool European marble interior, has the best, and probably the most expensive, food in the area. In the past, Niagara-on-the-Lake was a culinary wasteland. Now, thankfully, a farsighted Italian textile magnate and his wife, Signor and Signora Dalavalla, have created a first-class hotel. Polished Italian marble, gleaming brass, black leather, and an extravagant use of glass give the inn a feeling of ultramodern luxury.

The 10 guest rooms tend to carry on the minimalist style of the rest of the hotel with their clean lines and modern lighting.

Wisely the Dalavallas have a contract with a dedicated young Italian, Mario Prudente, who makes sure that the hotel runs like clockwork. He always seems to be on deck and he truly loves the business. Although he has little formal training, he used to travel to great hotels and watch the management. It has paid off.

Like many Italians, the Dallavallas and Prudente recognize the wonders of fine food. The kitchen is expansive, the chefs well trained. Daily during the theater season, and Tuesdays through Sundays during the rest of the year (see below for specific dates), fabulous Italian food is served. Taste is of prime concern, with presentation a close second. Plump snails (*lumache* in Italian) are sautéed in olive oil and butter and served surrounded by grilled golden polenta strips, rich red tomato, and a sprinkling of finely minced deep green basil. Other appetizers include marinated swordfish, prosciutto, smoked goose breast with sautéed mushrooms, or the staple of every good Italian restaurant, *carpaccio*, but this time served with brightly colored marinated vegetables.

Entrées include many superb dishes. The best buy in the house, though, is the fresh pasta, which, when supplemented with one of the inn's soups, will satisfy most moderate gluttons among us. The *conchiglie* (snail-shell pasta) is stuffed with ricotta and smoked salmon, then finished with a herbed butter sauce. Sage and rosemary season the *tagliatelle* in a lamb sauce, a most interesting combination.

Skip another course if you have to in order to enjoy dessert. Besides a heavenly *tiramisu*, there is the soufflé *freddo al Grand Marnier*. When the plate comes to the table, it looks like an abstract painting. A chilled Grand Marnier soufflé sits lightly in a bitter chocolate shell. Fresh fruit is scattered randomly over a pool of *crème fraîche* and strawberry *coulis*. The French do deserve a little credit for inspiring this marvelous dessert.

In the summer, a table d'hôte luncheon is served. The four courses guarantee that their guests will not only dine in style, but also will not miss the opening curtain.

The town of Niagara-on-the-Lake was the first capital of Upper Canada. Settled by Loyalists, it was the scene of much bloody fighting during the War of 1812. It was sacked and burned by the Americans in December 1813. Nonetheless it is without question one of the best-preserved 19th-century towns in North America. Several houses date from the year 1800.

Wilson's Hotel, now the Gate House, witnessed the founding of the Law Society of Upper Canada in 1797 after the introduction of English common law into the territory. In 1832, the society moved its offices to Osgoode Hall in Toronto, where it still functions as the regulatory agency to set standards for lawyers throughout the province and to grant them the right to practice in Ontario.

The Shaw Festival, founded in 1962 in the old courthouse, has played every summer since. Queens, princes, prime ministers, and presidents have come to its productions. For tickets or general information call 416/468-2172. If you are planning to visit the town during the festival, it is essential that accommodation be booked well in advance. For special plays and on weekends, one should call several months ahead.

For history buffs, Fort George (built 1796–99) has been restored, and during the summer it is open seven days a week. It played a vital role in defending Upper Canada and, in fact, prevented the capture of British North America by the Americans.

Shopping in Niagara-on-the-Lake tends to be expensive, so try the markets of nearby St. Catharines and Port Dalhousie. For gardeners, Stokes Seeds is one of the sites for the All-American trials. For beer lovers, Sculler Breweries has tours of their small facility.

***

Gate House Inn/Ristorante Giardino is in the center of Niagara-on-the-Lake. The town may be reached across the Lewiston Bridge from New York State or from Toronto along the Queen Elizabeth Way. Pearson International Airport (Toronto) is serviced by many major U.S. and international carriers. Ground transportation to Niagara-on-the-Lake is readily available from there.

Address: *142 Queen St., Niagara-on-the-Lake, Ont. L0S 1J0, tel. 416/468-3263, fax 416/468-7400.*
Amenities: *European Plan with complimentary coffee in the morning. Special dietary requests can be handled with advance notice. Meeting facilities consist of one small seminar room for up to 12 people. Dining room is fully wheelchair accessible as is one bedroom. Smoking is permitted throughout the inn but dining room has a nonsmoking section.*
Rates: *double (excluding tax) $125 Sept.–Dec. and Mar.–June, $145 July–Aug. MC, V.*
Restrictions: *No pets. Closed Jan.–Feb. Dining room closed on Mondays from the end of the Shaw Festival until Easter. No luncheons served during that time. Otherwise, open daily.*

Grape Expeditions

Wine country is an unfamiliar term in the Canadian vocabulary. But in the past decade a new breed of grower/vintner has taken over the fertile Niagara region: determined, energetic men and women with the grit to develop what are now being recognized as some of the finest wines in North America.

The older grape varieties (_Vitis labrusca_) are quickly giving way to the noble European grapes (_Vitis vinifera_) like Cabernet Sauvignon, Gewürztraminer, Riesling, Pinot Chardonnay, Pinot Noir, and Sauvignon Blanc. Several wineries are cultivating more obscure vinifera like Pinot Auxerrois, Pinot Gris, and Aligoté as well as hardier North American hybrids like Vidal, Seyval Blanc, and Baco Noir.

White-grape plantings are now mature, outnumbering the slower-growing reds. And this is where we shine! With the help of a cold northern climate, vintners can now create buttery Chardonnays, fruity Rieslings, and apricot/honey icewines.

***

The Niagara region of South Central Ontario has vineyards that are more than a century old, and _all_ wineries offer free tastings.

In 1989 the Vintners Quality Alliance (VQA) was established in the region—a bold move designed to place the Ontario wine industry firmly on the leading edge. The VQA is styled on the French Appellation Controlée system with myriad stringent winemaking and viticultural rules, the consumers' real guarantee of quality. It is the first such solid guarantee of quality to exist in Canada.

This tour has been designed for anyone who is staying at an inn within driving distance of the region. It travels north to south. Exit off the Queen Elizabeth Way as quickly as possible below the city of Hamilton at Fifty Road, and literally head for the hills. This ancient ridge, the Niagara Escarpment, was once the beach of an ice-age lake.

The first winery is Stoney Ridge Cellars (tel. 416/643–4508). Jim Warren and partner Murray Puddicombe have a combination tasting room, farm market, and delicatessen. At the farm market, begin assembling a picnic with fresh fruit from Puddicombe's farm; great cheeses from Hanon, just over the escarpment; Criveller chocolates from Niagara Falls; and Jack Beemer's orchard-gathered honey.

Jim built his reputation as a medal-winning amateur winemaker. His Chardonnays are among the best in Niagara, with a blast of concentrated flavor. Try all of them from various vineyards about the Stoney Ridge acreage—Lenko, Eastman, Guttler, and Puddicombe. A specialist in small batches, Jim makes one barrel every year of a perfumed port he calls Jasmine.

Traveling south on Highway 81, you wind through peach orchards toward the beginning of the Beamsville Bench growing region. Tom and Len Penachetti, of Cave Springs Cellars (tel. 416/687–9633), believe that this is the best 19 miles (30 km) of growing area east of the Rockies. The escarpment, on the right of the highway, varies in height from 90 to 150 feet (30–50 m) and acts as a natural buffer for the onshore Lake Ontario winds. The frost damage is minimized here because of the warming convection currents that wash over the vineyards.

Even to the uneducated palate, Cave Springs Chardonnays are exquisite. Several years ago, Clone 77 of that particular grape was discovered in the vineyard. A Cave Springs exclusive, it had the characteristics of a muscat grape, hence the new name, Musque. Unlike most Chardonnays, this one has no secondary fermentation. The wine is citrussy, with just a hint of green apple, and it's a multimedal winner. Indian Summer is a smooth-sipping, carefully made, late-harvest Riesling.

Visit Vineland Estates (tel. 416/562–7088), just off Highway 81 near Jordan, to experience an autumnal view of the softly rolling countryside with acres of vines drooping with this year's harvest. Vineland Estates is the prettiest winery in the region, and winemaker Alan Schmitt can guide you through his beautifully balanced Rieslings and Chardonnays while you lunch on a grapevine basket of breads, cheeses, and smoked meats on their Wine Deck.

Farther down the road, Henry of Pelham's (tel. 416/684–8423) winemaker is vinifying a full-bodied Baco Noir that is being served in Canadian Embassies around the globe. At no time is the dedication of the small vintners more apparent than on one subzero night last winter, when the precious drops of icewine juice were still being pressed outdoors at 1 A.M.—by hand! Two years ago, four rows of Seyval Blanc were discovered after the harvest, so perfect that the grapes were left in their golden clusters for an extra few weeks. Hand-picked and crushed, they yielded a late harvest wine never before made. Continue, following directional signs, around St. Catharines until you come to Château des Charmes (tel. 416/262–5202), the dreamchild of Paul Bosc.

A hands-on winemaker, Bosc has built his reputation on high-quality Frenchstyle wines. In 1988 he was named the Niagara Grape and Wine Festival's Grape King, an honor reserved for the region's best grape grower of the year. Bosc was the first vintner to wear the crown in the annual mid-September party. To celebrate his monarchy, and because he happened to have his best crop of Chardonnay grapes ripening on a little sandy knoll near his home, he created Le Roi, a superb Chardonnay that when you close your eyes and inhale, smells lightly of "buttered corn on the cob." Another one of his favorites, a grape he calls "the future of Niagara," is Pinot Auxerrois. Its vines are strong, perfect for the fickle Ontario climate. The wine is fruity and meant to be enjoyed young, and it needs no barrel-aging, a real plus when 100 new French oak barrels just cost the winery $70,000.

Three years ago Bosc entered his méthode champenoise Brut in a blind tasting in Ottawa. It takes courage to throw your hat into the ring with the great French champagne houses. He won! It's an exceptional wine, with fine streams of bubbles and a wonderful, breadlike champagne nose.

Bosc, like all the other top Niagara vintners, is looking free trade squarely in the face and reveling in the opportunity. His new winery, to be opened later in 1992, will be tucked carefully under the escarpment, complete with a theater and huge underground aging cellars.

North of Niagara-on-the-Lake are the meticulously cared for vineyards of Herbert Konzelmann (tel. 416/935–2866). After 25 years of producing wines in Germany, he came to Niagara and planted 30,000 vines in 1983. His skills lie in making beautifully rounded German-style wines. A Konzelmann Gewürztraminer is as fine an example of that grape's adaptation to Canada as you'll find. For a special dessert wine, try the Late Harvest Vidal, a bouquet of flavor. Although blush wines have fallen from most people's favor, Konzelmann makes a fruity Pinot Noir Rosé that should be tasted.

Klaus Reif (tel. 416/468-7738), a 13th-generation winemaker, was one of the youngest applicants ever to be accepted to the world-famous winemaking university at Geisenheim. In partnership with his uncle, Reif makes delightful German-style wines. A German hybrid, Kerner, is balanced and fruity. His 1988 Vidal Icewine is legendary, winning a string of medals.

Perhaps the most daring of all Niagara's young vintners, Reif is now culturing his own supply of yeast, a first for the Canadian industry. His huge oaken barrels are cooled by another innovation, narrow coils of filament directly connected to a computer that monitors the temperature of each vintage and adjusts its temperature to the optimum coolness for fermentation.

Down the quiet lane and around the corner is Inniskillin (tel. 416/468-2187), the granddaddy of them all. In 1975, Donald Ziraldo was granted Ontario's first wine license since 1929. He is unquestionably the driving force that has propelled the industry toward its present vitality. A University of Guelph agriculture graduate, he returned to the Niagara with a dream—a small estate winery. Ziraldo is the consummate marketing genius. He took a flagging industry and wove the basic threads of today's amazing network of wineries.

Karl Kaiser, Inniskillin's winemaker and cofounder, is expanding his repertoire with experimental wines. Walk into the cool tasting salon enveloped in the fragrance of oak and fermenting grapes, and sip and swirl an easy-drinking Gruener Veltliner, or one of their clean, well-made Chardonnays. Inniskillin's Icewine is so good that there's a prerelease waiting list. It is Niagara's best icewine. Their Cabernet Franc, if it has been bottled when you read this, is the richest Canadian red I've tasted. Karl Kaiser has done it again.

Gather up your grapey treasures and head homeward, tanned and certainly glowing after an intoxicating sip of Canada.

For information on Niagara events and accommodation, contact: **The Region Niagara Tourist Council,** 2201 St. David's Rd., Box 1042, Thorold, Ont. L2V 4T7, tel. 416/685-1571. **The Niagara Grape and Wine Festival,** 164 St. Paul St., St. Catharines, Ont. L2R 3M2, tel. 416/688-0212.

The Kettle Creek Inn

Gary and Jean Vedova purchased the remains of the Garden Inn in the early 1980s. After major renovation the Kettle Creek Inn was open for business by 1983, a real tribute to the vision these innkeepers had. The parlor has a fireplace that is particularly welcome during the winter and early spring, when weather can be damp. The first rooms to be dressed up, complete with duvets and custom-made bedsteads, have shared bathrooms and saunas. In 1990 eight additional suites were added in two guest houses. It's in these rooms that the Vedovas have pulled out all the stops. They are named after local artists whose works hang in each suite. They all overlook the mounds of flowers in the English-style garden that doubles as a fair-weather dining terrace.

Good food is the order of the day at Kettle Creek. Five varieties of lettuce are tossed with a balsamic vinaigrette. New York sirloin is served with red wine/shallot butter melting over it; Ontario lamb chops, with rosemary au jus. The yellow perch, which Port Stanley is known for, is breaded and deep-fried. Desserts are seasonal and contain as many of the fresh fruits and berries as chef Pat Boehme can find.

Just down the road on George Street is Floridel Gardens. Orchids have been cultivated there since 1973. It is easy to see why the flowers have an international botanical reputation. More than 700 varieties bloom in the two main greenhouses. Although much of the store's trade is wholesale, the public is most welcome from Tuesdays through Saturdays from 9 A.M. to 5 P.M. The starter plants are from all over the world but are mainly tropical in origin—most now come from Hawaii. Before

Mother's Day in early May, the greenhouses are bursting with a riot of color. Some flowers, like the popular moth orchid, a native of Central America, are three to four inches (7½–10 cm) in diameter and last for weeks. Plants are for sale and include growing instructions to supplement the verbal guidance that flows freely.

Another grower, Moore Water Gardens, just north of Port Stanley, specializes in water lilies and everything else that it takes to create your own pool, complete with fish and fountain. Visitors are welcome from Monday to Friday, in the mornings from October to March and from 9 A.M. to 5 P.M. during the late spring and the summer.

Locals will tell about Hawk's Cliff, east of the village, which is part of the hawk migration in mid-September. Better still are the monarch butterflies that congregate here on their journey to the wintering forests in Mexico.

The L&PS train makes its historic run most days in the summer and on weekends the rest of the year. It chugs its way from Port Stanley to Union, a distance of three miles (five km). A longer run, to St. Thomas, is also scheduled. The schedule is available at the Kettle Creek Inn or by writing the railway at Box 549, Port Stanley, Ont. N0L 2A0 (tel. 519/782-9993).

Port Stanley is the largest natural harbor on the north shore of the lake—it is a working port well-known for its large fishing fleet. Fresh pickerel, perch, and salmon may be purchased along the waterfront, and tours of the fish-processing plants can be arranged.

Like all the Great Lakes, Erie has dozens of shipwrecks. And because it is such a shallow lake, only 200 feet (64 m) deep, many of them are accessible to divers. Port Stanley has a scuba sales, service, and charter shop that specializes in wreck dives. This same shop is an Ontario Underwater Council–approved air station.

The area is dotted with small fishing villages, beaches, fruit stands, and pick-your-own farms. It generally has a more moderate climate than the rest of the province, so the growing season is longer and gentler. If you can, load up on strawberries, raspberries, apples, peaches, tomatoes, or corn from local farms or roadside stands. There are also several excellent farmers' markets in the area as well. Aylmer Sales Arena is open year-round on Tuesdays from 9 A.M. until 9 P.M. Tillsonburg Farmers' Market runs from May until November on Saturdays from 8 A.M. until noon. Horton Market in St. Thomas operates on Saturdays from 7 A.M. until noon, year-round.

***

The Kettle Creek Inn is in the village of Port Stanley, 28 miles (45 km) south of London. Exit from Highway 401 at Wellington Road South and take Highway 4.

Address: *Main St., Port Stanley, Ont. N0L 2A0, tel. 519/782-3388.*
Amenities: *Breakfast is included in room rate. Specials diets can be accomodated with appropriate notice. The inn has one large board room for up to 30 with audiovisual equipment, private dining room and walkout to the garden. Dining rooms and two guest rooms are wheelchair accessible. Dining rooms have smoking and nonsmoking sections.*
Rates: *All exclude sales tax. Main Inn: 9 guest rooms with shared bath and sauna, single $50, double $60–$70; Guest House: 5 guest*

rooms with private bath, queen-size bed, single $80, double $90; Guest House: 2 suites with private whirlpool, living room, queen-size bed, gas fireplace, single $115, double $125; Designer Suite: all of the above with king-size bed, single $140, double $150. Additional person add $10. Inn Escape Package includes two nights, dinner each evening, plus breakfasts: $220–$380 per couple. DC, EnRoute, MC, V.
Restrictions: *No pets.*

Langdon Hall
Country House Hotel

Hidden in 40 acres of woodland, close to Highway 401 and the hamlet of Blair, is the former country estate of U.S. multimillionaire Langdon Wilks, a direct descendant of John Jacob Astor. Very few locals even knew that the huge American Revival–style mansion existed, but when William Bennett, the architect who so perfectly restored the Millcroft Inn (*see* p. 167), saw it in 1978, he began to dream.

Now, 11 years later, his vision and that of his partner, Mary Beaton, has been fulfilled, and Langdon Hall Country House Hotel has thrown open its gates to welcome discriminating travelers. The hotel, in turn, has been welcomed as the newest member of the country's Relais et Châteaux. There is no other inn, or country house hotel, like it in Canada.

Two main buildings are the focus for activity—Langdon Hall itself, proud and sedate, and the Cloisters, a series of bedrooms and meeting facilities connected to Langdon Hall by an underground tunnel. The accommodation includes 36 first-class rooms and seven elegant suites, each with its own character, 38 with working fireplaces. The woodwork has been handcrafted to Bennett's exacting specifications by local artisans.

Dr. Leslie Laking, former head of the Royal Botanical Gardens in Hamilton, was coaxed out of retirement by Bennett to oversee Langdon Hall's intricate plantings. When a little more mature, the gardens will be a regional showplace of botanical beauty in an area known as Carolinian Ontario. The climate is exceptionally mild, and thus plants that would normally grow only in the southern United States, such as papaw, sassafras and skunk cabbage, flourish in quiet woodsy corners.

Outdoor recreational facilities include a tennis court, a croquet lawn, and a heated swimming pool. Indoors, guests are able to work out before enjoying a sauna and a whirlpool. Or they may choose the gentler pastimes of cards and billiards.

Chef Nigel Didcock, who trained both in London and with the Troisgros brothers in France, tempers his classical French cuisine with Canadian country cooking. When he came to the area, almost a year before the hotel was to open, he spent most of his time learning about the climate and haunting the nearby farmers' markets in search of local produce. Fresh asparagus comes from down the road in the spring. Ontario's best *chèvre* (goat) cheese is made less than 20 minutes away. Didcock must lead a charmed life— low and behold, morels started popping up right on the property.

Hidden behind a high fieldstone wall is the magnificent kitchen garden. Softly tilled earth grows tomato plants that are staked higher than five feet (1.5 m). Masses of dill, huge feathery clumps of fennel, asters, zinnias, flowers for drying, and row upon row of translucent green lettuce bask in the sun. A sprawling patch of (bug-free!) nasturtiums with leaves the size of tea plates creep toward the mounds of fresh herbs. Chefs across Canada would kill for a garden like this one.

The joy is that Nigel Didcock is a superb chef. The garden salad really is just that, with torn bits of kale and a scattering of flower petals. Small mouthfuls of sea scallops have been marinated to serve as a counterpoint to lemon fettucini, and the lacy leaves of sweet cicely add a sweet licorice touch. In the summer the foods are seasonal and light, with a genuine harvest flavor. In the winter, they are heartier; again, the chef uses ingredients that make us aware that we are in Ontario. Cabbage, a vegetable that is looked down upon by many, often appears on the menu, as do sweet winter squash and the province's great potatoes.

In the autumn, thick, juicy peach pie is served with inn-made mint ice cream. Chunks of apple are covered with golden sweet strudel topping.

The accompanying wine list is well chosen and moderately priced. Some of Ontario's best wines are featured.

The dining room, overlooking the green, is centered on a quiet pool of lily pads and strategically placed grasses that seem to bend on cue in the breezes. An old-fashioned wooden swing hangs in the portico of the Cloisters, a place for contemplation beside the reflecting pool.

Tea is served on fine Limoges china in the glass-surrounded conservatory, which overlooks another of Dr. Laking's gardens. Phlox and old roses perfume the courtyard.

Because it is so close to the historical and culinary heart of the province, Langdon Hall is an exquisite base from which to explore. This is Mennonite country, and three of the five farmers' markets that are within driving distance reflect that heritage. The most famous of these is in downtown Kitchener, where every Saturday (and Wednesdays during the summer), shoppers can purchase everything from maple syrup and the Brethren's goose-down pillows to smoked pork chops and shiitake mushrooms. North of Waterloo, two competitive markets have developed over the past decade. The first, the Waterloo County Farmers' Market, was founded by disgruntled Mennonites when the old Kitchener market was "renovated." They simply left. There you will find a lot more true farm produce. It's a very busy market. If you have never been to a market before, you should be prepared to spend a few hours and take your camera. Across the road are the stockyards—where good buys can be found for large quantities.

All the villages in the area are fun to browse in. St. Jacobs and Elmira, near the Waterloo County Farmers' Market, are the centers for the Mennonite community. The Meeting Place, in St. Jacobs, is operated by the church. They explain, by demonstration and film, the roots of the faith and how they practice in Canada.

The Mennonite Relief Auction is held on one Saturday in late May to benefit the poor in other countries. All year long congregations sew quilts. The auction is Canada's best quilt show and sale. But the added bonus is the great country food, from icing-filled long-john donuts to fresh strawberry pie. Everything that is sold is donated—and so is the auctioneers' time.

From Langdon Hall, it's a short drive to the Stratford Festival (tel. 519/273-1600), which showcases the works of William Shakespeare from May to October every year, plus a host of other playwrights. Performances are held in the afternoon and evening at a number of venues around the city. On special days backstage tours can be arranged.

Other sites of interest are the Sea-gram Museum in Waterloo, where the curators will take you through the history of winemaking; Doon Heritage Crossroads, to glimpse life of early Waterloo County; the Kitch-ener-Waterloo Art Gallery; the oldest Mennonite home in the area, the Joseph Schnieder Haus; the Kortright Waterfowl Center outside Guelph; and the Royal Botanical Gardens in Hamilton.

Langdon Hall was built as the dream of a farsighted couple and is the epitome of elegance. Rituals such as dressing for meals are observed, so perhaps it is not the best place for the casual traveler. However, for those seeking refinement and style, Langdon Hall is the place to be.

***

Langdon Hall Country House Hotel is about one hour from Toronto, 45 minutes from Pearson International Airport. Take Highway 401 west past Cambridge to Exit 275 (Homer Watson Boulevard). Drive south on Fountain Street to Blair Road (second on the right). Follow the street signs to Blair. After the town tavern, take the second road to the right. Discreet signs mark the way. Turn left immediately into the driveway.

Address: *R.R. 33, Cambridge, Ont. N3H 4R8, tel. 416/338–8800 or 519/740–2100, Relais et Châteaux toll-free from North America 800/67–RELAIS.*
Amenities: *European Plan. Special diets can be accommodated but prior notice is appreciated. Full meeting and convention facilities are available for up to 50 people— the conference rooms open onto the Orchard. Smaller groups can be accommodated in various venues throughout the hotel. There are designated nonsmoking areas.*

Much of the inn is wheelchair accessible.
Rates: *$125–$275 (excluding tax and service) double. AE, DC, EnRoute, MC, V.*
Restrictions: *No pets.*

The Millcroft Inn

Adventure is everywhere in Ontario, and a visit to the Millcroft Inn is no exception. On warm summer evenings, guests can try their hand at hot-air ballooning. The balloons billow as they are filled in the early evening light. Brilliantly colored spheres, they slowly rise and drift over the Caledon countryside with the summer breezes. Wicker gondolas carry the passengers and pilot. Below, a tracking van chases over back roads. As the sun sets, they gently float earthward, champagne corks pop, the flutes are filled, and guests toast each other on their successful flight.

The Millcroft Inn was one of a series of old mills on the Credit River in the village of Alton. Surviving a major flood that destroyed many of the others, and several serious fires, it was purchased by an expert Toronto hotelier, George Minden, and his associates. Architect William Bennett was contracted to redesign and restore the old mill. In doing so, he won the National Award of Honor for Heritage Preservation. A true conservationist, Mr. Bennett continued to make his mark on Ontario's finest buildings when he took on the even more ambitious project of restoring Langdon Hall Country House Hotel (*see* p. 164).

What was once the Dods Mill, a factory producing woolen garments, now contains 22 beautifully appointed bedrooms, all individually furnished with a blend of Canadian and European antiques. The Dods residence has been returned to its turn-of-the-century glory as the Manor, a separate house that has 10 luxurious bedrooms, some with hot tubs and fireplaces. A series of 20 two-story chalets, the Crofts, was constructed on the other side of the Credit River; they feature sleeping lofts with living areas below, as well as private patios.

Mill-keeper Mark Harrison comes from a long line of restaurateurs and innkeepers. He hails from Devon, England, and you'll recognize him as the person running like a jackrabbit along the back roads near the inn. He meets most guests personally and sincerely tries to create the feeling at the inn of a "home away from home."

The chef at the Millcroft is Swiss-trained Fredy Stamm. He has worked with culinary guiding light Anton Mosimann, and he apprenticed in the Grand Hotel in Lucerne, the hotel made famous by César Ritz and Auguste Escoffier. Stamm has many fresh herbs and vegetables grown for him by local farmers. His wife grows the edible flowers. In the spring they harvest wild leeks, ginger, and fiddleheads for the inn.

Chef Stamm is king of the culinary empire at the Millcroft. He creates daily menus in addition to the seasonal table d'hôte. Caledon trout may be poached with woodland mushrooms and finished with a rosemary butter sauce. Medallions of Ontario pork tenderloin, reputed to be the best in Canada, are served with goat cheese *au gratin* and fresh tomato preserve. He strays somewhat from his Canadian focus in his offerings of gulf shrimp, Scottish smoked salmon, and U.S. lamb, but generally stays true to his philosophy of extreme freshness. No shrimp that has been transported a thousand miles can be fresh.

The desserts are wonderful. Pastry chef Luzia Felske offers a large selection of inn-made ices (such as honey-lemon, blueberry-yogurt, and pineapple-kirsch) and all-natural ice creams (for example, banana-nougat, coffee-toffee, and white-chocolate chunk). From fresh berries to "white-chocolate explosion," they are well worth trying.

One would expect an excellent wine and liquor list, and the Millcroft does not disappoint. It is well priced from inexpensive bottles to fine vintages; most are in the $20–$60 range.

Upon arrival, or earlier, guests are advised to reserve a dinner table in "the pod," one of the most unusual dining areas in the province. It's surrounded by glass and juts out over the falls. In the darkness, the water bounces and plays along in the glow of a small spotlight.

For summer activities, there are two tennis courts, a heated swimming pool and hot tub, volleyball, canoeing or punting on the pond, miles of walking trails, and, of course, jogging with Mark Harrison. Winter brings another dimension. The cross-country skiing and skating are excellent. Before hauling your skis along, it's best to check snow conditions. Each of the last four winters has been different, one having little or no snow.

***

The Millcroft Inn may be reached by taking Highway 401 west to Highway 410 north. Drive eight miles (13 km) to Highway 7 west. Travel west for one mile (1.6 km) to Highway 10. Turn right and follow Highway 10 north to the town of Caledon, approximately 15 miles (24 km).

At Caledon turn left on Highway 24 and go two miles (three km) to Highway 136; then go two miles (three km) to Alton. Turn left at the stop sign and then right into the entranceway to the inn.

The Millcroft is 40 minutes from Pearson International Airport in Toronto and an hour from downtown Toronto.

Address: *Box 89, John St., Alton, Ont. L0N 1A0, tel. 416/791–4422 (toll-free from Toronto) or 519/941–8111, fax 416/857–6130, Relais et Châteaux toll-free from North America 800/67–RELAIS*
Amenities: *A country Continental breakfast is included in room rate. Special diets can be handled but prior notification is appreciated. Meeting facilities at the Millcroft are exceptional. Four rooms accommodate up to 32 with full audiovisual equipment. The dining room is wheelchair accessible as is one guest room. Nonsmoking section in dining room but otherwise no regulations.*
Rates: *$155–$170 per room, single, double, or triple (where there's a built-in bed). Numerous special packages and weekend escapes are available. AE, DC, EnRoute, MC, V.*
Restrictions: *No pets.*

The Waterlot

Located in the small town of New Hamburg, the Waterlot is a small (three-bedroom) inn that is frequented by locals in search of a delicious meal.

New Hamburg was believed originally to have been a squatters' settlement on the grassy banks of the Nith River. Although a mill was built in the 1820s, the settlement and the mill-keeper were victims of a cholera epidemic. Apparently some of the victims' bones were discovered to the rear of the inn's property. Over the years, several waves of immigration changed the face of the region. First, of course, were the United Empire Loyalists and the Pennsylvania Dutch or Amish. Then came the Scots, one of whom actually built the Waterlot as his home, and still later a large influx of Germans. The city of Kitchener's original name, Berlin, was changed during World War I.

Without exception, the Waterlot has been the dwelling place of people who shaped the town, from a senator to two country doctors.

Attached to the building is the Waterlot store, a great place to shop for your picnic.

Breakfast is served to overnight guests, but "not too early," says innkeeper Gord Elkeer.

Dinner entrées range from quail stuffed with apricots and pine nuts to tenderloin of lamb baked in phyllo pastry with local goat cheese.

From the Waterlot, it is a short 15-minute drive to the city of Stratford where, at the Stratford Festival, from May to October, Shakespeare is king.

***

The Waterlot is 20 minutes west of Kitchener-Waterloo, and 1½ hours west of Toronto off Highway 7, which heads toward Stratford.

Address: *17 Huron St., New Hamburg, Ont. N0B 2G0, tel. 519/662–2020 fax 519/662–2114.*
Amenities: *Breakfast included. Special diets can be handled with advance notice. Meetings may be held in any of the five dining rooms, which accommodate from 10 to 40.*
Rates: *$70–$90 for the two rooms with shared bath; $115 for the room with private bath. AE, EnRoute, MC, V.*
Restrictions: *Not suitable for pets or small children. No smoking in guest rooms. Rooms not accessible by wheelchair. Restaurant closed Mon.*

Western Ontario
The Benmiller Inn

The Benmiller Inn is on the verge of being excluded from the list of great Canadian inns because it has become so corporate-oriented. It is operated by the Granite Group, business people who have devoted themselves to purchasing and restoring many of the province's heritage properties. It's a Catch-22 situation. Without their input, many of the resorts would have operated at a less efficient level, if they survived at all. But even though they try their best to add the small touches that make an inn special, visits are not as personally satisfying as they were when the "owner/innkeeper/sometimes chef" greeted guests at the door.

That said, The Benmiller Inn is still one of the most beautifully restored mills in the province. These old mills were crucial to the settlement of Upper Canada, and the economy was completely centered on such industry. Wherever there was a strong river and a good waterfall, a little town sprang up, and the hamlet of Benmiller was no exception.
A woolen mill was built in 1840, a period of great optimism and expansion. It operated until the 1940s, when technology caught up with it. Not until Peter Ivey, a London, Ontario, industrialist bought it, did it come back to life. The restoration was a work of art. A brother-and-sister team, Peter and Joanne Mazzoleni, let their imagination propel the project. Over the ensuing years,

other properties filled out a complex of country inns, each with its own personality.

The mill itself was built of cast limestone, an awesome task in an era when there was no electricity or gas-powered engines. The original beams and structure have been lovingly maintained.

The first addition during Ivey's tenure was the River Mill, a former flour mill, which opened in 1975 with large suites and river views. The next year, a swimming pool and tennis courts were added. In 1979 the Gledhill House was purchased. The Gledhill family had operated the woolen mill for four generations. It was in their home that Ivey installed his luxury suites—two have private saunas and marble whirlpools. Here a guest can fish from his balcony in the trout-stocked mill pond or simply inhale the heady fragrance of the forest.

The final property to be purchased was Cherrydale Farm, a magnificent old stone farmhouse (circa 1834) on 200 acres. It is the oldest building still standing in Colborne Township and is the perfect place to go when you need rest and solitude. Meals, with the exception of some light snacks during the ski season, must be taken at the main inn just down the road. The ingredients for a Continental breakfast are provided in each room.

Meals in the Benmiller's magnificent dining room (reserve a window seat) tend to focus on local, hence seasonal, ingredients. They purchase goat cheeses to fill their crisp phyllo pastry, which the chef then smothers with a warm tomato vinaigrette. Vegetables are from the region, as are rainbow trout, guinea hen (oven baked with black currants and port-wine sauce), and tender Ontario pork. There is always a daily pasta and lots of non-local seafood like scallops and British Columbian salmon.

The countryside around Benmiller is rolling and perfectly husbanded. It is rural Ontario at its best. Each small village serves its own particular farm community. The Maitland River rambles casually on its way toward Lake Huron, where miles of pebbled and sandy beaches have some of the best freshwater swimming in eastern Canada.

Guests are treated to a large choice of activities. Meander down back roads on the inn's bicycles, play tennis, fly-fish for trout or salmon in the Maitland River, or swim in the indoor pool. Hike on the nature trails that crisscross the property, or have a game of billiards or even darts. Cross-country skiing is excellent in the wintertime, and there's even an indoor jogging track.

Both the Stratford Shakespearean Festival (tel. 519/273–1600) and the Blyth Festival (tel. 519/523–9300) are within an easy drive from Benmiller.

***

The Benmiller Inn is a healthy three-hour drive west of Toronto and about the same distance from Detroit. From Toronto follow Highway 401 to Highway 8 at Kitchener. Take Highway 8 through Stratford for about 5 miles (8 km) past the town of Clinton. Turn right on Huron County Road 1—the inn is 1½ miles (2½ km) down that road. From Michigan, follow the Bluewater Highway 21 north through Forest and Grand Bend toward Goderich. Take Route 8 east for 4 miles (6½ km) to Huron County Road 1 and then follow the signs.

Address: *R.R. 4, Goderich, Ont. N7A 3Y1 tel. 800/265–1711 or 519/524–2191, fax 519/524–5150.*
Amenities: *Rates are for bed-and-Continental-breakfast or Modified American Plan for a two-night stay. Special diets are fine as long as some advance notice is given. Meeting facilities are excellent with four conference rooms for over 100 delegates. Complete audiovisual equipment is available. The inn has special conference rates and menus. Wheelchair accessible. No nonsmoking areas.*
Rates: *bed-and-breakfast: Jan.–Apr. and Nov.–late Dec., $99–$199 single or double occupancy; May–Oct. and last week in Dec., $125–$225 single or double occupancy. Additional person $15 per night for 12 years and older; children under 12 free. Does not include 8% provincial sales tax and 7% GST. Modified American Plan (per couple): winter rates (see above dates) $215–$314.50; summer rates (see above dates) $230.50–$336.25. Includes accommodation for two nights, Continental breakfast each morning, dinner both evenings, lunch one day, provincial and federal sales taxes. AE, MC, V.*
Restrictions: *No pets, but kennel facilities are nearby.*

The Little Inn of Bayfield

The old-fashioned village of Bay-field, on the eastern shore of Lake Huron, was laid out just after the War of 1812 by British naval officer and hydrographic surveyor Henry Wolsley Bayfield, at the request of Baron van Tuyll of Belgium. Van Tuyll never saw his offshore investment but Bayfield went on to chart lakes Erie, Huron, and Superior as well as much of the St. Lawrence River to Labrador. He was appointed an admiral in 1867.

Because the accepted mode of transportation was by water, the port of Bayfield prospered. It grew quickly and hence has a wonderful stockpile of period buildings. Clan Gregor Square was the hub of activity at one end of Main Street, which still extends down to the water, where the Marinas on Bayfield River make up the largest sail and power facilities on the Canadian side of Lake Huron. The Little Inn is situated on this tree-lined avenue in a sensible location to welcome both stagecoach arrivals en route between Sarnia and Goderich and those who journeyed on the water.

In 1981 the present owners, Pat and Gayle Waters, bought the inn. They had stayed there as guests and, like so many others, fell in love with the village. They have been true to the history of the old inn, carefully restoring the structure while upgrading and adding *en suite* bathrooms. They dug out old photographs and rebuilt the original two-story ginger-

bread-embellished porch carefully, leaving the huge willow tree that drapes across the front of the property.

In 1987 the Guest Cottage was constructed across the street. One would be hard-pressed to tell that the building is new. Inside, the Waters have situated their more sumptuous suites, several with their own whirlpools and fireplaces. The region has many cross-country ski trails and snowshoe paths, and the warmth and privacy of a dancing fire in your room after a day in the fresh Huron County air is about as close to heaven as you can get.

Over the years the village has been discovered by a number of artists and gallery owners. It makes treasure shopping, for anything from antiques and Victorian-style lingerie to native art and expedition gear, a year-round joy.

In the mid-'80s they were fortunate to have an ebullient chef, Richard Fitoussi, join their staff. Richard is simply never at a loss for words. Consequently, he didn't stay in the kitchen for too long. Now he is the general manager, a position for which he is infinitely well suited. The region has been his supermarket. He buys as much local produce as he can, and his chef uses it to create an imaginative mix of dishes on their menu. Locally smoked goose breast is layered on top of a celery-root salad, and there is also a lobster pâté with truffles. Ontario pork tenderloin is roasted in vine leaves, or you may order a swordfish creole.

Long-aged cheddar cheese oozes from the lunchtime omelets. The inn serves a ploughman's lunch, hearty sandwiches, and, the ultimate in comfort food, beef stew. On Sunday there's a very popular brunch from 11 A.M. until mid-afternoon. High tea, with Devon cream, scones, preserves, and homemade pastries, is served daily.

Desserts are without a doubt the Little Inn's forte. Bourbon pecan pie has an intoxicating filling, nestled in a buttery crust and mellowed with the rich, smooth flavor of Bourbon topped with toasted pecans. Their chocolate thunder torte has a deep, dark, and delicious filling of bittersweet chocolate, showered with chocolate chips. The pastry chef creates other minimarvels, from a traditional *crème caramel* to a sour-cream-and-honey cheesecake. All ice creams are inn-made and are usually served with a raspberry sauce.

The wine list is good in its attempt to promote Ontario's vintages. It reflects the province's strengths, and five of the 13 white wines are from the Niagara area. Their Château des Charmes *méthode champenoise* sparkling wine is the best that has been produced to date in Canada.

Exercise is essential after such a feast, and both golf and tennis are nearby. Tie a fly and try your luck on the river, which regularly has a good salmon run. Trout are there all year round, and lake fishing charters are available.

Blyth Summer Theatre (tel. 519/523–9300) and the Stratford Shakespearean Festival (tel. 519/273–1600) are both in full swing all summer long. The Grand Bend Players, just south of Bayfield, also present summer repertory theater.

One of the real joys of this region is taking a morning drive up Bluewater Highway 21. Explore and discover the area, and have a breakfast picnic on a beach or at a roadside table. Using the Little Inn as your base, you can travel any direction except, of course, west, and each will show you a different side of Ontario.

***

The Little Inn of Bayfield is located in the village of Bayfield, on Highway 21, about 135 miles (217 km) north of Detroit and 140 miles (225 km) west of Toronto. There is a small local airstrip, Sky Harbour Airport, 13 miles (21 km) away in Goderich.

Address: *Box 100, Bayfield, Ont. N0M 1G0, tel. 519/565–2611.*
Amenities: *European Plan or Modified American Plan. Special diets are available off the menu, but if advance notice is given, more choices can be provided. Meeting facilities: Guest Cottage Conference Room accommodates 35 boardroom style, or 50 theater style. Carriage House Conference Room will hold 30 board-room style, or 50 theater style. Smoking restrictions apply only to part of the dining room.*
Rates: *Double occupancy: from $95 for en suite in original inn to $185 for large suite in Guest Cottage. Single, seasonal, seniors, corporate, and government rates available. Packages: weekend MAP package $170–$250 per day per person; daily MAP Sun.–Thurs. in winter and spring, $75–$100 per person. AE, CB, DC, EnRoute, MC, V.*
Restrictions: *Pets can be accommodated with the approval of the management. A kennel is located 10 minutes away. Only the dining room is wheelchair accessible.*

Saskatchewan

THE
BANBURY HOUSE INN
EUROPEAN BED & BREAKFAST
PASTA RESTAURANT & LOUNGE

Saskatchewan

Saskatchewan summer—bushes hanging with ripening chokecherries, grain elevators glowing pink in the early morning light, stands of winter-stunted trees, an ancient threshing machine abandoned by a hedgerow, a horizon brimming with the gold of wheat; and yet, two years earlier this had been a swirling dustbowl, with plumes of parched prairie earth spiraling hundreds of feet toward the heavens.

These are the vicissitudes that prairie people have to cope with. It's a harsh, magnificent, and powerful reality.

To live in these provinces one must love them. Perhaps it's watching storms as they scour the earth coming toward you. Or maybe it's standing outdoors at night under an overturned, inky bowl of sky glittering with stars. It also could be the people, who are as genuine as any in Canada, good people who will turn aside whatever they're doing to help their neighbors.

This sunniest of all Canadian provinces is also a forested wilderness of more than 100,000 freshwater lakes, undiscovered by the traveling public and full of fish. It's a quarter of a million square miles (647,450 sq km) awaiting the advent of ecotourism.

***

For a copy of The Great Saskatchewan Vacation Book *and* Outdoor Adventure, *write or call toll-free:* **Tourism Saskatchewan**, *1919 Saskatchewan Dr., Regina, Saskatchewan S4 3V7, tel. 306/787-2300 (in Regina), 800/667-7538 (in Saskatchewan), or 800/667-7191 (in Canada/U.S.).*

The Regina Area
The Banbury House Inn

The Banbury House Inn could be transported to a small European town and fit in perfectly. Built in 1905 by E. A. Banbury, founder of Canada's huge Beaver Lumber Company, it is now a registered historic site.

Innkeepers Rosemarie and Ernest Boehme have furnished the inn with antiques, and all the guest rooms have private baths or showers. The corner Honeymoon Suite has a whirlpool.

On the main floor dining room, a European-style breakfast is available for overnight guests, featuring soft cheeses, fresh muffins, and jams that are made from fruits in the garden—the saskatoon berries from the wild bushes that flourish in the countryside, or the plums that regularly load the trees in the backyard.

Ernest and their youngest son, Patrick, are chefs at Le Parisien next door, another beautifully restored turn-of-the-century house. It is not uncommon to see limousines pulled up outside bringing diners from Regina or even farther afield.

Food is classic European. Pheasant may be served in pastry or in a consommé. Veal schnitzel is simmered in wine and cream. There are steaks with all sorts of herb butters. Homemade Black Forest cake, nougat and chocolate tortes, light lemon sherbets, and fresh local berries are the highlights of the dessert menu. It's a culinary oasis in the prairies.

Wolseley, Saskatchewan, was once a whistle-stop on the Canadian Pacific Railway main line. Early in this century, the small river was dammed to provide essential water to run the steam engines that threshed the grain. Once the grain was threshed, it had to be stored, so the first Saskatchewan Wheat Pool elevators were built in 1927. Forty years, and countless tons of grain later, the present elevator rose from its site, across the road from the Banbury Inn. Serving 80 to 90 farmers in the region, its capacity is 128,000 bushels, more than three times that of the original structure.

Regina is the center of life in the southern part of the province. The Saskatchewan Museum of Natural History and the Saskatchewan Science Centre are located there. Just north of the city, at Craven, is the annual Big Valley Jamboree, Canada's largest country music festival, which is held in mid-July. In late May, Regina celebrates Mosaic, a multicultural festival that samples the foods, songs, and dances of the city's many ethnic groups (go for the *piroshki!*).

The Royal Canadian Mounted Police training facility is in Regina. Every

Tuesday at 7 P.M. throughout most of the summer, young recruits perform the traditional Sunset Retreat, a throwback to the military tattoo of the 1700s. At 12:50 P.M. on weekdays, the Sergeant Major's Parade is held. For specific times it is best to call the public relations coordinator in Regina, tel. 306/780–5900.

At the end of July, Regina's answer to the Calgary Stampede, Buffalo Days, has the whole city in an uproar. More than 215,000 people attend this mammoth Western fair. It opens with the Pile O'Bones picnic and continues with a costume contest and lots of free live entertainment.

***

The Banbury House Inn is 45 minutes east of Regina on Highway 1 in the town of Wolseley. Turn at Weird Willie's Store and then turn right on Poplar Street. Cross the railway tracks and immediately turn left on Front Street. The inn is at the end, across from the grain elevators.

Address: *104 Front St., Wolseley, Saskatchewan S0G 5H0, tel. 306/698–2239 or 306/698–2801*
Amenities: *European plan. Vegetarian requests can be handled easily, but for other dietary requirements the kitchen would need advance notice. Small meetings may be held for between 10 and 15 people. Bathrooms are wheelchair accessible as are some guest rooms.*
Rates: *double $50–$120. Extra person $10. Breakfast $5 per person (excluding taxes). AE, EnRoute, MC, V.*
Restrictions: *No pets. Restaurant closed Mon.*

Alberta

Alberta

Alberta is a privileged province. All year round there are fabulous outdoor activities to lure travelers. The Canadian Rockies have traditionally provided the focus for tourism within the region, but little by little attention is widening. The sweeping foothills that roll into the crags of various ranges, the desertlike badlands that have yielded up Canada's greatest archaeological finds, and the sea of gold and green that is ranch country—all are undiscovered treasures.

Alberta is a young territory. It was only in 1905 that it became a province, although fur traders were crisscrossing rivers in the mid-1700s. Albertans still have the great optimism of their pioneer forebears, and the cities are new, clean, and sprawling.

Native history is traced back 6,000 years at the UNESCO world heritage site, at Buffalo Jump in southern Alberta. Because of the arid climate, many of the artifacts are well preserved. The Tyrell Museum of Paleontology near Drumheller is Canada's finest exhibit of dinosaur fossils, some dating back 70 million years.

Arts and culture flourish at the world-renowned Banff School of Fine Arts. The setting, right in the midst of the snow-capped Rockies, is magnificent. Elk and deer regularly stroll down the streets. Faculty and students from all over the globe come to the Banff School to study music, dance, fine arts, theater, and publishing. The result is a vital arts community that frequently stages productions and exhibitions.

***

For more information on traveling in Alberta, contact:

Alberta Tourism, *Box 1500, Edmonton, Alberta T5J 2Z4, tel. 800/661-8888 (toll-free from Canada and the continental*

*U.S.) or 800/222-6501 (toll-free from Alberta). Ask for
a copy of* The Alberta Adventure Guide.

*If you plan to fly to Calgary, Alberta, and rent a vehicle,
travel time is 2 hours from Vancouver; 3½ hours from
Toronto; 8½ hours from London, England; 9¼ hours from
Munich; 9 hours from Tokyo; 3½ hours from Seattle; 4½
hours from Chicago; and 3 hours from Los Angeles.*

The Kananaskis Region
Mount Engadine Lodge

Mount Engadine is one of the West's undiscovered jewels. Perched on the edge of a wide, boggy valley under the watchful eye of the mountain from which it takes it name, it is a refreshing stop for a day or a week. Those who have enjoyed it once invariably return.

From Calgary, you can take a half-day detour into the scenic Kananaskis Valley on your way to the lodge. Kananaskis is a 1,550 square mile (4,000 sq. km) recreation area that borders on the Great Divide. Cattle-crossing signs are posted throughout the region, and you can frequently see longhorns grazing freely throughout these ranges. In fact, in late September there are more cattle than cars. It is not a road to travel on a quarter-tank of gas, or in an old car.

The wide highway into Peter Lougheed Park follows a valley surrounded by sharp rocky peaks and sliced by deep gorges. This is the transitional zone between the rolling foothills and high, glacier-worn peaks. Each mountain has a personality of its own. Some are rippled with gravel-filled crevices, some are folded around pockets of snow, while others stand on a cockeyed angle, heaved up by a massive, prehistoric tectonic movement. Glaciers gleam silver-gold in the sun.

Innkeepers Rudi and Lisbeth Kranabitter have poured all their strength into the creation of their unpretentious European-style lodge. When he wasn't working as a guide, Rudi built all the furniture and cabinets. He then embellished the beams and

lintels throughout with small carved flowers.

Guests head to Mount Engadine to hike or to cross-country ski. In the summer there are meadows and bogs of wildflowers, including more than a dozen species of orchid. In the winter, hundreds of miles of telemark or nordic ski trails lace the mountains and valleys together. Some cross-country ski trails, like those at Mount Shark, are set to international standards, with symbols that denote the degree of difficulty.

Chef Wolfgang Zbinden is the third essential ingredient to the success of Mount Engadine. As a fully qualified mountain guide, he is as at home on the glaciers as he is in the kitchen. His hearty fare and willingness to turn his hand to any task reflect his Alpine heritage.

A mountain breakfast has to be a hearty affair. Rudi's lovely pine sideboard is loaded with homemade muesli, yogurt, fruits, and big muffins. Plates of cheese and cold cuts are ready for hikers to make their own lunches. Just when you think you've eaten enough, Wolfgang appears at the long communal table balancing plates of *Kaisershmarren* (emperor's pancakes).

After you've spent a day on the slopes or scrambling over rocks on some backwoods path, dinner needs to be wholesome and filling. Begin with oatmeal vegetable soup, a recipe Wolfgang borrowed from his Swiss mother. Follow that with roast lamb and all the trimmings—whipped potatoes, lightly steamed green beans with a hint of onion and bacon, a crisp salad, and a heap of garlic-laden potato salad. Make sure you save a bit of room for a slice of apple strudel before you take a moonlight stroll or lounge on the deck overlooking the mountains.

The dormlike rooms all have warm down duvets covering the bunk beds. Near the dining room is a comfortable lounge that's well littered with German and English magazines. A cuckoo clock chortles the hour. Outdoors, on its own private peninsula, is a hot tub that hearty souls use year-round.

If you want a little more luxury and a semiprivate bath, two new cabins have been built beside the lake, with a panoramic view of the Commonwealth Creek valley.

A number of guests arrange with the Kranabitters to go heli-hiking up to Tent Ridge. The chopper will pick you up on the helipad near Mount Shark, and then, with either Rudi or Wolfgang leading the way, the group will hike back to the lodge. With a license from the park warden, fishermen can try their luck at landing cutthroat trout in some of the stocked lakes.

Although most trails are safe, it is important to realize that this country is wild. Proper footwear and clothing are essential, and one should never hike alone. A small survival kit is recommended for anyone taking a longer hike, as are a map and a compass. For longer forays, a qualified guide is essential.

***

Mount Engadine Lodge may be reached via Highway 40 from Longview, or from Canmore via the Smith-Dorian/Spray Trail. The lodge is at the Mount Shark turnoff. It is about 1½ hours from Calgary and 30 minutes from Canmore.

Address: *Box 1679, Canmore, Alberta T0L 0M0, tel. 403/678-4080, fax 403/678-2109*
Amenities: *Full American Plan. Special diets are regularly handled with prior notification. Small meeting facilities for up to 32 people. Summer June 15–Oct. 15; winter Christmas–Apr. 15.*
Rates: *daily $65–$95 per person, excluding taxes. A number of 3- to 5-day packages are available. Seniors' discount of 10%.*
Restrictions: *No pets. No smoking. Limited wheelchair accessibility.*

The Banff–Lake Louise Area
Baker Creek
Chalets and
Bistro

The Bow Valley Parkway from Banff to Lake Louise is one of the prettiest drives in Canada. The parkway winds along the Bow River, through Banff National Park. No trucks or other commercial vehicles are allowed. Baker Creek Chalets is a small collection of pretty European-style chalets sitting in a hardwood forest located six miles (10 km) east of Lake Louise. Each is a self-contained, well-constructed wooden cabin. Some have lofts and wood-burning fireplaces, and all have down quilts and kitchenettes. Built, owned, and operated by Mike, Ann, and Kirby Huminuik, they have one distinct advantage—they also have one of the best little bistros in the area, run by chef Daniel Martineau, from Chibougamau in the far north of Quebec, and pianist Charlie Wake.

Charlie Wake graduated from Montreal's Concordia University in music. Now, finally, he will be playing again—on the old piano in the lounge. Guests can enjoy a vintage wine, sit by the river-stone fireplace, and listen to Charlie's tunes, from classical to rock.

In the kitchen Daniel is making music of his own. Admittedly, the chive blossoms that grow by the back door are about as close to local ingredients as one can obtain in a national park, but he has loosened his imagination to create an innovative, if limited, menu.

Scallops are quickly baked in a little oil, sprinkled with balsamic vinegar, and served on a bed of butter lettuce. Sweet red and yellow peppers garnish the dish. On every entrée, from grilled lamb chops with Dijon/ Meaux mustard sauce to trout fillets with orange rosemary butter, Daniel creates a surrealistic painting with six to eight different vegetables. A crumbly topping covers the apple cake. Their chocolate almond torte is so rich it's sinful.

The short wine list is good and getting better. It's also refreshingly inexpensive.

The Baker Creek Chalets and Bistro is a perfect base from which to explore Banff National Park. Cross-country skiing and hiking trails lead right from the property. Mountain climbing, heli-hiking, the country's best alpine skiing—virtually every outdoor activity a national park can offer is within a short drive or cross-country skiing distance.

The bistro is open seven days a week, from the end of May until Canadian Thanksgiving in early October. Between Christmas and Easter it is open for business only on weekends. Other times, you have to fend for yourself in the cabin, a relatively easy but far less delicious task.

***

Baker Creek Chalets and Bistro is located 6 miles (10 km) east of Lake Louise on the Bow Valley Parkway.

Address: *Box 66, Lake Louise, Alberta T0L 1E0, tel. 403/522–3761 (chalets) or 403/522–2182 (bistro).*
Amenities: *European Plan. Chalets open year-round. Bistro open daily, May to Canadian Thanksgiving; Fri.–Sun., Christmas to Easter. Special diets can be accommodated but prior notice is appreciated. No smoking allowed in dining room, but it's fine in lounge.*
Rates: *Single room and one-bedroom, $75–$96 for two; two-bedroom, $120 for four. Dinner averages $50 for two, excluding wine. MC, V.*
Restrictions: *No pets. No meeting facilities. Not wheelchair accessible.*

Lake O'Hara Lodge

Reaching Lake O'Hara Lodge is no easy feat. In the winter, one has to strap on all one's belongings and ski uphill, an elevation rise of 1,500 feet (460 m), for 7 miles (11 km) along a logging road. In the summer, the shuttle bus leaves a base parking lot four times a day, but reservations at the lodge are essential. The lodge has an astounding 100 percent occupany rate. Many of the bookings are made the year before by guests who are returning for their 10th or 20th time. Without question, a vacation must be planned around a vacancy at the lodge.

The first rugged adventurers, men and women who founded the Alpine Club of Canada, believed that Lake O'Hara was made for climbers and hikers. Lake O'Hara Lodge should be reserved for only those who want to understand the history of the Rockies and the alpine pioneers who climbed the mountains, broke the trails, and built lodges like this one.

When British Columbia was enticed to join the Canadian Confederation, its people were promised a railway within 10 years. In 1881, the famous last spike was driven into the rail bed and the West was open for business. The history of Lake O'Hara Lodge is thoroughly tied to that of the railways. The graceful chalet was built by the Canadian Pacific Railway in 1920 with logs shipped from the British Columbian coast. The alpinists who stayed there later

lent their names to the 50 miles (80 km) of trails and mountain meadows that encircle the lake.

Today the lodge, which sits in Yoho National Park, is jointly owned by Marsha and Michael Laub and their partners, Tim and Leslee Wake.

The Laubs and the Wakes greet guests with a full orientation. The avalanche lecture and telemark ski lessons are Tim's task.

Following the trail maps, summer hikers can climb above the tree line or stroll from one sunny rock to the next. Over the years, flat boulders have been crowbarred into place over gushing streams. The gentle circuit around the lake takes about one hour and winds through the mossy, mushroom-filled forest.

Inside the main building, guests dine and lounge on the main floor. A wide balcony, onto which eight guest rooms open, runs the circumference of the upper floor, giving the whole lodge a spacious, airy look. Old photos and original oils outside the rooms form a gallery that make one want to linger. Old Colonel Robert O'Hara, the first "tourist" to reach the region after its discovery in the 1880s, looks sternly out of his picture frame. Old-fashioned bathrooms are shared by the guests. A box of chocolates sits on the pillow, and a feather duvet covers the bed.

Around the cold, unearthly blue lake, a string of log cabins enables up to 55 guests to stay at the lodge during the summer. Unlike the main lodge, the cabins have private showers and vacuum toilets. They are cozy and warm in summer but buried deep in snow in winter. Because they are on the Great Divide, it is snowy at Lake O'Hara even when other places are green. The weather is also quite fickle. A landscape over the stone fireplace in the main lodge is of a snowstorm on July 19, a few years ago.

It's little wonder that nonguests ski and trek into the lodge for meals. Because the logistics of shipping premade convenience foods up a fire road into a national park are too complex, all the meals are created from scratch on the premises. The kitchen is presided over by chef Hannes Hortenhuber. He and his wife, Erika, who does all the baking, make the most elegant mountain food that I've tasted. Fresh pasta is served often at lunch, sometimes with bits of salami in a blue cheese, cream, and sage dressing, or as baked cannelloni. Lamb and eggplant team up in a casserole, or chicken is braised with almonds, honey, and sesame seeds.

After hiking, but before dinner, there's afternoon tea, which features Erika's pastries and lots of lemonade. Because the air is so dry at these altitudes, one is always quite thirsty. Even the log-fired sauna has a bucket of beer outside in the winter.

Dinners are lighter and more refined than the lunches. A crisp garden salad may be topped with grilled scallops. Chanterelles and oyster mushrooms are sometimes made into a terrine. Melon slices are wrapped in *Bunderfleisch*, the Swiss air-dried beef. Tender sliced duck breast is served in an Armagnac sauce with glazed shallots. Salmon, veal, and Alberta beef and lamb all appear at least once a week on a rotating table d'hôte basis. Refreshing fruit desserts end the evening meal—if you want homemade ice cream or custard-filled puff pastry, you'll have to be at the lodge for lunch. Guests are urged to make preferences and allergies know to the innkeepers before arrival. Picnic lunches are provided for those who sign up early in the morning.

Fishing in the lakes is allowed. Catches are limited by park officials and must be reported. The cold water slows the growth rate of fish, but anglers have caught good numbers of cutthroat trout, which can be identified by their prominent orange line and black spotting on the tail, and rainbow trout. In Lake O'Hara, there is also a unique rainbow/cutthroat cross.

Yoho National Park is a photographer's paradise. Wildlife still roams free, and the air is so clear that it somehow seems to make a professional out of even an Instamatic user. Take lots of film. Everywhere one looks there's a new collage of flowers, lichen, and mushrooms, all framed in a background of rich green mosses.

Before or after a stay at Lake O'Hara Lodge, anyone who wants to deepen their understanding of the mountains should visit the Whyte Museum of the Canadian Rockies (tel. 403/762-2291), on Bear Street in Banff. Its displays, archives, and art gallery chronicle life from the early days until the present. The little gift shop has dozens of limited-edition books about the region.

When you successfully make a reservation at the Lake O'Hara, the Laubs or the Wakes will give you final instructions on what to bring. Special steel-edged telemark-

style skis can be rented in Banff for
the winter trek in. Warm clothing
should be packed, even in summer.

***

Lake O'Hara Lodge's entrance parking lot is 8 miles (12 km) from Lake
Louise, off the Trans-Canada Highway at its junction with Highway
1A. Turn right just past the CPR
tracks into the lot and either wait
for the bus or start to ski. A valid
parking ticket from the National
Parks office is required for any vehicle parked in the Lake O'Hara lot.

Address: *(summertime) Box 55,
Lake Louise, Alberta T0L 1E0, tel.
604/343-6418; (Oct.–May) Box 1677,
Banff, Alberta T0L 0C0, tel.
403/762-2118*
Amenities: *Full American Plan.
Special dietary requirements are
handled easily if advance notice is
given to the chef. Summer
mid-June–Sept., winter mid-Jan.–
mid-Apr.*
Rates: *$225–360 per couple, includ-
ing all meals, taxes, and bus fares.
No gratuities necessary. Personal
checks and cash only.*
Restrictions: *No pets. No smoking
is allowed anywhere in the buildings because of the fire hazard. Not
wheelchair accessible.*

The Post Hotel

Expect nothing less than perfection from the Post Hotel, Canada's newest western member of Relais et Châteaux. The names André and George Schwarz have been synonymous with fine Swiss-style hospitality for several decades. The reincarnation that the Post has undergone is not much short of miraculous. The original log building was left intact, but the rustic feeling is long gone. All 93 rooms (it's admittedly a little large to be a true country inn) are decorated with floral bedspreads and have hundreds of small touches courtesy of André's wife, Barbara: a bouquet of fresh flowers, a grapevine wreath, an Inuit painting, a carved owl on the banister, window boxes on the cabins full of annuals in summer or evergreen boughs in winter. The style is so personal.

Two luxurious log cabins, a 20-step walk from the door to the lobby, sit beside the Pipestone River. The fire is always prepared, a leather sofa in front of it; the queen-size bed is covered with what seems to be mandatory in the mountains, a huge, soft duvet. The Schwarzes seem to have thought of everything—even the inlaid bathroom floor tiles are toasty warm. In the summer, just down the grassy embankment, glacial water tumbles over the rocky riverbed. But in the winter, it freezes into a soft white cross-country ski trail.

The Post Hotel was once owned by Sir Norman Watson, a colorful player in the Rockies' history. Wealthy and, according to the locals, a bit eccentric, Sir Norman had dreams that were decades ahead of their time. He married for the first time, at the age of 79, but his wife detested Canada. She forced him to sell his many Canadian assets. The last to go was the Post Hotel. He sold it to the Schwarzes, who, like himself, had a more expansive vision of what it could be. André, Barbara, and George Schwarz came to the Rockies in the early '70s. They have made a lasting mark.

Swiss-trained chef Kenneth Titcomb lives up to every expectation. He laments that truly local ingredients are difficult to obtain. He does, however, find sources for the fine lamb for which Alberta is famous, farm-raised Arctic char, the best beef in Canada, and tiny unusual greens. The stroganoff on the menu reflects the owners' European heritage, but the perfectly cooked poached salmon with sun-dried tomatoes, sweet peppers, and baby vegetables is reminiscent of California. The wine list is excellent, with a number of good half bottles. I did expect that the waiters in this supremely hospitable province would be a little friendlier.

The Post's breakfast buffet is legendary. Cheerful waitresses fill the cups with steaming coffee. Creamy muesli, sweet braided breads still warm from the oven, bacon-fried potatoes, platters of specialty sausages, fried eggs on *rosti*, and

golden apple fritters help you begin
the day.

Coming to the Post in the winter
and not skiing is a sacrilege.
A shuttle bus leaves from the main
lobby every morning for Lake Louise, a ski area that reaches more
than 8,000 feet (2,400 m) skyward.
More than 30 runs, (25 percent novice, 45 percent intermediate, 30 percent expert) are serviced by seven
chairlifts and two high-speed quads.
The longest run is a curving five-
miler (8 km). For those who have
never skied the mountain before, the
Friends of Lake Louise are a group
of volunteers who act as orientation
guides through the back bowls and
down the runs. In a good year, skiing lasts easily until mid-May.

Horse-drawn sleigh rides and skating
are based at Château Lake Louise,
Canadian Pacific's mammoth hotel
that sits up the mountain road from
the Post.

The Schwarzes are justifiably proud
of their swimming pool, which is
cleansed by a state-of-the-art "hypo-
cell purification system." A whirlpool and a steam room are in the
same glass-surrounded area, from
which you can watch the snow fall
and fall.

The inn can arrange horseback riding expeditions and guided fishing
trips for its summer guests. Bicycle
rentals and white-water river rafting
are available nearby. The Lake Louise gondola operates until mid-
September, whisking you to the summit for spectacular, uninterrupted
views of the Victoria Glacier and the
Bow range.

The off-seasons are the best times to
drive the Icefields Parkway north of
Lake Louise toward Jasper. One glacier after another pours down the
mountain slopes. Lakes of cerulean
blue feed the rivers that irrigate
much of Alberta.

***

The Post Hotel is three hours west
of Calgary. Take the Trans-Canada
Highway (#1) west to the Lake Louise exit. At the first intersection,
turn right, and over the bridge, turn
left into the parking lot.

Address: *Box 69, Lake Louise, Alberta T0L 1E0, tel. 800/661–1586
(toll-free in North America) or
403/522–3989 fax 403/522–3966, Relais et Châteaux toll-free from
North America 800/67–RELAIS.*
Amenities: *European Plan. Special
dietary requirements can be handled with advance notice. Executive
meeting facilities are among the
best in western Canada. Two conference rooms in a private facility
can accommodate up to 100. The
hotel is wheelchair accessible. No
nonsmoking regulations.*
Rates: *(excluding taxes) rooms
$105–$290, depending on style chosen; cabins $195 and up. Packages
are available. No additional charge
for children. AE, MC, V.*
Restrictions: *No pets. Closed Nov.*

Storm Mountain Lodge

From the verandah you can see Storm of course, and all the burnt-cinder pinnacles, the long slag walls of the Sawback Range with cloud shadows drifting across them—grey, violet, mist-colored, black. Castle Mountain too. And, looking down the road to the southwest, peak after peak, peak after peak, treed or treeless, black or snow-crowned—vista after vista. . . . It has an austere grandeur that makes it kin to these snowbound miles far above timberline that few people but the Swiss guides ever see." (From a 1923 Canadian Pacific Railway pamphlet on Storm Mountain Lodge.)

Near the Castle Mountain junction, at an elevation of 5,600 feet (1,700 m), sits Storm Mountain Lodge, a rustic log building dating from 1922. The lodge is owned and operated seasonablly by George Schwarz, the co-owner of Lake Louise's opulent Post Hotel, who candidly admits that Storm Mountain is his favorite place.

The lodge has a feeling of yesteryear with the old Chinese lantern hanging in the main lodge, a remnant from the workers who built the railway. A ram's head, with a full curl on its horns, hangs over the fireplace.

The 12 cabins are furnished in ancient Rocky Mountain style—old bedframes (which may be the originals) and wicker furniture. Cozy duvets and wood-burning fireplaces, a necessity for the cool nights, add to their warmth.

The dining room serves standard fare with the odd homage to the region—Alberta beef and Rocky Mountain trout. Swiss chef Tony Spoerri was the sous-chef at the Post, and now he alternates between Storm Mountain and a heli-ski lodge. Every morning he provides a full breakfast with muesli and at least one special. Lingering over coffee at one of the window tables overlooking Vermillon Pass is a relaxing interlude or a great beginning to a day of hiking, climbing, or exploring the park.

Storm Mountain Lodge is a convenient, clean, and affordable stop for a few days or just an overnight in the mountains.

***

Storm Mountain Lodge is 20 minutes from either Lake Louise or Banff on Highway 93 south, which runs from the Trans-Canada to Radium Hot Springs at the Castle Mountain Junction.

Address: *Box 670, Banff, Alberta T0L 0C0, tel. 403/762-4155*
Amenities: *European Plan. Special diets can be accommodated. No nonsmoking areas.*
Rates: *double $110 (taxes excluded) AE, MC, V.*
Restrictions: *No pets. No meeting facilities. Not wheelchair accessible. Closed late Sept.–late May.*

British Columbia

British Columbia

At least once every February when our village is deep in snow or suffering a sleet storm, one of our so-called friends from Vancouver Island calls to let us know that the crocuses have finished blooming and the tulips are up. They really do count the flowers in Victoria, the province's capital city, every February. The last tally was upward of 80 million blossoms. The southern coastal region is one of the mildest areas in Canada.

British Columbia is the home of many native tribes who for millennia have enjoyed the bounty that the rich coastal region provides. Their trading routes extended from Alaska to Oregon. Because of this wealth they were able to develop very beautiful art forms that reflected their sophisticated religious beliefs. The presence of our first peoples is more strongly felt here than in any other Canadian province.

The fur trade in sea-otter pelts drew the Spaniards and the British to this coast in the early 1800s. Many place names are obviously linked to the Iberian peninsula. Cortes, Valdes, Esperanza, Estevan, and San Josef can all be found on a map of Vancouver Island. The British were their competition, and Captain Cook made the first official landing on the West Coast, at Nootka in March 1778.

With the building of the Canadian Pacific Railway, British Columbia became part of Canada. The railway changed the province's face in many ways. Thousands of laborers were required to construct the massive line. They came from China. Living in appalling conditions, many died but those who remained settled in the southern mainland of the province. Jobs were plentiful in the salmon canneries. Their presence is still strongly felt in that area where the Fraser River delta has created an alluvial plain dotted with Chinese market gardens. The city of Vancouver has the second-largest Chinatown in North America and, because of the recent influx of Hong Kong business people, it has the finest Chinese restaurants in Canada, if not the continent.

The interior of British Columbia is a region of mountain ranges and long, sheltered valleys. The climate is harsh but the skiing is the best in the country. Whistler-Blackcomb, the resort 1½ hours north of Vancouver, was just named number one in North America. Others such as Fernie, without the glitz, rely only on natural snowfall for their powdery slopes.

The fabled Strait of Georgia divides the mainland from Vancouver Island. It is world renowned for spectacular scenery and superb salmon sportfishing. At Campbell River the Strait narrows, and the tidal flow aerates the cold water to create a perfect habitat for this red-fleshed Pacific fighter.

British Columbia has something for everyone. Museums and art galleries, scuba diving and paragliding, skiing and heli-fishing—they are all part of the package.

***

For additional information on travel in British Columbia, contact: **Ministry of Tourism,** *Parliament Buildings, Victoria, B.C. V8V 1X4, tel. 800/663–6000 toll-free in North America.*

The Mountains
Bugaboo Lodge

Bugaboo Lodge, one of the Canadian Mountain Holidays group, is Hans Gmoser's original (*see* p. 197). Vowell Glacier is the predominant skyline feature, pouring down the mountain around the dark Bugaboo spires, which seem to stretch heavenward. At its base, hikers can study the action of this living glacier. Heli-hiking here is usually done in three-day segments, with special programs such as the photography workshop being longer.

"F-8 and be there!" That's Patrick Morrow's motto. The second Canadian to reach the top of Mount Everest and an accomplished photographer, Morrow has begun offering week-long photography workshops at Bugaboo Lodge. The many alpine meadow lakes and cascading waterfalls make a spectacular photographic studio.

Along with medal-winning cinematographer Roger Vernon from the Banff School of Fine Arts, Morrow is leading hikes into the surrounding mountains to teach "nuts and bolts" photography. Polaroid slide film is used, to ensure that the participant's work is critiqued the same day. Cameras are the only thing that is not provided for the guests. During the week both Morrow and Vernon give lectures and slide shows on areas that they have explored all over the globe. These men are among the best in Canada today, and this is a wonderful opportunity to meet and work with them.

***

If traveling by car, head toward Spillimacheen, 25 miles (40 km) north of Radium on Highway 95. Turn west near the Spillimacheen General Store on West Side Road. Cross the railway tracks and the river, and turn left again on West Side Road. The heliport is 1,000 feet (300 m) on the left.

Canadian Mountain Holidays has its head office in Banff, Alberta, although all of its lodges are in British Columbia. Reservations must be made through CMH in advance for any of the packages or day trips.

Address: *CMH Box 1660, Banff, Alberta T0L 0C0, tel. 800/661-0252 (toll-free from North America) or 403/762-7100, fax 403/762-5879.*
Amenities: *Full American Plan including all transportation, use of equipment, meals, tips, and taxes. Special diets can be accommodated if chefs are given advance notice. Excellent meeting facilities at all lodges for up to 44 people. Heli-hiking late June–mid-Sept.; heli-skiing mid-Dec.–early May.*
Rates: *$200–$372, per person 1- to 6-day overnight packages. Heli-skiing: 7-day (Sat.-Sat.) all-inclusive packages, $2,900–$5,100 per person. MC, V.*
Restrictions: *No pets. Smoking is allowed in public areas at all lodges, although there is no smoking in the rooms. Not wheelchair accessible.*

Canadian Mountain Holidays

Samuel de Champlain said that "all adventurers need is a place to sleep in safety." Hans Gmoser has taken that dictum and carried it a long way. Modesty seems to be a predominent trait of Gmoser, founder and guiding light of Canadian Mountain Holidays, Canada's premier group of mountain inns. Their unquestionable specialty is adventure. Their clients arrive from every continent.

In the 1950s helicopters were used in geological surveys. In 1963, Gmoser, an accomplished mountaineer and back-country skier, was engaged by a Calgary geologist, Art Patterson, to take a group down an eastern slope near the coal-mining town of Canmore. Although because of the high winds the event was not considered a success, a former U.S. Olympic skier, Brooks Dodge, approached Gmoser to organize a week of alpine touring in conjunction with two days of helicopter skiing. An old lumber camp in the Bugaboo Mountains was their base. Eighteen rugged skiers took part, lugging along their own sleeping bags and air mattresses. This was the beginning. The following year, 70 skiers came; the next year, 150. With borrowed money and a dream, Gmoser built Bugaboo Lodge in 1967–68.

The lodge has a shallow-sloped roof that can withstand the weight of 200 pounds per square inch. Gmoser didn't fool around with the elements.

In the deep Canadian winters heli-skiing, often through waist-deep snow on powder-covered glaciers, lures guests year after year. There are skiers who have made the circuit of all of the CMH lodges and others who are now in the esteemed "million-foot club," great amateur athletes who have skied more that 1,000,000 vertical feet (304,800 m). A husband-and-wife pair leads the list at 14 and 12 million feet, respectively.

Guests are transported to snow-draped peaks, set lightly on the ground, and guided earthward down virgin slopes; they weave tracks with precision into ropes that seem to connect the heavens with the jagged tree line below.

In the summer, *hiking* and *interpretative mountain walking* are the bywords. Fewer lodges are used, and the activities can be as strenuous or as laid-back as the hiker wishes. These summer lodges are the ones included here, for several reasons: They are approachable by car, and they are attractive for that large segment of the traveling public who want to get completely away, be pampered, and have a unique, exciting, educational holiday.

There are no happier chefs than those at the CMH lodges. They are given total freedom to purchase the finest ingredients—food costs are added up only at the end of the year. All the baking is done on the premises by specially trained pastry chefs, and the executive chefs prepare the fabulous entrées. Breakfasts are gargantuan affairs—lots of fresh fruit, homemade breads, muffins, and at least one main special such as French toast with maple syrup, sausages, and bacon.

Summertime lunches consist of barbecue picnics in secluded mountain hideaways over fires fed by bits of wood that the guides have gathered. The fresh air and exercise whets even the pickiest appetite. Over a half barrel filled with coals, the cook grills locally made bratwurst and juicy, Dijon-spiked hamburgers to serve on lodge-made buns. On the side there is usually a Greek salad loaded with cheese, sweet peppers, olives, and oregano; chilled pasta in a peppery olive/lime vinaigrette; and a bowl full of creamy, old-fashioned potato salad. There is always fresh fruit, juices, an urn of lemon-spice tea, and, of course, pure mountain water. The pastry chef may send along date squares, cookies bursting with chocolate chips and pecans, or poppy-seed lemon loaf.

Dinners at the lodges are equally well prepared. Each menu is up to the particular chef, but I have tasted thick Alberta beef filets, seen a chef deboning a perfect Pacific coho, and watched as skewers of beef kabobs were threaded before being marinated in wine and herbs.

All the lodges are licensed, and the wine lists are good but limited. This is the only extra charge CMH levies.

Top-quality leather hiking boots are supplied, as are wet- and cold-weather gear.

The guest rooms have little or no decoration, save the woodwork and the down-filled comforters that sit puffed on each bed. Some share bathrooms, but most have private baths and showers. Environmentally friendly soaps, shampoos, and toilet papers are provided.

Information and reservations for all programs, including heli-skiing, can be obtained from Canadian Mountain Holidays Inc., Box 1660, Banff, Alberta T0L 0C0 tel. 403/762-7100.

Bobbie Burns Lodge

he large white flowers of the western anemone and shrubby mountain heather carpet the meadows and hollows of the International Basin. Woolly pussy-toes and blazing fireweed are scattered in clumps here and there at these elevations. You get the feeling that you could walk forever.

At Iceberg Lake the constant pull of gravity forces the Malloy and Conrad glaciers to calve small chunks of ice.

The five-day program at Bobbie Burns, one of the Canadian Mountain Holidays lodges, attracts serious hikers and people who want to immerse themselves in a high mountain summer.

Like at the other lodges, hikers are divided into four groups, depending on interest and skill level. They are flown to various drop points; at lunch, when the helicopter brings the picnic, anyone can return to the quiet of the lodge to simply relax for the remainder of the day.

Fishermen can be dropped off for a day at an alpine lake. Because of the high altitude, the mineral content of the lakes is low and there are not as many fish as at lower elevations.

The highlight of a trip to Bobbie Burns is the exploration of the Conrad Glacier and its crevasses. Flowing for 6 miles (9 km) from the summit of Mount Conrad, it provides hikers with the opportunity to learn more about glaciation.

***

Bobbie Burns is 195 miles (314 km) west of Calgary. To get there by car, drive to Parson, which is 22 miles (35 km) south of Golden, British Columbia. In Parson, turn west on Sanborn Road and cross the river, and immediately after the crossroads you will see the CMH Heliport on the left.

See Bugaboo Lodge (p. 196) for Canadian Mountain Holidays' address, amenities, rates and restrictions information.

Cariboo Lodge

Paradise is sitting on top of the world! From the deck of Cariboo, the undulations of the Canoe Glacier are clearly visible, its millwells opening to allow streams to splash into the ancient depths.

The lodge, in the Canadian Mountain Holidays group, is located in the 10,000 foot (3,048 m) Premier Range, 80 miles (129 km) southwest of Jasper National Park.

This is the lodge where grandparents often bring their grandchildren for a two-day stay in the mountains. The beauty of Zillmer Canyon, with its high cliff walls and braided streams echoing through still air, keeps everyone enthralled. The ridge walk along Milk Punch, high above the tree line, follows a goat path. From the ridge, you can see both the North and South Canoe glaciers; the spire of Mount Robson, the highest peak in the Canadian Rockies; and the town of Valemount.

From the ridge, the hike leads to a marshy area spotted with false hellebore and fuzzy-leaved Labrador tea.

The lodge has a fishing pond that is stocked with trout. After a hot day, guests usually relax their muscles in the whirlpool, then plunge into this small lake.

One-day packages take off from Valemount and offer a full day of fabulous hiking and a mountain lunch with snacks in the late afternoon, before returning to the helipad in town. The two-day packages start after lunch on the first day and leave at midmorning on the third.

***

Cariboo Lodge can be reached by car from Valemount, B.C. 80 miles (129 km) southwest of Jasper, Alberta, via Highway 5. From Jasper, take Highway 16 west to Tête Jaune Junction and turn south on Highway 5 to Valemount. The heliport is 2 miles (3½ km) south of Valemount. The turnoff is at the next gravel road past the CMH Cariboo Lodge sign on the right-hand side of the highway. The heliport is visible from the turnoff to the left and is identified by the CMH Heliport sign.

See Bugaboo Lodge (p. 196) for Canandian Mountain Holidays' address, amenities, rates and restrictions information.

The Okanagan-Similkameen Region
Hatheume Lake Resort

The rates include both 110-volt power and your own belly boat. Sound interesting?

Hatheume Lake Resort was built in the remote mountains of south-central British Columbia by and for people who love to fish. It took Tim and Janet Tullis and their partners, Leni and Gus Averill, five years to find this perfect location on a chain of eight freshwater lakes, each with a different ecosystem. The lodge sits beside Hatheume, a lake so full of trout that the water ripples with them. The two-bedroom guest cabins are built with hand-hewn logs, and each has its own fireplace. A chilled bottle of Okanagan wine awaits you—a gift from the innkeepers. Because this lodge is not licensed, any additional wine or beer has to be transported in when you come.

Superb fly-fishing is the order of the day. The Kamloops rainbow trout are feisty, deep-bodied creatures; if kept (there is a heavy emphasis on catch-and-release), they make delicious eating. Tim's specialty is a unique, and secret, method of smoking the fish. His recipe is much sought after by other lodges, but he won't oblige. One has to visit Hatheume to enjoy it.

Before breakfast, Tim brings hot coffee to each cabin. Meanwhile Janet and Leni are serving up a huge ranch-style breakfast—eggs, sausages, hash browns, toast, and lots more coffee. Tim and Gus chat with everyone to assess skills and needs. Lakes are assigned and, if requested, lessons in fly-fishing, from tying to casting, are given. For those who have chosen to fish from a belly boat, otherwise known as a float tube, a quick rundown on how to maneuver them is provided, along with a pair of flippers.

To reach the more remote lakes, guests drive Jeeps over old logging roads. It is unusual not to see at least some of the local wildlife. Moose, deer, and coyote are the most common, but there are also lynx and the odd cougar about. Eagles soar above the trees, blue herons fish the shallows, and the Canada jays chatter and scold.

Boats with motors sit waiting at various tie-up points on the spring-fed lakes. Spin-casting with freshwater shrimp is the most commonly used method of landing the three- to five-pounders (1.4 to 2.3 kg).

The lodge has its own pro shop, a necessity for those who have forgotten their favorite lure or need a license. Tackle of every description is available, including Loomis rods, a variety of reels, fly line, and a wide selection of locally tied flies in special Hatheume Lake patterns.

A fleet of mountain bikes can be used on the 18 mile (30 km) Jeep trail system. Beyond that are hundreds of miles of logging roads on which one could conceivably ride for days.

Meals at the lodge are homespun and hearty. They are served family style, and guests have an unequaled opportunity to tell their particular fish stories to a whole new audience. Roast turkey with all the trimmings and meat loaf are the most popular meals. All the baking, from cinnamon rolls to peach pie, is hot from the oven.

In the first week of June, a fly-fishing school is offered. The instructors are real pros—the first, a biologist from Kamloops who teaches the ecology and entomology of the lakes; the second is a casting instructor from Oregon who expands on technique, equipment, fly-tying, and knots.

Autumn brings the annual cooking school, with chefs from various Northwest inns and restaurants. Local personality and Sumac Ridge Winery owner Harry McWaters gives a lecture on Okanagan wines.

***

Hatheume Lake Resort is one hour west of Peachland off the newly completed Coquihalla extension. From Vancouver, it is about three hours. Travel through Hope and then north toward Kamloops on the Coquihalla Highway 5. Turn east toward Peachland and continue for another hour. Follow directional signs.

Address: *Box 490, Peachland, B.C. V0H 1X0, tel. 604/767-2642 (year-round reservations) or 604/762-1148 (June–Oct., lodge), or ask operator for Kamloops Radio, Merritt Channel N699408.*

Amenities: *Full American Plan. Special dietary requirements can be accommodated, but advance notice must be given because shopping is done in town once a week. Meeting facilities are family style for up to 20 people.*
Rates: *$195 per person, excluding taxes. Minimum two-day stay. Children under 12, $130. Cash or check only.*
Restrictions: *No pets. No smoking is allowed in the dining room. No cigars or pipes in lodge. Innkeepers coach guests on the hazards of fire in such a remote area. One cabin is wheelchair accessible as is the dining room. Three lakes may be fished with the assistance of the innkeepers. Closed Nov.–May.*

Okanagan Valley

The wine valleys of sun-soaked central British Columbia are a mere 3½ hours from Vancouver and far less from Hatheume Lake Resort. Few regions on earth can boast more spectacular scenery. For 80 miles (130 km), Lake Okanagan slices north to south at the same latitude as the Champagne region of France and the Rhine Valley in Germany. Its glacial waters provide necessary irrigation for the almost desertlike conditions that exist on the steep, gravelly slopes.

In British Columbia, Premium Wine Standards have been adopted along with Designated Viticultural Areas. As in Ontario, a vigorous attempt is being made to establish, maintain, and encourage the production of better-than-average wines. The Vintner's Quality Alliance (VQA) stickers can be seen on many great British Columbian bottles, thereby assuring the consumer that the following criteria have been met:

Wines bearing the label designation "Product of British Columbia" are produced from 100 percent British Columbian–grown grapes.

Wines bearing the name of a particular viticultural area (for example, Okanagan, Similkameen, Fraser Valley, or Vancouver Island) are derived from a minimum of 85 percent grapes grown in the named area.

Wines bearing the designated name of a grape variety are derived from a minimum of 85 percent of the variety.

Where a vintage date appears on the label, at least 85 percent of the grapes were obtained in that harvest year.

"Estate bottled" means that the wine was made from grapes grown, crushed, vinified, and bottled in that winery.

All VQA wines are tested and approved by a wine-tasting/grading panel.

Farm-gate wineries, tiny growers who make and sell up to 10,000 gallons (37,854 l) per year, can now be licensed. Signs are hung at gates and visitors are welcomed throughout the province. Relatively untried in the commercial market, these wines are left up to the traveler to sample and determine which are the best.

The newly completed Coquihalla Highway soars, and at times plummets, toward the Okanagan and Similkameen valleys. Summerland is the entry point off the Coquihalla near Hainle Vineyards Estate Winery (tel. 604/767–2525). This is your first stop in the valley.

"A labor of love" best describes the vineyard of Tilman Hainle. His Alsatian-style wines include a bone-dry Riesling and an icewine that is a rarity in B.C. The Hainle estate can claim the only 17 acres in the province devoted to organic production. In 1989, his nonoaked Chardonnay was one of the best ever made in the Northwest. His Lemberger Trollinger is one of the few good reds made in the province, and his Kerner is excellent.

Journey south on Highway 97 toward Oliver to begin the tour in earnest. There you will be able to visit several very different wineries in one day.

The first, Gehringer Brothers (tel. 604/498–3537), produces German-style wines, rounded and high in fruit. You must taste their prize-winning Dry Riesling and an excellent Muller Thurgau.

Heading northward, you'll drive through Penticton, which takes turns each year with Kelowna as the home of the Okanagan Wine Festival (early October), a celebration of winemaking. It's harvest time, and at the wineries you can watch the crush. In town, teams roll up their pant legs and stomp grapes while international experts judge the past year's vintages. A marathon consumer wine-tasting is the climax of the festival at the new convention center. A state-of-the-art computerized tally system counts the votes before the sought-after medals are awarded.

Heading north, take some time to tee off among the Riesling vines at B.C.'s only vineyard golf course, at Sumac Ridge Estate Winery (tel. 604/494–0451). Play nine holes in the sunshine before sipping Chancellor Reserve, a steely light red. Even if you can't sample it, you should inquire about Sumac Ridge's *méthode champenoise* sparklers. Their best, named after B.C.'s provincial bird, the Steller's jay, is outstanding.

Directly across the lake is Cedar Creek Estate Winery (tel. 604/764–8866), the most beautifully landscaped of all the wineries and an absolute must-see on any tour. If you haven't eaten, pick up picnic ingredients at Ilichman's Deli in Kelowna and feast under the spreading grape arbors at Cedar Creek. A chilled bottle of their Gewürztraminer is absolutely essential. If it's available, sample their Dry Riesling.

At Mission Hill (tel. 604/768–7166), on the west bank of the lake, look for the limited-edition brandies. This large winery was established in 1981 and has won more than 200 international and national awards. There are so many good products that it is difficult to choose. They make an oaked B.C. Chardonnay. If you enjoy the herbaceous, grassy flavors of Sémillon, taste it as well.

Wind up your B.C. odyssey in Vernon by visiting Trudy and George Heiss's Gray Monk Estate Winery (tel. 604/766–3168). Gray Monk is undoubtedly one of the top four wineries in B.C. and certainly one of the prettiest. It is the oldest of the cottage wineries, which have a reputation for quality. They have pioneered the vinification of Pinot Gris, a grape that flourishes from Alsace to Austria. Recently returned from Germany, the Heisses' son has taken over the winemaking responsibilities and has created a wonderful Pinot Auxerrois. Unique to the Northwest is their Gewürztraminer Reserve made with an Alsatian clone.

The valley's farm-gate wineries that have excelled at vinifying certain grapes are Quail's Gate, at Westbank (Reisling); Hillside Cellars, at Penticton (Clavner or Muscat Ottonel); Wild Goose, at Okanagan Falls (Gewürztraminer); and Lang Vineyards, near Hillside (Maréchal Foch).

For information on the Okanagan Wine Festival, contact: **Okanagan-Similkameen Tourism Association,** Unit 104 - 515, Highway 97 South, Kelowna, B.C. V1Z 3J2, tel. 604/769–5959, fax 604/861–7493 or **The British Columbian Wine Institute,** 1864 Spall Road., Suite 5, Kelowna, B.C. V1Y 4R1, tel. 604/762–4887, fax 604/862–8870.

***

The Mainland
Durlacher Hof

Durlacher Hof is a small, authentic Austrian-style inn. White stuccoed walls are set off by an intricate natural wood balcony, well laden with brillant flowers in the summertime. Located just outside the beautiful village of Whistler, it's very peaceful, and with innkeeper Erica Durlacher at the Aga cooker, the meals are hearty and excellent.

A basket of hand-knit slippers sits beside the front door. Choose a pair and quietly pad upstairs to unpack. In the guest rooms, solid pine furniture is combined with patchwork-quilt coverlets on the duvets. The balconies have unsurpassed mountain views. The small bouquets placed neatly on the dresser make it clear that this innkeeper really cares.

But it's in the kitchen that Erica's concern for her guests shows the most. This is Austrian comfort food. As in the mountains of her home country, a bountiful breakfast is the kind of meal that will keep a skier or climber going till mid-afternoon. It begins with stewed or fresh fruits: perhaps half a grapefruit broiled with raspberry sauce or a baked apple with cranberries. The blueberry scones, apple Danish, and wholegrain and sourdough breads are made daily. She steals from the French for her *pain au chocolat*, hot and oozing. Then there's the daily entrée. Try the fabulous *palatshinken* (baked layers of crepes stuffed with cheese). On other days it might be a mushroom

strudel or a baked German apple pancake.

Most guests return to Durlacher for dinner. These meals are equally hearty and true to Erica's roots. She prepares *zwiebelrostbraten* with Tiroler *knödel* (sirloin steak smothered with onions and Tyrolean dumplings) on one night, smoked *kassler* with *spatzle* and *rotkraut* (smoked pork chops with noodles and red cabbage) the next. Lighter dishes are offered in the summer, and Erica often barbecues a rich red British Columbian salmon. Her meals seem to cry for a good beer like the Munich-style lager made in town by the Whistler Brewing Company.

The sea-to-sky highway leading to Whistler Village and Blackcomb Mountain is a real adventure in itself. Like the fabled Route 66, it's littered with horizontal and vertical panoramas.

It begins officially at Horseshoe Bay—the terminal for B.C. ferries' Nanaimo–Vancouver run. With the waters of Howe Sound dancing on the horizon, it heads north. After 40 minutes, it's time to stop for a wreck dive at Porteau Cove. The currents are gentle here, so a scuba experience can be leisurely.

Zoom along, windows down and hair drying, past Brittania Beach, once the home of the most productive copper mine in Canada. Stop beside Shannon Falls, the province's third highest, created, according to myth, by a sea serpent that decided to leave its watery home to slither up the mountain.

The Chief looms powerfully on the right, a solid granite monolith that has attracted climbers from all over the world. The Grand Wall is often speckled with daring souls. If you have packed your courage, break out the chalk bag and challenge this formidable peak. It's nice to know *after* the climb that in height it's second to Gibralter in the British Commonwealth.

There's wild white-water rafting, dry and comfortable, on the Squamish and Cheakamus rivers just up the road. The rafting company even provides waterproof camera boxes.

Mount Garibaldi and Diamond Head oversee the Garibaldi Provincial Park, with its huge network of hiking trails winding around Black Tusk, a 7,598 foot (2317 m) volcanic core. Ten minutes later you are at Whistler, named the number-one ski resort in North America by *Ski* magazine. In the summertime, it's a gorgeous hike to reach the summit; in the winter, well, let's just say you'll never forget your first run.

The combinations and permutations of a Whistler vacation are almost endless. At some point, however, one must tackle the mountain. Ski the glacier—it stays open until midsummer and reopens in late autumn. Rent a mountain bike, take it to the top, and thunder down the incline. Erica can tell you how to arrange a heli-picnic. Take paragliding lessons and soar over the valley in tandem or by yourself, golf at the Arnold Palmer–designed course; or simply stroll through this magnificent little village.

But you haven't yet reached your final destination—Seventh Heaven, the ski run at the summit of Blackcomb that boasts North America's

sharpest and fastest vertical drop. You must take one last chairlift to the top of Blackcomb Mountain. Slowly, quietly, the village fades and the mountain's silence enfolds you. Higher and higher until you really are in paradise—a breeze-washed snowfield atop the world.

***

Durlacher Hof is about 1½ hours north of Vancouver and five minutes from the center of Whistler Village. Follow Highway 99 north to Whistler; instead of heading into town, continue until you see Nesters Road on the left.

Address: *7055 Nesters Rd., Whistler, B.C. V0N 1B0, tel. 604/932-1924, fax 604/938-1980.*
Amenities: *A full Austrian breakfast is included. Special dietary requests can be accommodated with advance notice. Meeting space is available for small groups of up to 20 people, with a good roster of business facilities, including secretarial services. Wheelchair accessible.*
Rates: *double (taxes excluded) $79–$169. Packages available for special weekends and ski weeks. MC, V.*
Restrictions: *No pets. This is a non-smoking inn. Closed several weeks in May and Nov.*

The Park Royal Hotel

Take one sound kayak. Toss it into the swiftly running, glacial waters of the Capilano River. Hop aboard and negotiate the boulders, fisherpeople, and rapids as you tumble toward the ocean. About half a mile (.8 km) from the river's mouth, beach the craft on a grassy, azalea-rainbowed bank. Slosh up to your suite at the Park Royal Hotel and drink champagne while changing into evening wear. Ravenous, head to the dining room and feast on slate-grilled Pacific salmon. Pop music will drift up from the bar, where you might have a nightcap. Or simply stroll the softly lighted gardens, inhaling the fragrance of flowers and newly mown grass. Fall into bed. Sweet dreams!

The reality of this situation is that this magical day has just occurred within Canada's third-largest city, Vancouver.

The Park Royal Hotel, like many other Vancouver-area buildings, was built in the 1940s, on a bush road in the wilds northwest of the city. Now located within the city limits, the Park Royal began life as the private home of a Danish boat builder, but by the 1950s it was too large for the family. It was turned into a guest house, and when Mario Corsi and his partners bought it in 1974, there was a large Motel sign on top. The sign came down. Mario and Angelica Corsi have been at the helm ever since.

Mario was born near Rome and began his career as a lift operator in that city's Ritz Hotel. The dining room drew him because he loved good food. He knew that he needed to broaden his language base, so he worked all over Europe to acquire a working knowledge of French, Flemish, German, and English. It was while he was in Germany that he heard about Vancouver. Going there sounded like a great adventure, so he took off, leaving his girlfriend, Angelica, behind. When he landed, about the end of April, Vancouver was in full bloom. "I had never seen a more beautiful city. I called Angelica and told her that I had found Paradise," Mario says.

Mario is not a shy man. He is totally involved in the life of his city. He has been chairperson of the Cancer Society campaign and instrumental in organizing a huge Italian festival. He looks almost bullish, which he no doubt is about life. His voice is rich and resonant, like a fine bottle of wine.

The 30 rooms at the inn are elegant and warm. Oriental carpets have hardwood floor halos. Some bedsteads and wardrobes are matching antique pine. Some rooms are decorated around beds of brass and porcelain. All bathrooms, which are perfectly appointed, are private. The rooms that face the river are slightly more costly than those that overlook the quiet cul-de-sac, Clyde Street, where a silver Rolls-Royce is parked by the hotel's front entrance.

The Tudor Dining Room and Garden Lounge (the terrace) have a different atmosphere—more elegant and serious. The day may begin with a simple muffin or something as complex as a wild-rice pancake stuffed with cold-smoked salmon and bathed in a fresh basil sauce. Their signature breakfast dish is a West Coast version of eggs Benedict using smoked salmon and salmon caviar as a salty garnish.

The Park Royal is known for its executive business lunches, which last for 1½ to two hours—is there really that much to discuss? The weekly menu always features two to three kinds of fresh fish, including salmon and, often, black Alaskan cod, one of the finest of coastal fishes. The best Pacific prawns are caught in deep, icy waters during the autumn. Their flesh is sweet and firm, so good that they are simply grilled with garlic and butter. In season, the omelettes will be stuffed with chanterelles.

The soups, made by an "old-fashioned Portuguese mama," are chunky and hearty. Nothing drives away the winter dampness better than a dish of her bean soup with garlic-laden *chorizo* (sausage) and potatoes.

From midafternoon until late in the evening, the downstairs pub is alive and hopping with Vancouverites who like the Old World atmosphere. Mario says that it's one of the most successful bars in the city. Five or six local beers are on tap from cottage and microbreweries. You can sample Granville Island Lager or Horseshoe Bay Pale Ale. Okanagan Springs makes a great St. Patrick Stout and an Old English Porter. There is also a healthy selection of imported beers. Pub-style foods such as fish-and-chips or steak-and-kidney pie complete the menu.

Chef Hans Schaub does super things with seafood. His cooking is simple and basic, respecting the ingredients. No sole stuffed with shrimp mousse and lobster sauce here. Instead you will find a hearty *cioppino*, Italy's answer to *bouillabaisse*. Basil and most of the other herbs are from the inn's organic garden. Lamb comes from nearby Saltspring Island; venison, boar, and buffalo are purchased from other provincial producers.

For dessert, there's the classic tiramisu, lots of fresh fruits and sherbets, and, when they are not too busy, *cannoli*, the crispy rolled wafer stuffed with sweetened cream or berries, depending on the whim of the pastry person.

Wines are a very big part of the Corsi tradition. Their selection is extensive, focusing on three major growing areas—California, France, and Italy. "I buy the best I can afford" says Corsi. They always have eight to 10 wines by the glass so that guests can explore new and unlisted vintages.

The city grew but never swallowed up the Park Royal. The grounds still fall down to the Capilano River where you can fish every day of the year. When the dam, higher on the river's course, is opened you can indeed kayak. You can hike the trails that lead by the river up to the salmon hatchery or downstream to Ambleside Park and the par-3 golf course by the ocean.

The train to Whistler/Blackcomb, North America's number-one ski resort, is five minutes from the Park Royal. This station is also the base for the Royal Hudson, a steam train that hugs the shore on its journey to Squamish. Passengers then board a ship, the M.V. *Britannia*, for the return trip to Horseshoe Bay.

Grouse Mountain is like a backdrop for the stage that is Vancouver. It is a mere 10 minutes from the inn, and because it has an elevation of 3,000 feet (900 m), the skiing lasts late into the spring. In the summer, a cable car soars to the summit and affords a fabulous view of the city at work, boats plying her harbors and skyscrapers pushing upward.

The Park Royal is five minutes, if there's heavy traffic, from Stanley Park, a 1,000 acre rain-forested preserve set aside by a very wise planner many decades ago. There you can stroll or cycle along the 7 miles (8 km) of seawall along the park's circumference, or go through the shaded park where small red squirrels will eat from your hand. The Vancouver Aquarium, with its world-class marine displays, is located there. Plan to spend at least half a day in this facility.

Up the canyon from the Park Royal is the Capilano Suspension Bridge, the longest suspended footbridge in the world. Not for the faint of heart or the weak of knee, this graceful span sways only a little at 230 feet (70 m) above the rushing river.

***

The Park Royal Hotel is located just west of the Lions Gate Bridge in West Vancouver. Take Marine Drive west and exit almost immediately to the right onto Taylor Way, then another right onto Clyde Street. From the Horseshoe Bay ferry terminal, drive into the city on Highway 99, taking the Taylor Way exit. Clyde Street is on the left just before Marine Drive.

Address: *540 Clyde St., West Vancouver, B.C. V7T 2J7, tel. 604/926-5511, fax 604/926-6082.*

Amenities: *European Plan. Coffee and a newspaper are delivered to your room in the morning. Special dietary requirements pose no problem. Meeting facilities are excellent and can accommodate up to 50 persons. A special area in the diningroom in reserved for nonsmokers.*
Rates: *All exclude government room tax and service. Single $95–$120 Clyde St. side, $105–$165 Capilano River side; twin $105–$120 Clyde St. side, $130–$165 Capilano River side; queen/double $105–$130 Clyde St. side, $130–$165 Capilano River side; suite $185 single on Clyde St. side, $225 double on Capilano River side. Off-season rates available Oct.–Apr. The VIP Tudor Evening Package is $150 for two, including champagne on arrival, a five-course meal, a room at the inn, and coffee in the morning. AE, DC, EnRoute, MC, V.*
Restrictions: *No pets. Limited wheelchair accessibility.*

Special Attractions in the Vancouver Area

You should never come to such a vital city as Vancouver without some idea of the things that a traveler might enjoy:

Chinatown, the second largest in North America, is the home of great Oriental restaurants and the Dr. Sun Yat-sen Gardens, the first classical Chinese garden built outside China.

Granville Island Public Market is full of regional foods that are perfect for a picnic lunch, plus a cooperative restaurant called Isadora's. A whole series of boutiques, high-quality art shops, and a brewery have sprung up in the immediate vicinity.

Stanley Park and the Vancouver Aquarium, where orca whales have been successfully coaxed to reproduce, is well worth a visit.

The Museum of Anthropology provides a superb trip through the native history of British Columbia.

The Vancouver Art Gallery has mounted shows from all over the world, and has an excellent permanent collection.

There are many festivals in the city, including the International Film Festival, the International Folk Music Festival, the Dragon Boat Festival, and the Vancouver Fringe Festival for comedy at its weirdest.

For more information on the city of Vancouver, contact: **Vancouver Travel InfoCentre, Dept. C.B.**, Pavilion Plaza, Four Bentall Centre, 1055 Dunsmuir St., Box 49296, Vancouver, B.C. V7X 1L3, tel. 800/663–8555 (from U.S.) or 604/683–2000.

The Gulf Islands
April Point Lodge

It must have seemed the end of the earth for Phil and Phyllis Peterson and their four children when they founded April Point Lodge on Quadra Island in 1944. Since then it has become one of the oldest family establishments in British Columbia, with three children (Warren, Eric, and Joy) and several grandchildren (including Carl and Heidi) in various posts around the lodge. Phyllis, affectionately known as Mrs. P., is still in the kitchen, daily supervising the baking of her famous sticky buns and pans of Nanaimo bars, those sweet layered confections that are named after a town that is down Vancouver Island from April Point.

April Point is a red cedar lodge built on a Kwakiutl Indian midden, a six- to eight foot (2.4 m) deep layer of crushed oyster shells. Infront of the lodge a colorful array of marine traffic flows by, from cruise ships like the *Pacific Princess,* festooned with twinkling lights in the evening, to barges loaded with all the worldly possessions of a family on the move, or half a forest. Their destination? The Queen Charlotte Islands or Alaska.

This region has long been known for its salmon fishing. Vancouver Island and the mainland are barely separate here, and the Pacific Ocean pushes through Discovery Passage with all its force. Intense tidal action aerates the cold water, providing a perfect deep-water habitat for a number of different species of fish. Oyster farms abound, and these line-cultured, buttery soft shellfish are often on the lodge's menu. Another favorite is salmon—blue-backed coho that sparkle in the sun.

Nowadays April Point has salmon-fishing guests from every corner of the world. Eric, the son who acts as host when he's not off exploring exotic places like Outer Mongolia, has developed programs that allow guests to fish as well as cook with some of North America's finest chefs. Sinclair Philip of Sooke Harbour House (p. 225), John Bishop of Bishop's in Vancouver, and even John Folse of Lafitte's Landing in Louisiana have all given weekend sessions.

But fishing *is* the name of the game, and by 6 A.M. excitement is building on the dock. Clutches of guests almost dance about in the northern air anticipating their adventure, while guides collect the final bits of gear. By noon, they'll all be back on the dock, ravenous and ready to regale anyone and everyone with newly invented fish stories.

Eji Umemura, one of April Point's 65 superb guides, demonstrated *gyotaku,* the Japanese art of fish printing that allows the image of any trophy-size fish to be preserved while its flesh can be eaten—an ecologically correct way of remembering your tyee (over 30 pounds/14 kg) or even a small, perfect coho.

Eric and his crew are heavily involved in a salmon-enhancement program. In April and May, smolt (baby salmon) are held in pens at the lodge's marina. Not just a few hundred—around 350,000 of them are cared for by shifts of volunteers. If you arrive in those months, you'll surely see them being fed, and if you're very lucky, you'll see them being released in a roiling silvery mass.

All summer long, heli-picnics can be arranged that take guests to Friendly Cove on the far side of Vancouver Island, where Captain Cook first landed.

Accessible only by boat or chopper, Friendly Cove is an idyllic place to spread a picnic blanket among the Indian paintbrushes. Crack open your first course of steamed Dungeness crab while your guide grills fresh prawns over an open fire. Chilled wine, lodge-baked bread, and fresh salads will emerge from the basket. Explore the solitary little chapel with its magnificent stained-glass windows, donated by the Spanish government to commemorate the Spaniards' involvement in the region. Pick a handful of blackberries from the vines entangling the old town site before returning to your blanket for "just a sliver" of Mrs. P's apple pie. The food both on the picnics and at the lodge is honest fishing-lodge fare and is often organically raised right on the island.

Heli-fishing for steelhead in high mountain rivers or a mountain meadow hike can also be arranged at the lodge.

In late September, guests don wet suits, masks, and snorkels. Eric or one of the staff then drives them to the headwaters of a salmon river where they float downstream with the current in a watery free-fall as the salmon spawn in deep gravel pools below.

The lodge is filled with Indian artifacts and is close to one of British Columbia's best native museums at Cape Mudge, where potlatch memorabilia that has been recovered by the band from various governments is proudly on display. Petroglyphs also can be found on the island.

Although swimming at April Point is almost nonexistent, there is excellent, challenging scuba diving. Rentals and air fills are available in Campbell River. You can meet Cruncher, the wolf eel, which lives about 30 feet (9 m) below the ferry terminal in Quathiaski Cove.

Nature lovers can photograph everything from killer whales that feed on salmon to a whole family of playful harbor seals. Hummingbirds literally fly into your room, and bald eagles can be fed leftover baitfish. Around the lodge, delicate Easter lilies and salal cascade down the steep banks into the water where white plumose anemones, red sea urchins, and a huge variety of seaweeds flourish.

There's a working lighthouse at Cape Mudge and a neat pub at Herriot Bay, where the ferry connects to still another island, Cortes.

Cycling (bring your own bike) is wonderful on Quadra, and if you have an extra minute, visit Quadra Foods—a most eclectic grocery store. They handle everything from organic produce and stamps to wines and macrobiotic ingredients.

If there is one major drawback that the Petersons have to put up with, it's the pulp mill across the channel. Although the breezes rarely blow the sulfurous smell over the lodge, it is, however, truly an eyesore on the western horizon.

The rooms at the lodge vary from basic to luxurious, with cooking facilities available in some. On the dock side, they can be a little noisy when the Petersons' fleet of Boston Whalers leave and arrive. Others, nestled in the trees, provide a perfect retreat with only eagles whistling overhead. April Point is a busy, fun place to learn to love salmon fishing, Indian art, and northern British Columbia.

***

April Point Lodge is located 165 miles (265 km) north of Victoria on Quadra Island. Drive up Highway 1 and take a B.C. car ferry on its hourly crossing. By air, scheduled service connects Campbell River to Vancouver, Victoria, and Seattle. By water, private boats can be moored at the April Point Marina.

Address: *Box 1, Campbell River, B.C. V9W 4Z9, tel. 604/285-2222, fax 604/285-2411.*
Accommodations: *38 rooms, including six suites that have king- and queen-size beds. All have private baths. Sixteen guest houses, with one to six bedrooms—several are very luxurious with outdoor hot tubs overlooking a private bay. Most have whirlpools, hot tubs, and fireplaces.*
Amenities: *European Plan. Special diets can be accommodated if advance notice is given. Courses are available on Northwest cooking (guests forage for foodstuffs with the chefs), Cajun cuisine, and the art of gyotaku, in which students are required to catch their subject. The all-inclusive cost is $199 per person per day. One large conference room can accommodate 25–250 people and can separate into three smaller rooms. The lodge can sleep 110. Most of the lodge is wheelchair accessible. There aren't any smoking restrictions, but the lodge is so airy that it should not be a problem. Rates are for accommodations only. All meals are extra although reasonable in price ($25–$35 per person for dinner).*

Some cabins have cooking facilities. Lodge is fully licensed. Guided fishing trips and heli-picnics are extra, but all gear is supplied. It is customary to tip your fishing guide. Smoking, canning, and freezing services are available.
Rates: *double $99–$395. Extra guests $30. Children under 14 free. Discount rates of 25%–50% off apply to Apr. and Oct., and very reasonable early or late season all-inclusive packages are available. AE, DC, MC, V.*
Restrictions: *Pets? "Love 'em!" says Eric. Closed Nov.–Mar.*

Cliffside Inn on-the-sea

Pender Island is one of those lovely places that take some effort to get to but are very, very hard to leave once you are there. From the Otter Bay ferry terminal, the lanelike road winds through old fern-filled forests and patches of wild trailing blackberries that threaten to grab the car. Yellow broom and sweet peas form natural hedgerows.

Cliffside Inn is down one such road, firmly attached to the high bluff overlooking Navy Channel and has a wooden stairway that plummets to the rocky shoreline. A perfect romantic hideway, it is more suited to adults than to children. Innkeeper Penny Tomlin, a romantic herself, has attended to every detail, from pink place mats to brass beds with piles of pillows. The Rose Hip Suite has a king-size Japanese soaker tub surrounded by candles. A hidden outdoor whirlpool is sheltered from the breezes and is surrounded by gardens and watery vistas. Lace and flowers, good food, and, above all, privacy are the watchwords.

From their window seats, guests watch winter storms course around the islands and over Mount Baker. In the summer, Penny provides pails and shovels for clam-digging on the beach.

Every day during the spring and the autumn, Penny feeds the eagles from her Cliffhanger Deck. Four or five of the big birds swoop down to catch salmon in midair.

Each morning she serves breakfast to her guests in a tiny dining room filled with sunlight and local art. There may be hot rhubarb stew or baked apples, eggs Benedict or a fluffy omelet.

Her well-executed dinners are served every second night and only to guests as part of a two-day package. The limited menu may include lamb braised, then baked with red wine and mushrooms, or steak topped with Szechwan peanut sauce, or lightly marinated in lime juice and gin. The vegetables are from an organic farm "down the road" and from Penny's hydroponic greenhouse. She regularly picks berries from her four 100 foot (30 m) rows of raspberry bushes, and heads to Vancouver Island to purchase fresh fish and jumbo prawns at the Sidney fishermen's market.

Penny can arrange boat charters that will drop guests at deserted beaches for an afternoon of seclusion. Because Cliffside is unlicensed, guests are allowed to bring their own favorite wines or purchase them at the B.C. Liquor Store in the Driftwood Centre.

The two islands that make up Pender are connected by Canal Bridge the, one-time site of an archaeological dig. Between them, they have 17 hidden coves and accessible beaches, more than any other of the Gulf Islands. Besides a great little nine-hole golf course, there are miles of superb cycling trails. The fisherperson in your family can catch perch all day long from the Port Browning Marina Dock, and then at 4 P.M., as is the custom, feed them to the awaiting eagles. The restaurant in the same marina has the best hamburgers, fish-and-chips, and homemade tortes on the island.

Pender has a large collection of fine artists. Cris Allen at the Silver Forge has created spoons for the Princess of Wales's children. One should not miss Malcolm and Marie Armstrong's Marine and Wild Bird Art Gallery near the Port Washington Dock; it's surrounded by Marie's 80 bird feeders.

The Hope Bay Craft Outlet sells only the works of local artisans. Browse through the hand-spun wool while sipping a cup of cappuccino. Rolley's Antiques, Collectibles and Japanese Tea Garden can be found on 17 acres of forest and sculpted trees near Otter Bay.

***

Cliffside Inn on-the-sea is 2½ miles (4 km) from the Otter Bay Ferry Terminal. Take Otter Bay Road to Bedwell Harbour Road. Turn left to Hope Bay dock, then follow Clam Bay Road to Armadale Road. Turn right and you will see the Cliffside sign on your right, approximately 600 feet (182 m) from the turnoff.

Address: *R.R. 1, Armadale Rd., Pender Island, B.C. V0N 2M0, tel. 604/629-6691.*
Amenities: *Two breakfasts and one four-course dinner for two are included in the package rates. Bed-and-breakfast-only rates are also available. Special diets can only be accommodated with lots of advance notice. Not suitable for meetings.*

Rates: *double (excluding tax) $150–$195 for two nights. Single-day rates are also often available. MC, V.*
Restrictions: *No pets. Not wheelchair accessible. Smoking permitted in outdoor sheltered areas.*

Fernhill Lodge

Mayne Island is not a place to do, it's a place to be!" So says Mary Crumblehume, of Fernhill Lodge. Sit on the swing and watch her and her effervescent husband, Brian, working in their magnificent herb gardens. The lodge's gardens have a definite bent toward history. The Crumblehumes have created an Elizabethan knot garden and a medieval garden of physic, and Brian is working on the hillside to develop a Roman garden. The property, at a high point in the middle of the island, has more than 150 fragrant herbs—from the common ones like mint (12 strains) and oregano (six varieties) to anise hyssop, a licorice-flavored perennial with purple brushlike flowers, and pineapple sage, a tender perennial that has sweet scarlet blooms. There are yards of perky camomile blooms and long borders of lavender.

Brian has only one request of his guests—"Rub the leaves; they're sensual."

With Brian at the stoves, they have been preparing authentic "historical dinners" for over half a decade. Brian calls it gastronomic time travel. From Roman times to the Renaissance, the Crumblehumes create accurate renditions of unusual dishes like *hedgehogges in sawse verte* (balls of spicy pork with almond quills and sorrel sauce), which is served on trenchers, the baked-bread plates of the Middle Ages. The Roman dinners may include *porcel-lum lasaratum*, (pork ribs in ginger sauce served with *dulcia*—dates fried in honey—and olive oil, then sprinkled with pepper). Renaissance dinners are a little more refined. Slivers of smoked eel are served in a fruit sauce, and a cheese tart is flavored with marigolds and herbs.

The menu has something on it for those who would rather stay in the 20th century. Handfuls of fresh herbs from the garden are used to spark a large selection of vegetables as well as entrées like salmon, shrimp, lamb, and chicken.

Breakfasts are old-fashioned in only one sense—they are huge. Scones, muffins, amazing omelets, eggnog, and cappuccino are all available every morning.

Fernhill is constructed of raw golden wood. Each guest room is decorated in a particular period theme: 18th-century French, Jacobean, Oriental, or Canadian, all with *en suite* bathrooms. The conservatory has a scented geranium that is at least eight feet (2.5 m) high. There's a quiet corner for reading, and a dining room overlooks the forest.

Play the piano or the medieval game of skittles, read a book from the inn's library, or travel farther afield to hike the island's arbutus-filled woods or tidal pools.

Spring is a wonderful time to visit Mayne. The island was the center for a daffodil-farming industry before World War II. These farms were owned by Japanese who diligently worked them until, in one of Canada's darker moments, they were interned in the interior of the province. After the war the farmers didn't return, and today Mayne has tens of thousands of wild daffodils blooming in early April.

The beaches are accessible by foot and are a paradise for photographers. Catamaran charters can be arranged, and if you have your own scuba equipment, Brian can point you to the best dives. Cycling on the island is superb, and numerous galleries simply beg to be visited.

The most important of all the artists is Don De Roussie, who carves in local woods and soapstone. He also happens to be the keeper of the Active Pass Lightstation, known officially as Georgina Point. He is always working on pieces, most of which have been commissioned. If you are lucky, you may also get a tour of the lightstation.

***

Fernhill Lodge is about five minutes from the ferry dock at Village Bay. Follow the Village Bay Road until you see the post office on the left-hand side. You will come to a T intersection, which is Fernhill Road. Turn right and continue until you see the Fernhill Lodge sign.

Address: *Box 140, Mayne Island, B.C. V0N 2J0, tel. 604/539-2544.*
Amenities: *Breakfast is included. Brian views special dietary requests as a real challenge—and he always welcomes a challenge. Small meetings for groups can be accommodated.*
Rates: *double (excluding tax) $75–$120, single $60–$100. Cash.*
Restrictions: *No pets. No smoking inside. Not easily wheelchair accessible.*

Hastings House

Pamela and Hector de Galard have been blessed with an inn that is every hotelier's dream. Hastings House, a proudly Tudor country-house hotel, stands on Saltspring Island, far enough from city life to be a true hideaway, yet close enough for guests to make the trip. Their acreage is on prime waterfront, with sailing vessels constantly gliding on the horizon. They have a fine chef who has brought home gold more than once for the Canadian culinary team at the Frankfurt Olympics. Their loyal veteran staff constantly make the inn's guests feel at home without being intrusive. And as if on cue, deer nibble grass around the old apple trees.

Peace and tranquillity must be etched on the cornerstones of Hastings House.

Better suited to adults than to children, Hastings House is just outside Ganges and is on the same lively harbor. The 30 acres are composed of meadows and forest. The latest parcel to be added was the small acreage of a local botanist whose all-engrossing interest was the wildflowers of Saltspring. Now, many species of native flora grow on the inn's property.

Executive chef Lars Jorgensen, who runs the kitchen with talented sous-chef Geoffrey Couper, is one of Canada's rising stars. His list of credits is long and impressive. He brings to Hastings House the energy of one who knows about great food—how to grow it, and how to prepare it.

He began in the garden, where he has expanded the range of edible flowers and exotic greens—by means of a high, deer-proof fence. Then the smokehouse was fired up to yield bacon, sausage, and fish. Geese and ducks have been given space to roam in the pastures along with the sheep and chickens.

Needless to say, most meals in Chef Jorgensen's dining room are cooked *à la minute* and with preparations that are in step with the seasons. The garden salad may have slices of inn-smoked goose breast with balsamic vinaigrette. The soup may be a creamy blend of garden sorrel, spinach, and beet greens, with a dollop of garlic-saffron mayonnaise. Wild sockeye salmon could be sliced so that it forms a pouch into which Jorgensen stuffs sea scallops and shrimp. Then the lily is gilded with a maple-butter sauce.

Fresh berries play an important part in the concert they call dessert. Blackberries are layered with the puffiest of pastry to make millefeuilles that float on a Cointreau cream. Blueberries are made into tarts and set off with a scoop of ginger ice cream. Or diners can choose to finish with a simple plate of cheese and a glass of vintage port.

The marriage of wine and food is given its due homage with a moderately long wine list. Older vintages, Bordeaux of 1978/1981/1982, and several of the earlier vintage champagnes are well represented. Although the wine list is not inexpensive, many of the bottles simply cannot be obtained any longer.

Like an English country house, the inn has many of its guest suites in small cottages scattered over the property. At one time they were the outbuildings for the farm. All the electrical and plumbing connections have been buried so as not to disturb the pastoral views. Fine floral fabrics cover the wing-back chairs, Persian rugs are scattered through some of the rooms, and dark Tudor beams are exposed in the manor house. Many have fireplaces and all are immaculate.

The inn will lend guests mountain bikes on which to ride the high country. (One note of caution: Check ferry arrival times, because the roads can be very busy for the 30 minutes after it slips into port.) A civilized game of croquet or a quiet time in the library is perfect for many who are really pining for peace.

The roads on Saltspring are lined with holly and fields of grazing lambs. There's a funky Saturday market at Ganges complete with crystal and incense vendors, delicious baked goods (try Barb's Buns), and whatever else the island's vendors think needs to be sold.

Life on this largest and, some say, most beautiful of all the Gulf Islands can be as laid-back and '60s-ish or as upscale and elegant as one wants to make it.

***

Hastings House may be reached in a number of ways. By car, take the Saltspring Island ferry from either Tsawwassen (you'll need a reserva-

tion) or Swartz Bay, north of Victoria. Guests arriving without a vehicle can be met at the ferry terminals or float-plane base. Scheduled and charter air service are provided by Harbour Air between Vancouver and Saltspring Island.

Address: *Box 1110, Ganges, B.C. V0S 1E0, tel. 604/537-2362, 800/661-9255 (toll-free in U.S. and Western Canada), and 800/67-RELAIS (Relais et Châteaux reservations), fax 604/537-5333.*
Amenities: *Modified American Plan, which includes breakfast or Sunday brunch and afternoon tea. Special diets can be prepared if advance notice is given. Please note that a dress code is in effect for the evening meal; gentlemen are asked to wear jackets. Meeting facilities are available for up to 15 people.*
Rates: *single or double (excluding tax) $200–$420. Additional person $40. On weekends there is a two-night minimum stay; on holiday weekends the minimum is three nights. AE, MC, V.*
Restrictions: *No pets. One suite is wheelchair accessible but must depend on a very efficient room service for meals. No smoking is allowed in the dining room. Closed Dec.–mid-Mar.*

Oceanwood Country Inn

Oceanwood is the new kid on a block of fine inns and is definitely worth watching. Though only two years old, Oceanwood has already garnered kudos from food critic John Doerper of *Pacific Northwest Magazine* and broadcaster and oenophile Jurgen Gothe, who led a wine-tasting weekend at the inn not long ago.

For Jonathan and Marilyn Chilvers, the inn was an opportunity to escape the trauma of life in the city. By either good luck or good management, they acquired chef Ranada McAlister, who has a penchant for regional foods and a solid knowledge of how to cook with them. She is well versed in the joys of Northwest cuisine, which she happily shares with the inn's guests. On Mondays there's always an island-made herb pasta, sometimes topped with juicy scallops and shrimp in a fresh basil sauce, or perhaps a thyme-and-fennel-spiked tomato sauce with chunks of perfect Pacific snapper. The four-course, table d'hôte menus during the rest of the week may include a French sorrel soup or a salad of mixed greens in a blackberry vinaigrette; poached salmon with scallop mousse in a white-wine-and-chive sauce, or chicken with balsamic vinegar and wild mushrooms. Desserts run the gamut from a lemon hazelnut tart to raspberry mousse with fresh berries.

Marilyn greets guests with a smile and, when things get busy, clears the tables. Jonathan, a gregarious and fun-loving character, works the full bar. Flowered tablecloths and Mexican tiled floors give both the dining room and the lovely solarium an earthy feel.

The Chilvers' wine list is perfectly in tune with Ranada's meals. It is organized by grape varietal, and only two of the champagne selections come from regions other than California, Oregon, Washington, and British Columbia. Jonathan offers many of these superb wines by the glass, so that it's possible to sample a whole range of vintages before leaving. He has also developed an excellent selection of dessert wines, far better than most multimillion-dollar hotels.

For years, even before they thought of opening Oceanwood, the Chilvers traveled the country inns of the world. This is the reason so many aspects of the inn are well thought out. Not only does the establishment have a large common living room; each of the guest rooms has space in which to sit and read. Marilyn has chosen to decorate each suite with a personality all its own. In the Geranium Room, the bright blossoms splash fabric and prints alike. Sometimes wicker furniture is used; other times it's rich mahogany or country pine. Three have their own fireplaces and whirlpool baths. Guests can throw open the wide French doors onto the garden terrace or closet themselves in the privacy afforded by California shutters. The inn is more suited to adults than to children.

Oceanwood Inn has been the scene of a number of outstanding spring and autumn events, which focus on everything from the vintages of a particular winery with the winemakers as their special guests, to a weekend on healthful eating, featuring a food writer/media star. The inn is incredibly popular; local British Columbians fly over Friday night via Harbour Air and return in time for work on Monday. It is on these weekends that Chef McAlister really shows her culinary mettle.

The hot pool and sauna are open both in winter, with snowflakes falling, and in summer, surrounded by flowers. Situated on the terrace between the inn and Navy Channel, it's a wonderful spot to get the knots out of the old muscles after a stressful week.

Guests are provided with bicycles if they want to leave the property to tour the island and visit its crafts people. Both Marilyn at Oceanwood and Mary Crumblehume from Fernhill say that the following should *not* be missed—the Artery (landscapes/pottery), the Treasure Chest (silver/gold made-to-order jewelery), the House of Taylor (weaving/island crafts), and the Charter House (weaving/hand-spun wool).

Tennis courts are available on the island, as well as sailing and salmon-fishing charters. A short ferry ride is all that is needed to reach Pender Island's nine-hole golf course.

***

Oceanwood Country Inn may be reached by ferry from either Tsawwassen (Vancouver) or Swartz Bay (Victoria). There are also daily scheduled flights via Harbour Air from downtown Vancouver. From the Village Bay ferry terminal, head up Village Bay Road just until Dalton Road leads to the right. Turn right. This road leads almost immediately onto Dinner Bay Road. Follow Dinner Bay Road until you reach the inn at the end.

Address: *630 Dinner Bay Rd., Mayne Island, B.C. V0N 2J0, tel. 604/539-5074, fax 604/539-3002.*
Amenities: *Breakfast and afternoon tea included in rates. Special diets can be prepared with advance notice. Meeting facilities include a dedicated conference room with good audiovisual equipment and can accommodate 10 around a board-room table.*
Rates: *double (excluding tax) $95–$170. Minimum stay two nights on weekends, three nights on holiday weekends. MC, V.*
Restrictions: *No pets. Limited wheelchair accessibility. The inn has one designated smoking area. No smoking in dining room.*

Woodstone Inn

Woodstone Inn, more suited to adults than to children, is located on 22 mile-long (35 km) Galiano Island, a 50-minute ferry ride directly from Tsawwassen. It sits surrounded by nine acres of forest, which is well interlaced by hiking trails. The innkeepers, Rosemary and Bob Walker, Connie Kennedy, and Mike Hoebel, have tried to think of everything, including gumboots for their guests who like to tramp through the woods on self-guided nature walks.

All of the wicker- and antique-decorated rooms have been named after the flowers that bloom on the property—foxglove, lupin, lily, sunflower. They alternate between a view of the peaceful valley with cows grazing, or the rich green forest. The Lilac Room, which opens to a private patio and has its own fireplace, is completely wheelchair accessible. The large soaker tub and queen-size bed are just added bonuses.

Chef Dean Mollon provides a limited, well-cooked menu. Breakfast features a different specially prepared dish every day. It may be poached eggs with Galiano smoked salmon in a bath of Béarnaise sauce, or a steaming stack of orange-laced pancakes with island-made herbed sausages.

Galiano is an island to explore. The Ixchel craft shop, named after the Mayan goddess of women's endeav-

ors, usually has the work of jewelry artist Haidee Leif. She creates whimsical designs in silver wire, beads, and shiny chunks of seashells.

Galiano has miles of old logging roads and trails to hike. The timber was stripped but then taken over as a tree farm by one of the lumber giants, MacMillan Bloedel. At the moment, the Galiano Conservancy Society is attempting to discourage the sale and massive development of the island.

***

Woodstone Inn is west of the ferry dock on Georgeson Bay Road. Follow the directional signs; the inn is on the left.

Address: *R.R. 1, Georgeson Bay Rd., Galiano Island, B.C. V0N 1P0, tel. 604/539-2022.*
Amenities: *Rates include breakfast and afternoon tea. Special dietary requirements can be handled if advance notice is given. Meetings may be held at the inn for up to 17 people. One suite is wheelchair accessible, as is the dining room.*
Rates: *double (excluding tax) $75–$125. MC, V.*
Restrictions: *No pets. Smoking is permitted outdoors only.*

Vancouver Island
Fairburn Farm
Country Manor

airburn Farm is nestled in the lush Cowichan Valley of coastal British Columbia, tucked away among fields where lambs graze.

Anthea and Darrel Archer preside over and farm the 130 acres on which he grew up. A mile away from their nearest neighbors, they provide guests with a chance to touch the earth.

The 19th-century manor house has a wide porch that overlooks rail-fenced fields and gardens. Most of the food that is served in the farmhouse kitchen is organically grown by the Archers. The hens donate the eggs, and the Brown Swiss and Guernsey cows give their milk. Butter is churned in the kitchen to spread on the home-baked breads or atop the freshly picked vegetables. Anthea has also perfected the art of making creamy white cottage cheese.

Peppery watercress flourishes in the fresh running water that spills out of their overflowing well. Nettles are gathered to use in soups. Maple sap is tapped and boiled into syrup. Later in the summer, wild blackberries are made into jam. An old quince tree gives enough fruit to make jelly. The apple orchard that was planted before 1920 is still producing some of the antique varieties—Gravenstein, wealthy, russet, and Jonathan king. The wheat that

they harvest in the autumn is made into flour—hard wheat for bread, soft for pastry.

These people are so self-sufficient that they have their own sawmill in which they fashion the trim for their house from the dead or dying trees that Darrel finds in the forest. Alder, maple, and Douglas fir are all used.

Guests are encouraged to become as much a part of the day-to-day life on the farm as they want. They can help gather the eggs and shear the lambs, or simply sit on the veranda and meditate.

The house has six guest rooms, two with their own fireplaces and whirlpools. A third has an *en suite* bath with shower, while the other three have private baths down the hall.

Breakfasts at Fairburn Farm are among the best of any served at Canadian inns. Homemade granola or hot porridge is followed by pancakes with a wild berry sauce—salal, blackberry, raspberry, or Oregon grape. Homegrown bacon and sausages are cooked to go with the free-range eggs and toasted homemade bread or muffins. Although there's lots of coffee, farm-gathered mint is brewed for a refreshing tea.

Lunches can be packed for travelers, but at noon the big farm table is again laden. Homemade soups, sometimes full of fresh herbs, are served with more fresh-baked bread.

Dinner in their unlicensed dining room is the same sort of wonderful fare—real food made by hardworking, friendly people.

Kelvin Creek meanders through the property for a mile. There's a natural swimming hole and two kayaks to paddle. Mountain bikes, horseshoes, and badminton provide a few of the on-site alternatives to doing the chores.

In nearby Duncan the Native Heritage Museum has been recently opened. It features some of the finest art and handicrafts that I've seen in one place. Argillite carvings and basketry of uncommon quality are both on display and for sale. A traditional salmon dinner is served in the potlatch theater while native dancers perform.

Because of its relatively gentle climate, likened to the Moselle valley in Germany, the Duncan area is home to several brand-new farm-gate wineries (*see* p. 203). There are two to watch. Zanatta Vineyards (tel. 604/748–2338) has eight acres of grapes in production. Winemaker Loretta Zanatta has just completed her master's degree in oenology in Pacenza, Italy, and is concentrating on white wine production. The second winery, Venturi-Schulz Vineyards (tel. 604/743–5630), is operated by another Italian, Giordano Venturi, and his wife, Marilyn. They are died-in-the-wool purists and flatly refuse to sacrifice the quality of their wines in order to hurry their entry into the farm-gate program. Meanwhile, they are the only makers of balsamic vinegar in Canada. Some barrels of this walnut-colored vinegar have been aging for 18 years.

Bastion City Wildlife Cruises (tel. 604/753–2852) leave Nanaimo on a 66 foot (20 m) motor launch. The ship circles the small islands that are scattered along the shores while passengers watch for bald eagles and sea lions. The boat goes out to the sandstone cliffs of Gabriola Island, and on to Elephant Rock and Dragon's Mouth.

The *Meriah* (tel. 604/748–7374), sailing out of Cowichan Bay, takes both day and evening cruises to islands like Saltspring, and excursions to Maple Bay, where passengers stop at the Brigantine Inn for a drink.

***

Fairburn Farm Country Manor is halfway between Victoria and Nanaimo on Vancouver Island. From Victoria, head north on Highway 1 toward Duncan for 33 miles (53 km). Turn left at Koksilah Road and head west past Riverside Road and Howie Road. The next on your left is Jackson Road. Turn left and continue to the farm.

Address: *R.R. 7, Jackson Rd., Duncan, B.C. V9L 4W4, tel. 604/746–4637.*
Amenities: *Breakfast is included. Special diets can be handled if guests call ahead. Small seminars are regularly held for up to 10 people.*
Rates: *double (excluding taxes) $80 (small twin room) to $120. MC.*
Restrictions: *No pets. No smoking indoors. Not wheelchair accessible. Closed Nov.–Mar. for lambing.*

Sooke Harbour House

Sooke Harbour House stands on its own as the most innovative restaurant in Canada. It has been said by one member of the West Coast media that innkeeper Sinclair Philip has done more for Vancouver Island tourism than any other single individual. It could be true.

Sooke Harbour House is a sparkling white clapboard country house. Wild, fiery nasturtiums and starry flowered borage roll down a slope, a dusty purple mound of lavender forms a huge spiky powder puff outside the dining room, and shiny-leaved salal bushes hang with ripening berries. At night, whimsical seashell lights softly illuminate the faces of the Johnny-jump-ups.

Inside the inn, Frederica Philip has stationed huge wildflower bouquets all around. Seaweed jewelry and mobiles made of old cutlery somehow seem right for her eclectic gift shop.

Over the years, each guest room has been given a unique theme—the Icthyologists' Study has every kind of fish motif that Frederica could find. The Edible Flower Room is a lesson on which flowers are safe to throw into your salad. A local artist was commissioned to paint the bathroom tiles with all the flowers from the Sooke Harbour House list of edible flowers. The Victor Newman Longhouse suite is used often as the honeymoon suite because of its size and the double whirlpool bath. It was

named after the man whose art fills it. Victor Newman is a soft-spoken Kwakiutl Indian who lives in Sooke, and his dance masks are outstanding! The red cedar backsplash that he built and painted for the bath is a sweeping collage of sacred symbols.

Every room has an ocean view, most have supremely private terraces, and some have outdoor hot tubs. They all have flowers and lace and fine artwork. Even in the summer, the fireplaces are laid to take the chill off the cool night air. A small basketful of herbal teas is ready to be brewed, and on the night guests arrive there is usually a plateful of homemade cookies.

Antiques from all over Canada furnish the rooms and braided rugs are scattered on the golden hardwood hallways, from where you can view bearded Byron Cook, busily transplanting and weeding all year round.

Kitchen life focuses on the gardens and on the sea. The chefs are outside a dozen times a day. They may choose a head of ruffled peacock kale for a soup, some unopened lavender flowerettes for a batch of popovers, a handful of blue rosemary flowers to scatter on a sauce, or a work bowl full of vibrant blooms for a salad.

The chefs also head to the saltwater holding tank with a washbasin at the ready. With great care they lift out spiny red and purple sea urchins for a sensuous soup, or a Dungeness crab that simply couldn't be any fresher. If there's a clump of fat gooseneck barnacles, they will be scrubbed and steamed to serve as finger food.

What cannot be grown and collected on the property is gathered from neighboring organic farms. Once Frederica even put an advertisement in the local paper for wild berries. She had to buy three used freezers to store the harvest that arrived—bagfuls of juicy wild blackberries; sweet, somewhat dry salal berries; and a healthy basket of salmonberries.

The chefs are becoming experts on wild foods. With constant consultation with Dr. Nancy Turner, an ethnobotanist from the Royal British Columbia Museum in Victoria, a series of pit-cooking extravaganzas have been organized. Chunks of halibut and butter clams, sword fern fronds, skunk cabbage leaves, and salal branches are layered with the tender growing shoots from some of the native plants like Indian celery and salmonberry bushes. The pit is then covered with earth, and the party continues for several hours before the food is removed and served.

The athletic maître d', Michel Jansen-Reynaud, is an avid outdoorsman and mycologist. Normally sedate and very French, he becomes completely animated when he has returned from a foraging expedition in the rain forests, where he stalks chanterelles and angel wings, boletuses, and oyster mushrooms.

Dining at Sooke Harbour House may be, as the food critic for *Philadelphia Inquirer* put it, "the best restaurant dinner" you'll ever have. If not, it will come very, very close.

Overnight guests are part of what has been christened the Canadian Plan. A full breakfast and elegant lunch are included with the room rate. Although the menu may change with the mood of the morning chef, you may be offered heart-shaped hazelnut waffles with fresh fruits, maple syrup, and venison sausages, or buckwheat crepes filled with Bramley seedling apples. Whatever the choice, it is bound to be delicious and beautiful. Lunches are light, airy affairs. The dining room is flooded with sunlight, and the sea gulls wheel just below the eagles. The constantly changing menu always has a soup (perhaps sorrel or nettle) with thick slices of nutty grain bread warmly wrapped in a woven kelp basket; always a fabulous mixed green salad, perhaps strewn with calendula petals; and always a dessert—with luck it's Frederica's favorite chocolate torte.

It is absolutely essential that dinner reservations be made as far ahead as is possible. If a particular table is desired—try one in the new alcove or in the windowed corner of the main dining room—one must call days ahead. It's only a minor inconvenience for such an evening.

The pine tables are draped in white linen. The candles are lit, the tide is out, and the table is set. A drink perhaps before your meal? The wine cellar is full of Northwest treasures, so you may want to choose from it. All the waiters are knowledgeable, but if you are able to call upon Sinclair, you'll learn a bookful about the various vinifera grown from California to the valleys of British Columbia.

The basic menu is always supplemented as fresh seafood becomes available. The sea-urchin soup, splashed with B.C. Gewürztraminer, is made with the roe of the spiny shellfish that Sinclair collects off the shore in his scuba gear. The warm sea-cucumber salad with tuberous begonia dressing has the same source. Island lamb, salmon, black cod (a delicacy that rarely reaches Canadian tables), wolffish, rabbit from a farm in nearby Metchosin, and Dungeness crab are all on the menu frequently. But no matter how they are prepared, the meal will surely be memorable!

The spit of land that curves oceanward in front of the inn forms the basin that was known by natives who traveled this way as "the camping place." It's wild and wonderful and deserted. Nootka roses bloom on the higher levels, surrounded by white cockleshells. Seaweed and salicornia color the shores.

If you can pull yourself away, and I admit that it is very difficult, the Sooke and District Regional Museum is worth a few hours of time. This area was raw wilderness with only a small settlement until the turn of the century. Old photos and displays make one marvel at the tenacity of the pioneers.

In August the Sooke Fine Art Show attracts visitors and entrants from all over the province. After a juried competition, the art is available to be purchased. Many of the best pieces have ended up at Sooke Harbour House.

All who travel to Sooke must come via Victoria, Canada's most British city. There are dozens of great attractions, but if your time is limited you must visit the Royal British Columbia Museum. It is one of the finest museums Canada has, full of northwest Indian treasures and totems. If you have an extra few minutes, walk up Fort Street to buy some Victoria Creams from Rogers' Chocolates and some tea at Murchies, or browse for a few minutes (or hours) in Munro's Books.

***

Sooke Harbour House is located west of Victoria on Highway 14. From Victoria, follow Highway 1 north to the Highway 14 intersection. Follow signs to Sooke. About 1 mile (1½ km) after the main intersection and stoplight, turn left onto Whiffen Spit Road. The inn is on the right, next to the ocean.

Address: *1528 Whiffen Spit Rd., R.R. 4, Sooke, B.C. V0S 1N0, tel. 604/642-3421 or 604/642-4944, fax 604/642-6988.*
Amenities: *Canadian Plan— breakfast and lunch included. Special diets can be handled with advance notice. Meetings for up to 20 can be accommodated with lots of advance notice. Several rooms and the dining room are wheelchair accessible. Eight guest rooms are nonsmoking as is the dining room.*
Rates: *double (tax excluded) $125– $270. No charge for children under 12. Additional persons in room, $25 each. AE, MC, V.*
Restrictions: *Well-behaved pets are allowed with prior arrangement for $10/night.*

Yellow Point Lodge

For more than half a century, the words *Yellow Point* and *West Coast hospitality* have been synonymous. It began in the early 1900s when a young man, Gerry Hill, was sailing the east coast of Vancouver Island. The point ahead was a mass of yellow broom flowers spilling down a bank covered with bleached oyster shells. Thirty years later he hand-winched massive logs into place to build his lodge on this 180 acre bit of heaven. Amid the forest and beside 1½ miles (2.4 km) of waterfront, the guests who came year after year felt as much a part of it as did Gerry's son, Richard. The bond of loyalty became so strong that they banded together, 65 strong, to form the Friends of Yellow Point (FOYP). Every year they travel from all over British Columbia to renovate and repair. Their fee is merely room and board.

Gerry Hill truly loved life and approached it with vigor. In 1988, fire destroyed the entire lodge. Everything from the recipes to its famous sprung dance floor was cinders. He was 90 but immediately he began to rebuild. The FOYP rolled up their executive sleeves and pitched in. Pictures show them peeling logs in the snow. The massive stone fireplace was redesigned by nine engineers. Little by little, Yellow Point was reborn. When he was sure that Richard was going to take over, Gerry would argue that the old lodge had been better—after all, Richard did

use a crane. After a year of living in the new lodge, Gerry died.

This is much too brief a summary of a man's life, but it will give you some sense of where the lodge fits in to the short history of Vancouver Island.

Today, Richard and his wife, Sandi, are at the helm. The sprung floor is again the scene of dances, and the large round tables are filled with guests, who must be over 16. The proportions are still expansive. The lounge and lobby is 30 feet (9 m) by 60 feet (18 m), with vaulted ceilings 17 feet (5 m) high. Chairs are overstuffed. Picture windows open onto a breathtaking view of Stuart Channel, framing the Gulf Islands, surrounded by the shimmering water or veiled in mist.

In some cases the accommodations can be likened to summer camp for big kids. *Rustic* would almost be too kind for a few of the old cabins and barracks, originals that for the sake of memory were not dismantled. The best rooms are very luxurious, so there's something for everyone. Choose between little cabins in the meadow or rooms in the lodge. The only problem could be getting a reservation. Former guests *always* get first dibs.

Millie, the lodge's executive cook, has been with the Hills so long that she has her own cabin. She and her sidekick, Bernice, were the ones responsible for resurrecting all the recipes after the fire—no easy feat, for there were certain dishes that guests simply expected to taste a particular way. Millie and her crew start in the early morning, baking muffins for breakfast. Any that are left are put out with coffee at 11. Treats like banana bread, spicy tomato-soup cake, and chocolate banana loaf are served for afternoon tea. These are homespun recipes with two secret ingredients—love and butter.

Breakfasts always have one special, such as apple-walnut pancakes with raspberry butter, but there's a choice of half a dozen other dishes, including any style of eggs you want. Buffet lunches, after the coffee break and a couple of moments before teatime, always have a soup like thick seafood chowder, warming turkey soup, clam chowder, or borscht.

Every night there is a different main course. It might be Millie's legendary oven-barbecued spareribs, roast turkey from a farm up the road, or huge roasts of beef. In the summertime, the old stone barbecue is fired up next to the saltwater swimming pool. Big fillets of salmon, fresh off a local trawler, and sirloin steaks are grilled. Instead of sitting in the dining room, guests find themselves outside at long trestle tables, much like being at a community picnic. Bowls of salads made with island-grown organic vegetables and inn-baked rolls round out the menu. That is, until dessert. Pans of apple-rhubarb crumble are served with cream. There are blueberry pies and rhubarb pudding cake—all old-fashioned desserts that have many heading back for seconds. Wine is available for those who care; the fresh air is intoxicating enough for most.

A sauna and hot tub are in a copse near the 200 foot (60 m) pool. Ca-

noes, rowboats, and a sailboard or two can be used off the point to investigate myriad coves that hold otters, seals, and who knows what other sea creatures. Mountain biking is available, as are tennis, volleyball, or badminton.

These extras are wonderful, but the very best gift Yellow Point Lodge gives its guests is a sense of camaraderie and of worth—an honest chance to become its friend.

***

Yellow Point Lodge may be reached from either Victoria or Nanaimo. Vancouver's Horseshoe Bay ferry runs to Nanaimo. From there journey south on Highway 1 for 3 miles (5 km) before turning left onto Cedar Road for another 10 miles (16 km). The lodge will pick up guests at the ferry, at Cassidy Airport near Ladysmith, and at the bus station.

Address: *3700 Yellow Point Rd., R.R. 3, Ladysmith, B.C. V0R 2E0, tel. 604/245-7422.*
Amenities: *Full American Plan, including three meals and three snacks. "Medically necessary" diets can be handled if lodge is called well in advance. Several cabins are wheelchair accessible. The lodge has designated smoking areas.*
Rates: *$52–$72 per person for cabins on the shore without running water; $72–$102 per person for other rooms and cabins. MC, V.*
Restrictions: *No pets.*

The Northern Coast
Nimmo Bay Lodge

"To fly is human, to hover divine!"

The sweeping melodies of David Foster's grand piano fill the stereo headphones, and the chopper *is* hovering divinely—over a clear blue lake ringed with snow—beside a 5,000-foot (1,525 m) waterfall. The meltwaters from Mount Waddington and Silverthorne cascade down the cliffside, and the fish are biting.

This is the art of heli-fishing at Nimmo Bay.

Craig and Gloria Murray chose to station their lodge in north coastal British Columbia at the foot of a waterfall for a very practical reason. They needed a source of hydroelectricity. The lodge is dwarfed by the encircling peaks. A wide deck outlines the cedar-sided building, and a narrow gangway leads to the huge outdoor hot tub where worn-out anglers hash over their latest batch of fish stories.

Inside the lodge, a massive wood stove is situated between two picture windows, and the walls are loaded with paintings, carvings, and photographs of other notables who have run away to Nimmo Bay.

Destroying fish is not the goal of those who stay at the lodge. It's the struggle of a steelhead in a glacial river and the fight of a bullish salmon that guests pay to experience.

Murray says, "When we started helicopter sports fishing we realized that we did not want to kill fish, we wanted to catch them. We realized very soon that to continue fishing this way we would have to have a catch-and-release policy." For this type of dedication to the environment, Craig Murray has been inducted into the International Order of St. Hubertus, founded in 1692 to prevent the extinction of any species of animal or fish.

Guests are whisked up into the mountains to special drop points to fish. These drop points are actually given phony names by the lodge to prevent overfishing. If the bite isn't on in one area, the pilot gathers the anglers and flies them to the next spot. More actual fishing is done in two days than most people do in a month.

Fishing and art are inseparable at this lodge. A fly being cast with precision is an art form on its own. But Murray has taken it one step further and launched a program he calls "Flying Colours." With his friend and local watercolorist, Gordon Henschel, he lifts painters into some of the most spectacular and undiscovered scenery in the world. Here guests come face-to-face with surging rivers, plant life from the coastal beaches and alpine meadows, and animals like mountain goats, killer whales, and sea lions.

Homeward bound on the final flight
of the day, a pilot may sometimes
land and pick up a bucketful of still-
wriggling sweet prawns. Gloria's
seafood is excellent! Her secret is
simple—she uses the freshest fish
you'll find west of Grand Manan.
The cold waters and abundant food
allow fish to grow to their succulent
best. Farm-raised chinook is smoked
for guests to take home with them
for snacks. Gloria even makes her
own homemade ice cream.

***

Nimmo Bay Lodge is reached only
from Port Hardy flying via the
lodge's aircraft.

Address: *Box 696, Port McNeill,
B.C. V0N 2R0, tel. 604/956-4000,
fax 604/956-2000.*
Amenities: *European Plan. Special
diets can be handled, but several
weeks of advance notification is
needed to prepare. For business
meetings, the lodge can accommodate up to 12. Both lodge and heli-
adventures are wheelchair accessible.*
Rates: *Start at $3,850 U.S. for four
days and four nights (tax excluded). V.*
Restrictions: *No pets. Smoking is
not allowed in the bedrooms.
Closed Nov.–Mar.*

Directory

Notes

Notes

Notes

Notes

Notes

Notes

Notes

Notes

Notes

Notes

Fodor's Travel Guides

U.S. Guides

Alaska	Las Vegas, Reno,	Pacific North Coast	Texas
Arizona	Tahoe	Philadelphia & the	USA
Boston	Los Angeles	Pennsylvania	The U. S. & British
California	Maine, Vermont,	Dutch Country	Virgin Islands
Cape Cod, Martha's	New Hampshire	Puerto Rico	The Upper Great
Vineyard, Nantucket	Maui	(Pocket Guide)	Lakes Region
The Carolinas & the	Miami & the	The Rockies	Vacations in
Georgia Coast	Keys	San Diego	New York State
The Chesapeake	National Parks	San Francisco	Vacations on the
Region	of the West	San Francisco	Jersey Shore
Chicago	New England	(Pocket Guide)	Virginia & Maryland
Colorado	New Mexico	The South	Waikiki
Disney World & the	New Orleans	Santa Fe, Taos,	Washington, D.C.
Orlando Area	New York City	Albuquerque	Washington, D.C.
Florida	New York City	Seattle &	(Pocket Guide)
Hawaii	(Pocket Guide)	Vancouver	

Foreign Guides

Acapulco	Cancun, Cozumel,	Italy 's Great Cities	Paris (Pocket Guide)
Amsterdam	Yucatan Peninsula	Jamaica	Portugal
Australia	Caribbean	Japan	Rome
Austria	Central America	Kenya, Tanzania,	Scandinavia
The Bahamas	China	Seychelles	Scandinavian Cities
The Bahamas	Czechoslovakia	Korea	Scotland
(Pocket Guide)	Eastern Europe	London	Singapore
Baja & Mexico's Pacific	Egypt	London	South America
Coast Resorts	Europe	(Pocket Guide)	South Pacific
Barbados	Europe's Great Cities	London Companion	Southeast Asia
Barcelona, Madrid,	France	Mexico	Soviet Union
Seville	Germany	Mexico City	Spain
Belgium &	Great Britain	Montreal &	Sweden
Luxembourg	Greece	Quebec City	Switzerland
Berlin	The Himalayan	Morocco	Sydney
Bermuda	Countries	New Zealand	Thailand
Brazil	Holland	Norway	Tokyo
Budapest	Hong Kong	Nova Scotia,	Toronto
Budget Europe	India	New Brunswick,	Turkey
Canada	Ireland	Prince Edward	Vienna & the Danube
Canada's Atlantic	Israel	Island	Valley
Provinces	Italy	Paris	Yugoslavia

Wall Street Journal Guides to Business Travel

Europe	International Cities	Pacific Rim	USA & Canada

Special-Interest Guides

Bed & Breakfast and	Cruises and Ports	Fodor's Flashmaps	Smart Shopper's
Country Inn Guides:	of Call	Washington, D.C.	Guide to London
Mid-Atlantic Region	Healthy Escapes	Shopping in Europe	Sunday in New York
New England	Fodor's Flashmaps	Skiing in the USA &	Touring Europe
The South	New York	Canada	Touring USA
The West			